THE
CRIMINAL
CONSPIRACY
TO ELECT
HILLARY
PRESIDENT

BERT AMECHE

Copyright

Dedication

To: Cathy and Mom

Table of Contents

Preface

"As [Emerich de] Vattel says himself... 'All the tranquility, the happiness and security of mankind rest on justice, on the obligation to respect the rights of others.'" --Thomas Jefferson

This book contains perhaps the largest factual evidence repository of government crimes committed in the Clinton email investigation, the Clinton Foundation investigation, and the Trump campaign/Russia investigation. The evidence for all three investigations should be considered together for understanding the magnitude, pattern, context, and interrelationships of the conspiracy to elect Hillary Clinton president and harm Donald Trump.

Andrew C. McCarthy is a former assistant U.S. attorney for the Southern District of New York. He led the 1995 terrorism prosecution against Sheikh Omar Abdel Rahman and eleven others. The defendants were convicted of the 1993 World Trade Center bombing and of planning a series of attacks against New York City landmarks. McCarthy is a contributing editor of National Review. During the last two years, McCarthy has written many articles on the Clinton investigations and the Trump/Russia collusion investigation. He is by far the best investigative journalist on these investigations, and perhaps the best investigative journalist period! McCarthy should be considered an American hero for exposing the biggest scandal by far in US history. I refer to the evidence and legal analysis in McCarthy's articles extensively in this book.

Evidence of a Conspiracy

An abundance of compelling substantial evidence indicates that the Obama administration's Department of Justice (DOJ), and FBI committed multiple felony offenses to wrongfully exonerate Hillary Clinton in the email investigation. They also terminated the validly predicated Clinton Foundation investigation before the election.

The FBI and DOJ's misconduct in the Clinton email investigation drastically changed the 2016 presidential election results. The Democrats would have had a different presidential candidate if Clinton had been indicted. Former FBI Director, James Comey, former Attorney General, Loretta Lynch, and others violated multiple laws during the justice process to exonerate Clinton. For example:

- Illegally permitted Clinton's aides to represent her as attorneys
- Conspired with defense attorneys to hide obstruction of justice evidence
- Permitted a false attorney-client privilege between Clinton and her aides
- Conspired with defense attorneys to destroy evidence
- Permitted subjects of the investigation to attend Clinton's interview

The DOJ and FBI headquarters hindered and ultimately terminated before the 2016 election the investigation into Hillary Clinton's abuse of power to enrich the Clinton Foundation even though there was a factual indication of wrongdoing.

In 2015, the Democratic National Committee (DNC) began researching Donald Trump's relationship with Russia. When the DNC discovered that their computer network had been hacked in April 2016, they hired the cybersecurity firm, CrowdStrike. CrowdStrike identified the Russian government as the hacker. Hillary Clinton and the DNC, chaired by Debbie Wasserman Schultz at the time, plotted to blame the hack on the Trump campaign colluding with Russia. The Clinton campaign and the DNC hired Fusion GPS, headed by Glenn Simpson, to create false evidence of Trump/Russia collusion. Simpson hired

Christopher Steele, a former British intelligence officer, to fabricate the evidence. Steele created 35 reports, known as the Steele dossier, containing the false evidence. Simpson and Steele provided the dossier to the FBI, the DOJ, the State Department, and the media in order to help Clinton win the election.

Sergei Millian is a Belarusian-American small business owner and con artist. Millian's allegations in Steele's dossier are the genesis of the story and the sole "evidence" that the Trump campaign coordinated with the Russian government to steal the emails from the DNC servers and post them on WikiLeaks to harm Hillary Clinton in the presidential election. Millian's allegations were recited thousands of times by the media, was harped on by Hillary Clinton, her campaign, and the Obama administration throughout the 2016 election campaign, was used to obtain a warrant to surveille the Trump campaign team and to prepare the Intelligence Community Assessment, was the focus of multiple congressional investigations, and was the origin of the Trump/Russia counterintelligence investigation that morphed into Mueller's Special Counsel investigation. For this reason, Sergei Millian has undoubtedly been the most influential person in the United States for the past two years.

The Obama administration used the Clinton/DNC Steele dossier to harm Donald Trump and they worked with foreign nationals to vilely set up and frame innocent people in the Trump campaign as "evidence" of Russian collusion. Chapters 6 through 21 describe in detail how the conspirators set up many people in their quest to get Hillary Clinton elected president.

Rosenstein and Mueller join the conspiracy

Deputy Attorney General Rod Rosenstein wrote a memo on May 9, 2017 that strongly supported firing FBI director James Comey. On May 9, 2017, President Trump sent Comey a termination letter stating that he accepted Rosenstein and AG Jeff Session's recommendations to fire him. Trump later stated that he had already decided to fire Comey before receiving Rosenstein's memo.

The Democrats seized on Trump's firing of Comey as an opportunity to accuse the president of obstructing the FBI's Russia investigation and they assailed Rosenstein for his memo justifying the firing. The New York Times wrote that Rosenstein "grew concerned that his reputation had suffered harm," and he "became angry at Mr. Trump."

On September 21, 2018, a NY Times article, based on anonymous sources, said that FBI officials, including then-acting director Andrew McCabe, wrote internal memos documenting meetings with Rosenstein. Rosenstein suggested in several conversations with multiple FBI and Justice Department officials that he or a top FBI official, such as McCabe, would secretly record President Trump. The Times' sources said Rosenstein's intent in recording the president would be to expose him as being "unfit for office" in order to force his removal under the 25th Amendment. James Baker, Comey's top FBI counsel, later confirmed this in congressional testimony.

Unbelievably, a few days after his memo justifying firing Comey, Rosenstein told FBI officials that he wished Comey were still FBI Director and that he hoped to get Comey's advice on the appointment of a special counsel.

Comey testified that he asked a friend to leak his memos on meetings with the president to get a special counsel appointed. The friend illegally leaked the memos to the NY Times. On May 16, 2017, the Times ran a story titled "Comey Memo Says Trump Asked Him to End the Flynn Investigation."

McCarthy writes "When Democratic pressure to appoint a special counsel reached fever pitch with the Times' publication of its report, based on a Comey leak, that Trump had pushed for the FBI to drop the Flynn investigation, Rosenstein decided to appoint a special counsel without specifying any crime against Trump."[i]

Robert Mueller was friends with James Comey, so he was probably angered by Comey's firing. On May 16, 2017, Mueller rode with Rosenstein to the White House for his job interview with the president for the FBI Director position. The next day, on May 17, Rosenstein appointed Mueller Special Counsel to investigate "any links and/or coordination between the Russian government and individuals associated with the campaign of President Donald Trump." This was only 8 days after Comey's firing on May 9. Rosenstein had openly wished to get Comey's advice on the appointment of a special counsel, so one can deduce that he asked Mueller's advice in the car ride.

Peter Strzok was FBI agent in charge of the Clinton email investigation and the Trump/Russia investigation. As evidenced by his texts, he held a deep animus toward Donald Trump. The day after Mueller's appointment as Special Counsel, he recruited Strzok. After the recruitment interview, Strzok texted his lover, Lisa Page, that he could "fix and finish" the "unfinished business" he "unleashed" with the Clinton email exoneration, because the Special Counsel investigation could result in "impeachment?" Rosenstein wanted President Trump removed from office, and he openly contemplated using wiretaps to prove Trump was "unfit for office," so that he could be removed by the 25th Amendment. One can surmise from Strzok's reference to "impeachment" that Mueller and Rosenstein, perhaps in their car ride to the White House, discussed and decided that the best way to remove the president was an unbounded Special Counsel investigation to gather "evidence" for impeachment.

Donald Trump received more than 62 million votes to become president. Rosenstein was angry at President Trump for harming his reputation. Driven by his bruised ego, Rosenstein, in an extremely narcissistic act, plotted to void the election by getting President Trump removed from office less than 4 months after the inauguration.   Rosenstein found a willing partner in Mueller to reverse the will of the voters by aggressively investigating the president and his associates without any limits or probable cause to find evidence of some crimes so a democratic majority in Congress could impeach the president. Mueller and Rosenstein joined the conspiracy to harm President Trump by using the justice system as a political weapon.   All Americans should be truly concerned that a powerful person like Rosenstein, in a fit of anger, could so easily wage a vendetta against the president with complete impunity.

Mueller's own indictment evidence absolves the Trump campaign of Russian collusion

The Debbie Wasserman Schultz/DNC and Hillary Clinton plot to blame the Trump campaign for coordinating the DNC hack with Russia worked unbelievably well, and their hoax continues unabated with the Special Counsel investigation.

On January 6, 2017, the Obama administration published the Intelligence Community Assessment (ICA) on "Assessing Russian Activities and Intentions in Recent US Elections." At that time no definitive proof existed that the Russian military intelligence service (GRU) hacked the DNC and stole the emails as evidenced by the fact that the ICA preparers did not assign a confidence level to this assessment.

The FBI and NSA continued to investigate the hack, and eventually uncovered incontrovertible proof that the GRU hacked the DNC. In March 2018, Rod Rosenstein transferred the evidence and FBI agents involved from the DOJ to the Special Counsel. In this way, Mueller received undeserved credit and publicity for finding the DNC hackers when he indicted 12 Russian GRU intelligence officers on July 13, 2018.

The evidence in Mueller's indictment is extremely detailed. The FBI and NSA were able to trace the activities of specific GRU officers by day, and to a location in Moscow. For example, they found GRU officers capturing the keystrokes of DNC employees and taking pictures of their computer screens.

The NSA and FBI captured private messages between Assange/WikiLeaks and the GRU officers posing as Guccifer 2.0. Assange communicated the strategy to influence the election:

- On or about June 22, 2016, Organization 1 [WikiLeaks/Assange] sent a private message to Guccifer 2.0 to "[s]end any new material [stolen from the DNC] here for us to review and it will have a much higher impact than what you are doing."
- On or about July 6, 2016, Organization 1 [WikiLeaks/Assange] added, "if you have anything hillary related we want it in the next tweo [sic] days prefable [sic] because the DNC [Democratic National Convention] is approaching and she will solidify bernie supporters behind her after."
- The Conspirators [GRU/Guccifer 2.0] responded, "ok . . . i see."
- Organization 1 [WikiLeaks/Assange] explained, "we think trump has only a 25% chance of winning against hillary . . . so conflict between bernie and hillary is interesting."

The Russians and WikiLeaks were trying to sow discord between Clinton and Sander's followers, they were not trying to help Trump because Assange believed that he only had a 25% chance to win. House Intelligence Committee Chairman Devin Nunes said Mueller's indictment of 12 Russian officials looks "ridiculous" because it left out the fact that Russians unsuccessfully tried to hack Republican targets.

The Mueller indictment's evidence is "smoking gun" proof that no one in Donald Trump's campaign was involved in the GRU's hacking, and, therefore, Mueller's Special Counsel has no basis to continue its investigation of Trump campaign/Russia coordination. This evidence clearly demonstrates that Clinton and Wasserman Schultz created, disseminated and used the fraudulent Trump/Russia collusion story to help Clinton win the presidency.

The conspirators dramatically changed the 2016 presidential election outcome

The DOJ and FBI should have indicted Clinton based on the overwhelming evidence that Comey presented on July 5, 2016. Instead, they corrupted the federal justice process in a sham investigation to improperly exonerate Clinton in an attempt to get a criminal elected president.

The Obama administration's criminal conspiracy harmed all Americans of voting age, because the wrongful exoneration enabled Clinton to be the Democratic candidate instead of Bernie Sanders. I am an independent voter and I voted twice for Barack Obama, but I would not ever vote for Clinton because of her email and Clinton Foundation crimes. I only vote for either the Democratic or Republican candidate for president, so I would have loved to have had Bernie Sanders as a voting option.

All Americans, regardless of party affiliation, should be enraged that high-level Obama administration officials used the DOJ, FBI and Intelligence agencies as political weapons to help President Obama's preferred candidate and harm the candidate in another party. The Democrats should be especially furious. Polls showed Sanders doing significantly better than Clinton in a Trump matchup, so Bernie Sanders may well have been the president today instead of Donald Trump if not for the FBI and DOJ's criminal conspiracy.

Hillary Clinton, the DNC, and the Obama administration conspirators also changed the election outcome by widely disseminating the false narrative that the Trump campaign colluded with Russia to hack the DNC and steal the emails. This convinced unknown millions of people to vote for Clinton instead of Trump. If voters had known about the Clinton/DNC plot to falsely blame Trump for Russian collusion, an unknown tens-of-millions of votes would likely have been cast for Trump instead of Clinton.

The conspirators in the Obama administration swore an oath of office to "support and defend the Constitution of the United States against all enemies, foreign and domestic; that I will bear true faith and allegiance to the same." The conspirators are traitors who turned the justice system, FBI, and intelligence community into a political weapon to elect their preferred candidate, Hillary Clinton. This is the very definition of a "police state." The conspirators attempted to turn our government into a police state like China, Russia, Saudi Arabia, and Iran. If Clinton had won, the conspirators would have been rewarded, and their crimes covered up.

This is by far the biggest scandal in the history of the United States. President Trump should order Jeff Sessions to appoint a special counsel to investigate and prosecute these traitors for their felony offenses, including violations of the RICO law, so that it never happens again.

The Clinton/DNC Russian collusion scam may yet succeed

Unfortunately, the Clinton/DNC hoax is on the verge of succeeding in nullifying the 2016 election of Donald Trump. Mueller and Rosenstein's objective has always been impeachment, and they may well achieve this if the Democrats win majorities in Congress this November as some polls indicate.

This is by far the biggest scandal in US history. Why aren't the American people aware of it? The answer has three parts: 1) Rod Rosenstein, 2) the mainstream media, and 3) Democrats.

1. Rod Rosenstein

Donald Trump has been president for almost two years, so it is simply outrageous, but hardly surprising, that the DOJ and FBI have not even attempted to investigate the easily disprovable Clinton and DNC funded dossier allegation that the Trump campaign coordinated with Russia to steal and publish the DNC emails. Jeff Sessions unnecessarily recused himself from the Russia investigation, so Rod Rosenstein is in charge of the DOJ for all aspects of Trump/Russia collusion, including Mueller's special counsel investigation.

Rosenstein continually stonewalls requests by congressional committees performing investigations related to their oversight responsibilities. For example, Rosenstein delayed for many months disclosing documents requested by congressional committee chairmen, Rep. Devin Nunes and Senator Chuck Grassley, who are investigating possible DOJ and FBI misconduct. When Rosenstein finally releases documents to the committees, they are unnecessarily heavily redacted. When, upon congressional insistence, the redactions are disclosed, it is obvious Rosenstein made the redactions to protect the DOJ and FBI rather than for national security reasons. Rosenstein's tactic is obviously to buy time in hopes the Democrats take control of Congress and shut down the investigations.

Comey used Sergei Millian's false allegations to define the FBI's Trump/Russia collusion counterintelligence investigation. Rosenstein again used Millian's allegations as the Special Counsel's scope. Millian's allegations are easily disprovable, but neither Comey nor Mueller attempted to verify them. Mueller's investigations are solely directed at President Trump and his associates. The list of questions that Mueller wants to ask President Trump clearly demonstrates that Mueller is after the president for obstruction of justice. Mueller's friend, James Comey, is President Trump's obstruction of justice accuser. Comey committed multiple felonies, but Mueller does not investigate him. Mueller, a former FBI Director, does not investigate the FBI's misconduct in the Trump/Russia investigation such as the Carter Page FISA surveillance warrant that the FBI obtained without probable cause.

Rosenstein learned that FBI/NSA evidence incontrovertibly proved the Trump campaign did not coordinate the DNC email hack with Russia before March 2018 when he transferred the Russian hacking case to Mueller. Even though this evidence extirpates the very foundation of the Special Counsel's reason for being, Rosenstein dishonestly did not announce this or terminate the Mueller special counsel investigation.

2.The mainstream media

The mainstream media is a very effective propaganda machine for the Democrats. In October 2017, the Pew Research Center found the media was three times more negative and eight times less positive toward Trump than it was to Obama, and the media was also significantly more biased against Trump compared to presidents Clinton and Bush II. A Harvard study in May 2017 said Trump set "a new standard for unfavorable press coverage of a president."

The DOJ's Inspector General, Michael Horowitz, issued a report titled "A Review of Various Actions by the Federal Bureau of Investigation and Department of Justice in Advance of the 2016 Election."[ii] Horowitz found that officials in the FBI at "all levels of the organization" leaked information to reporters without authorization. The FBI's strict media relations policy on disclosures was "widely ignored" during the Clinton email probe and afterwards. The report said "We have profound concerns about the volume and extent of unauthorized media contacts by FBI personnel." A chart showed dozens of FBI officials who spoke to reporters without permission, including several special agents, special agents in charge, secretaries, management and program analysts, attorneys, an "FBI executive," a deputy assistant director and an assistant director.

The Obama administration's conspirators Andrew McCabe, Peter Strzok, James Baker, and Lisa Page all leaked classified information to the press to get stories disseminated in a beneficial way for them. James Comey, who committed multiple felonies, successfully leaked his memos to the press with the objective of getting a special counsel appointed.

The mainstream media allied with the conspirators and the Democrats to successfully cover up the biggest scandal by far in U.S. history. The New York Times and Washington Post publish stories handed to them by the conspirators, referred to as "anonymous sources," to deftly cover up the conspirators' wrongdoing and promote the Clinton and DNC's hoax that the Trump campaign colluded with Russia to hack the DNC. Sergei Millian's allegations are the raison d'être of Mueller's special counsel investigation. The mainstream media's many "investigative journalists" could have easily uncovered the facts about Sergei Millian and his false allegations, but did not. The mainstream media's objectives are to harm President Trump and help the Democrats achieve their impeachment goal, so disproving Millian's allegations would undermine these goals.

3. Democrats

The United States is unique in the world in its peaceful presidential elections and smooth transfer of power to the winner. The transfer from President Bush to President Obama went smoothly, but the transfer from President Obama to President Trump was marred from the beginning by angry protests, violence, and lawsuits.

Donald Trump won the election, but Democrats planned for his impeachment before the inauguration, when Democratic senators, including Elizabeth Warren, introduced a bill in

December 2106 to require a president to divest any assets that could raise a conflict of interest and failure to do so would constitute high crimes and misdemeanors "under the impeachment clause of the U.S. Constitution." Democrats formed PAC's as early as February 2017 aimed at Trump's impeachment because 1) his businesses had conflicts of interest that violated the Foreign Emoluments Clause, or 2) his coordination with Russia in the DNC hack to influence the 2016 election.

When President Trump fired James Comey in May 2017, the Democrats discussed impeachment on the grounds of obstruction of justice. On July 12, a Democratic representative introduced an Article of Impeachment in the House that accused the President Trump of obstructing justice in the Trump campaign/Russia collusion investigation. It did not pass, but the Democrats could conceivably impeach the president if they take control of the House in the midterm elections.

In furtherance of their impeachment strategy, Democratic senators and representatives try to impede congressional committees' investigations into potential Obama administration wrongdoing in the Clinton investigations and the Trump/Russia investigation. Rosenstein helps with this by stonewalling congressional requests for documents, and making unnecessary extensive redactions. The Democrats' goal is to cover up this scandal in the hope that they win congressional majorities in the midterm elections. When they are in the majority, the Democrats can terminate the congressional committee investigations into DOJ and FBI wrongdoing in the Clinton investigations and the Trump/Russia investigation.

After the midterm election, Mueller will issue a report of the Special Counsel findings that the Democrats in the majority can use to impeach President Trump.

It would be a grievous miscarriage of justice if the Democrats impeach President Trump under the pretense that he obstructed justice in an investigation that only exists because of the false Sergei Millian allegations in the Hillary Clinton and DNC funded Steele dossier. Mueller and Rosenstein know that Trump's campaign did not collude with Russia because of the evidence in their indictment of 12 Russian intelligence officers.

Donald Trump is the democratically elected president. The Democrats with the help of the mainstream media, Rosenstein, and Mueller are aiming to overturn the will of the voters by impeachment based on the false allegations of Sergei Millian – the most influential person in America.

The Steele Dossier – Real Russian Collusion

Hillary Clinton, through her campaign, and the DNC hired Fusion GPS and Glenn Simpson to create evidence to falsely blame the Trump campaign for colluding with Russia to hack the DNC and publish the stolen emails on WikiLeaks to hurt Clinton in the election. Simpson in turn hired a former MI6 intelligence officer, Christopher Steele, to fabricate the false evidence.

Steele, a foreign national, paid former and current Russian government officials to provide negative information on Trump that Steele used to create a 35-page dossier of false allegations against Trump and his associates. "The dossier quotes from a large number of anonymous sources. It cites 'a former top level Russian intelligence officer still active inside the Kremlin', 'a senior Russian foreign ministry figure' and "a senior Russian financial official'."[iii]

The evidence in Mueller's indictment of 12 GRU intelligence officers very clearly proves the absurdity of Steele's allegations in the dossier.

Hillary Clinton, her campaign, Debbie Wasserman Schultz, the DNC, Perkins Coie, Fusion GPS, Glenn Simpson, Nellie Ohr, Sydney Blumenthal, Cody Shearer, and the others involved in the Steele dossier conspired with a hostile nation, Russia, and a foreign national, Steele, to subvert a federal election. They received something of value from Russian government officials and a UK citizen in the form of the Steele dossier's false evidence. The conspirators used the Steele dossier's false evidence to influence the election to help Hillary Clinton win.

A partner at Perkins Coie, Robert Bauer, stated that a campaign finance law prohibits foreign nationals from providing "anything of value ... in connection with" an election and it is criminally enforceable.

Perkins Coie is one of the conspirators. They hired Fusion GPS for Clinton and the DNC. Very strong evidence indicates that Hillary Clinton was directly involved in the creation, dissemination, and use of the false Steele dossier allegations. For example, prior to the election the Perkins Coie attorney, Michael Sussman, a former DOJ lawyer, provided the FBI's General Counsel, James Baker, with documents and a thumb drive related to Russian interference in the election, hacking and possible Trump connections.[iv] Obviously Sussman would do this only at the instruction of his clients, Hillary Clinton and the DNC.

The conspirators in the DOJ, the FBI, the State Department, and intelligence community used the false Steele Dossier allegations and foreign nationals to help Clinton win the election so they could remain in power.

Hillary Clinton used Steele's false evidence of Trump/Russia collusion throughout her 2016 presidential campaign in ads, speeches, and the debates. Clinton and the DNC had their vendors, Fusion GPS and Steele, disseminate the false allegations to the media, the DOJ, and the FBI. Clinton and the DNC's scam lives on in the Mueller investigation, and it is by far the biggest scandal in US history.

Clinton, the DNC, and their co-conspirators betrayed the United States by subverting the democratic election process through fraud in order to gain power. Congressional Democrats and the mainstream media betrayed the United States by covering up the biggest scandal in US history. The conspirators actually did change the election results because an unknown millions of votes were cast for Clinton instead of Trump because of Clinton and the DNC's Trump/Russia collusion scam.

The Democrats are riding roughshod over President Trump and the Republicans

President Trump holds all of the aces – the truth! The truth is that the Obama administration, Hillary Clinton, and the DNC colluded with foreign nationals in the UK, Australia, Ukraine, Russia, Malta, and other nations to create and disseminate the false Trump/Russia collusion story to influence the 2016 presidential elections.

Most Americans do not know that Clinton and the DNC successfully perpetrated a huge fraud with the Trump/Russia collusion story. As a result, the Democrats are poised to possibly win congressional majorities in the midterm elections. President Trump, the Republican National Committee and Republican donors are sitting on the sidelines like deer in the headlights while the Clinton/DNC fraud continues with the Mueller investigation. They need to take urgent and drastic action.

The DOJ and FBI under the direction of Rod Rosenstein are protecting themselves by not disclosing documents requested by congress. President Trump needs to fire Rod Rosenstein for cause, and order the appointment of a Special Counsel to investigate crimes committed by Obama administration personnel in the Clinton email and Foundation investigations and the Trump/Russia collusion investigation. President Trump should order that the Special Counsel team be composed of the best prosecutors and FBI agents from different states in order to minimize bias and maximize talent. The team should not include anyone from Washington D.C. or New York.

Unbelievably, the DNC brazenly filed a lawsuit against members of the Trump campaign team for colluding with Russia to hack the DNC and steal the emails. The Trump/Russia collusion story is a hoax perpetrated by the DNC and Clinton with the Steele dossier. The Republican National Committee and Republican donors should take the following actions to expose the biggest scandal in U.S. history (refer to the chapter with this title for details):

- File a $100 million countersuit against the DNC.
- File a $100 million lawsuit on behalf of Carter Page and any other people surveilled against the conspirators that obtained a FISA surveillance warrant on false pretenses.
- File a $100 billion lawsuit on behalf of the American people against the conspirators for criminal actions to elect Hillary Clinton president and harm President Trump and his associates by subverting the justice process.

How this book came about

At the beginning of 2017, I realized there had been a conspiracy by certain Obama administration officials to unjustly exonerate Hillary Clinton in the email investigation and unjustly harm Donald Trump with the Trump/Russia collusion investigation. In June 2016, I began sending letters to President Trump's attorneys with the evidence I gathered on this conspiracy. On September 16, 2017, I sent letter to the DOJ's Inspector General, Michael Horowitz, requesting an investigation of the criminal conspiracy to elect Hillary Clinton president along with a 55-page document of evidence.

From May through September of this year, I sent more letters with new factual evidence to some of the president's attorneys along with recommendations, including recommendations for the president to fire Rod Rosenstein for cause and order a Special Counsel to investigate the criminal conspiracy to elect Clinton president. I never received feedback, so do not know if the attorneys even read my letters.

The midterm election is imminent and the Democrats are poised to take a majority in the house and/or senate. Most Americans will go to the polls unaware of the criminal conspiracy, so I decided to quickly copy and paste from my letters to make and self-publish this book.

The evidence I sent to the IG, Michael Horowitz, in September 2017 had extensive endnotes. Speed was my primary concern in the letters to the president's attorneys, so I did not cite references. I attempted to review and add references to this book, however, I surely missed some in my haste to publish the book as soon as possible because of the looming midterms. I sincerely apologize for any missed references.

Final thoughts

I am a former internal auditor with experience in financial, operational and IT audits. An auditor is a type of investigator. I used my audit knowledge and experience to research and gather facts from authoritative sources to objectively form conclusions. I am not a writer and have never published anything before.

My mother was a stenographer with the FBI in the early 1940's, and she brought me to an FBI headquarters tour when I was 10 years-old. I revered the FBI, and my fondest dream as a child was to become an FBI agent.

My mother and I were shocked and deeply saddened to discover how Comey; McCabe, Lynch, and the other conspirators betrayed their country and criminally corrupted our wonderful justice system in an unsuccessful attempt to get their favored candidate elected president and remain in power. They collaborated with foreign nationals to do this.

James Madison said "Justice is the end of government" and "ever will be pursued until it be obtained, or until liberty be lost in the pursuit."

I love my country and sincerely hope that President Trump appoints a Special Counsel to bring the traitors to justice and restore the great reputation of the DOJ, FBI, and intelligence community that Comey, Lynch, McCabe and the other conspirators tainted. The wonderful people working for these agencies to protect our country deserve this.

1. Biased Investigators

Introduction

Attorney General, Loretta Lynch, and FBI Director, James Comey, initiated and oversaw the Clinton email, the Clinton Foundation, and the Trump/Russia collusion investigations during the Obama administration.

Comey worked for Lynch, and testified he was "very close personally to that [email] investigation." If Comey believed that Lynch and others in the Department of Justice (DOJ) interfered to obstruct the FBI's investigation, he is obligated to resign and/or report it to his subordinates, Congress, an Inspector General, and/or, his supervisor (the Deputy Attorney General, Sally Yates). Likewise, Lynch should have acted if Comey and the FBI had done anything wrong in the investigations.

The DOJ and the FBI did in fact corrupt the federal criminal justice process, as the evidence summarized below indicates, to wrongfully exonerate Hillary Clinton in the email investigation. Comey was obviously a full partner with Lynch in this misconduct since he did not resign or report it.

The abundance of compelling, substantial public evidence indicates that Lynch, Comey, and others conspired to wrongfully exonerate Clinton when she was running to become the Democratic candidate for president. If the DOJ and FBI had conducted an impartial investigation, a grand jury and the DOJ would have indicted Clinton because the compelling evidence clearly demonstrates that Clinton was "grossly negligent." Clinton would not have been the Democratic candidate for president if she had been indicted.

The election would have been drastically different if Bernie Sanders had been the Democratic candidate. Lynch and Comey must have believed Clinton was guilty since they blatantly committed felony offenses, and violated ethical and procedural guidelines to exonerate her – in essence they conspired to get a criminal elected president.

Most of the legal points cited on the Clinton email and foundation investigations were drawn from articles by Andrew McCarthy, a former chief assistant U.S. attorney and Shannen Coffin, a senior lawyer in the George W. Bush Justice Department and White House.

Comey and Lynch assigned biased and conflicted people to the Clinton email investigation.

The conflicted Andrew McCabe oversaw the Clinton email investigation

The DOJ Office of Inspector General investigated the allegation that "the FBI Deputy Director, Andrew McCabe, should have been recused from participating in certain investigative matters."[v]

The allegation is that McCabe violated the Hatch Act by campaigning for his wife. The Hatch Act prohibits certain federal executive branch employees, including FBI employees, from engaging in partisan political campaigns. The FBI said that McCabe consulted the FBI's ethics experts prior to his wife's announcement of her election bid in March 2015, and that he followed the advice by taking no role in the campaign and avoiding work on public corruption cases in Virginia.[vi]

The Hatch Act prohibits the following:

- take an active part in partisan political campaigns,
- campaign for or against a candidate
- wear or display partisan political buttons, T-shirts, signs, or other items,
- post a comment to a blog or a social media site that advocates for a candidate,
- host a political fundraiser.

Beginning in the same month he met with the FBI ethics experts, McCabe violated all of these prohibitions. McCabe's wife, Dr. Jill McCabe, was a hospital physician and had never run for office. The Virginia governor, Terry McAuliffe, met with Andrew and Jill at their home on March 7, 2015 to recruit Jill McCabe to run for the Virginia legislature.[vii] McAuliffe is a longtime personal best friend of the Clintons, a former Clinton Foundation Board member and a major Democratic fundraiser. McAuliffe's briefing memo stated "This is a candidate recruitment meeting. McCabe is seriously considering running against State Senator Dick Black. You have been asked to close the deal." The briefing package included McCabe's FBI biography showing he was Assistant Director in Charge of the FBI's Washington Field Office responsible for investigations in northern Virginia.

Richard Painter, the former chief ethics lawyer for the White House, said the "question is why are you sending your bio from the FBI? Are you trying to do that to influence the campaign or is this something somebody wants for informational purposes? But if you're trying to use your position to get somebody to give money to a political campaign that is crossing the line." [viii] Andrew McCabe's meeting with McAuliffe was a de facto fundraiser for his wife because, as a result, McAuliffe's PAC and the Virginia Democratic party, heavily influenced by McAuliffe, donated $675,000 to Jill McCabe's campaign. Andrew McCabe was not running for office, which begs the question: why would a Governor personally recruit and spend so much money on a physician who never ran for office, and why would he have Andrew McCabe's biography with him?

Senate Judiciary Committee Chairman Charles Grassley (R-IA), in a November 2016 letter to the Justice Department inspector general, noted that in July 2015, around the time the Clinton investigation began, Andrew McCabe was promoted to associate deputy director at FBI headquarters. Grassley wrote, "the FBI asserts that Mr. McCabe did not have an 'oversight role' in the Clinton investigation until he became the number two in command in 2016. However, the FBI's statement does not foreclose the possibility that Mr. McCabe had a non oversight role while associate deputy director. Thus, even during the time period in which his wife's political campaign received approximately half a million dollars from Gov. McAuliffe's political action committee, and over $200,000 from the Virginia Democrat Party, he may have had a role in the investigation and did not recuse himself." Also, during this time,

Senate Judiciary Committee Chairman Charles Grassley (R-IA): "While Mr. McCabe recused himself from public corruption cases in Virginia -- presumably including the reportedly ongoing investigation of Mr. McAuliffe regarding illegal campaign contributions -- he failed to recuse himself from the Clinton email investigation, despite the appearance of conflict created by his wife's campaign accepting $700,000 from a close Clinton associate during the investigation," Grassley wrote in seeking the IG probe. (In another source: In his letter, Grassley noted the Journal reported "98% of the Gov. McAuliffe related donations to his wife came after the FBI launched the investigation." [ix]

Former Supervisory Special Agent Robyn Gritz, filed a complaint alleging McCabe violated the Hatch Act. She included as evidence social media photos showing McCabe wearing a T-shirt supporting his wife's campaign during a public event and then posting a photo on social media urging voters to join him in voting for his wife. Other social media photos in the complaint showed McCabe's minor daughter campaigning with her mother, wearing an FBI shirt, and McCabe voting with his wife at a polling station. [x]

Devlin Barrett wrote a Wall Street Journal article on October 24, 2016 about McAuliffe funding Jill McCabe's campaign. McCabe recused himself from the Clinton email investigation one week prior to the presidential election - after the investigation had already ended with Clinton's exoneration.

McCabe should have recused himself throughout the investigation.

McCabe was eventually fired in March 2018 for committing three violations of the FBI's ethics code. The violations were lack of candor under oath, lack of candor when not under oath, and the improper disclosure of non-public information to the media about the FBI investigation into the Clinton Foundation.

Two extremely biased FBI officials worked on the Clinton email investigation and Trump/Russia investigation

Peter Strzok was the deputy assistant director of the FBI's counterintelligence division. He was the FBI agent in charge of the Clinton email investigation and the Trump/Russia investigation. Lisa Page was the Counsel to Andrew McCabe. Strzok and Page were lovers and exchanged 50,000 text messages throughout the presidential election and first year of the Trump administration. Strzok and Page's texts displayed contempt for Donald Trump and desperately wanted Clinton to win the presidency. In one text, when Page asked if Trump would ever become president, Strzok replied, "No. No he won't. We'll stop it." A sampling of their texts demonstrates extreme bias:

Page - God Trump is loathsome human.

Strzok – Yet he many win.

Strzok – Good for Hillary.

Page – It is.

Strzok – Omg he's an idiot.

Page – He's awful

Strzok – God Hillary should win. 100,000,000-0.

Page – I know

Page – Also did you hear him make a comment about the size of his d**k earlier? This man cannot be president.

Strzok – Yes I did. In relation to this size of his hand. All the "Lil Marco" blah blah blah

Page – I can not believe Donald Trump is likely to be an actual, serious candidate for president.

Texting on July 19, 2016 about the Republican National Convention:

Page – And wow, Donald Trump is in an enormous do*che.

Strzok – Hi. How was Trump, other than a do*che?

07/26/2016, Strzok – And hey. Congrats on a woman nominated for President in a major party! About damn time!

07/27/2016, Page – Yeah, it is pretty cool. She just has to win now.

08/06/2016, Page – Jesus. You should read this. And Trump should go f himself.

08/09/2016, Page – He's not ever going to become president, right? Right?!

08/26/2016, Strzok – Just went to a southern Virginia Walmart. I could SMELL the Trump support...

Strzok texted in August 2016 "I want to believe the path you [Page] threw out for consideration in Andy's [McCabe] office - that there's no way he [Trump] gets elected - but I'm afraid we can't take that risk," "It's like an insurance policy in the unlikely event you die before you're 40."

10/20/2016, Strzok – I am riled up. Trump is a f***ing idiot, is unable to provide a coherent answer.

2. The FBI & DOJ Conducted a Sham Clinton Email Investigation

Comey, Lynch, Strzok, McCabe, Page and the other conspirators corruptly and criminally acted on their biases to protect Hillary Clinton and her associates from prosecution in the email investigation by shielding them in the following ways:

The DOJ/FBI did not use a grand jury

All major criminal investigations use a grand jury. The conspirators did not open a grand jury investigation in order to control the process and outcome. McCarthy wrote "it was Lynch's Justice Department that: refused to authorize use of the grand jury to further the Clinton e-mails investigation, thus depriving the FBI of the power to compel testimony and the production of evidence by subpoena."[xi] "Comey is like a guy who ties his own hands behind his back and then says he was powerless to defend himself.... in this investigation — unlike every other major criminal investigation in which the government tries to make the case rather than not make the case — the Justice Department declined to convene a grand jury. Regarding this highly irregular dereliction, there appears to have been no FBI pushback."[xii] McCarthy further explained that "(with exceptions not relevant to this discussion) the convening of a grand jury is a necessary precondition to the filing of a felony indictment."[xiii] Comey and Lynch avoided this prospect and kept the indictment decision for themselves by not using a grand jury.

The DOJ/FBI illegally allowed Clinton's top aides to represent her as attorneys

The DOJ and FBI illegally and unethically allowed top Clinton's aides Cheryl Mills and Heather Samuelson, both suspects in the investigation, to represent Clinton as attorneys.

McCarthy describes this as "a scheme to obstruct the investigation by concealing potentially incriminating evidence under bogus assertions of attorney-client privilege.... In a nutshell, the Federal Bureau of Investigation and the Justice Department permitted Hillary Clinton's aide Cheryl Mills — the subject of a criminal investigation, who had been given immunity from prosecution despite strong evidence that she had lied to investigators — to participate as a lawyer for Clinton, the principal subject of the same criminal investigation. This unheard-of accommodation was made in violation not only of rudimentary investigative protocols and attorney-ethics rules, but also of the federal criminal law." Mills and Samuelson used Clinton's email system when employed by Clinton at the State Department, so they broke federal law by acting as Clinton's private lawyers in order to influence the email investigation.[xiv][xv][xvi]

The DOJ/FBI allowed a false attorney-client privilege between Clinton and aides

The DOJ and FBI allowed Mills to refuse to answer questions about Clinton's private email server when Mills invoked a false attorney-client privilege. As Coffin notes "Mills' knowledge of facts learned while serving in a non-legal capacity at the State Department could not possibly be protected by an attorney-client privilege."[xvii]

The DOJ invoked false attorney-client privilege in advocating for Clinton's aides

In a shockingly blatant effort to impede the investigation, a Department of Justice (DOJ) attorney invoked the Clinton/Mills false attorney-client privilege to protect Mills during a deposition from answering questions about her knowledge of the email setup. Coffin writes that Mill's "communications with Clinton and other material witnesses also were actively protected by the Department of Justice throughout the criminal and civil investigations."[xviii]

The DOJ/FBI gave unnecessary immunity deals to protect Clinton's aides

Comey and Lynch gave Mills and Samuelson immunity deals to obtain their laptop computers. Comey told Rep. Ben Sasse (R-NB) that Mills needed the immunity "because without it, Mills would have fought investigators tooth and nail in an effort to withhold her computer." Comey and Lynch could have compelled them to surrender their computers through a subpoena or warrant. McCarthy said "the immunity grant was wholly unnecessary" and was done "because the Justice Department had no intention of prosecuting them."[xix] Comey had written a draft exoneration letter before 17 witnesses testified and prior to the immunity deals.

The DOJ/FBI granted unnecessary immunity to hide the destruction of subpoenaed emails

The DOJ and FBI granted immunity to Paul Combetta for nothing significant in return. Combetta used BleachBit to delete Clinton's emails from her private server on March 31, 2015, after he had a conference call with Clinton's staff on March 25. He had another conference call with Mills and Clinton's attorney on March 31st.[xx] On March 3, congressional "preservation letters" were sent to Clinton and to her email hosting company ordering them to protect, and not to destroy any records, and congressional subpoenas were issued on March 4, 2015 to preserve all emails on the personal server. Combetta's email destruction therefore was obstruction of justice, and any involvement of Clinton's aides and attorneys would amount to a conspiracy to obstruct justice. Combetta testified that he "was aware of the existence of the preservation request and the fact that it meant he should not disturb Clinton's e-mail data on the PRN server."

The DOJ/FBI conspired with defense attorneys to hide obstruction of justice evidence

The DOJ and FBI agreed to limit the search of Mills and Samuelson's laptops to no later than January 31, 2015. This prevented the FBI from discovering obstruction of justice evidence on the laptops related to the March 31, 2015 destruction of Clinton's emails. Strong evidence indicates Clinton's aides, lawyers, and a vendor worked together in March 2015 to delete more than 30,000 emails under subpoena.

On March 2, 2015, the New York Times revealed that Clinton used a personal email account as secretary of state. The Benghazi Committee did not know this, and on March 3, they sent "preservation letters" to Clinton and to her email hosting company ordering them to protect, and not to destroy, any records. On March 3, John Podesta sent an email to Mills stating "On another matter....and not to sound like Lanny, but we are going to have to dump all those emails so better to do so sooner than later."[xxi]

Mills sent Combetta an email on March 9 telling him about the Benghazi committee's preservation request. Combetta told the FBI that he did not remember it, then later told them he received it and understood that he should not delete the emails. The DOJ/FBI did not prosecute Combetta for this perjury. The FBI found a March 31 work ticket that referenced a conference call between Combetta, Mills and David Kendall, Clinton's attorney. Combetta was told not to discuss the work ticket because it was protected by attorney-client privilege.[xxii]

The Department of Justice (DOJ) obstructed justice by agreeing to terms requested by Mills and Samuelson's attorney, Beth Wilkinson, in two letters dated June 10, 2016 after the DOJ learned Combetta deleted the emails. The DOJ agreement restricted the FBI review of Clinton email archives to those dated between June 1, 2014, and Feb. 1, 2015.[xxiii]

McCarthy said "Combetta was obviously in contact with Mills and other Clinton team members from early February through the end of March 2015 — the period the FBI was barred from examining under the computer side deal." "When asked during last week's House hearing how he could believe Combetta, FBI director Comey pointedly replied that it was not a matter of believing Combetta; the problem was not having evidence that disproved Combetta's story. So, if the FBI was interested in finding such evidence, why would it agree (or at least abide the Justice Department's agreement) to an arrangement under which it was denied the ability to review documents on Mills' computer from March 2015, when Combetta, while in frequent communication with Mills, destroyed the e-mails?"[xxiv]

The DOJ/FBI conspired with defense attorneys to destroy evidence

The DOJ and FBI agreed to destroy Mills' and Samuelson's computers after the FBI concluded its search. McCarthy wrote "Finally (at least until the next shoe drops), why would the FBI agree to destroy the computers after conducting the (apparently highly limited) examination that was agreed to? The Federal Rules of Criminal Procedure explicitly provide (in Rule 41) that, when the government has taken custody of property for investigative purposes, a person who is somehow aggrieved by this deprivation may petition the court for the return of that property. .... it is always possible that new information could emerge that would revive the case. Under such circumstances, the computers could have had renewed relevance and their destruction would have been highly problematic. How would it help the FBI to have had a hand in that?"[xxv]

The FBI/DOJ granted unnecessary immunity to subjects of the investigation

The DOJ and FBI granted Bryan Pagliano, who set up Clinton's server, John Bentel, Huma Abedin, Samuelson, Mills, and Combetta immunity even though there was no grand jury. Judge Andrew Napolitano said this is "inexplicable... because immunity is only supposed to be given by a federal judge to induce testimony before a grand jury or a trial jury. The FBI didn't present a single piece of evidence to a grand jury, they didn't get a subpoena from a grand jury, they didn't get a search warrant from a judge."[xxvi]   McCarthy said that "The main subjects of the investigation could easily have been compelled to provide evidence and testimony — which is what investigators do when they are trying to make a case rather than not make a case. There was no valid reason for prosecutors to treat criminal suspects to an immunity spree. Mrs. Clinton's friends at the Justice Department chose not to subpoena Mrs. Clinton's friends from the State Department and the campaign. The decision not to employ regular criminal procedures — i.e., the decision not to treat the case like other criminal cases — was quite deliberate."[xxvii]

U.S. District Court Judge Royce Lamberth said he was "shocked" and "dumbfounded" when he learned that FBI had granted immunity to former Clinton chief of staff Cheryl Mills during its investigation into the use of Clinton's server according to a court transcript of his remarks:[xxviii]

"I had myself found that Cheryl Mills had committed perjury and lied under oath in a published opinion I had issued in a Judicial Watch case where I found her unworthy of belief, and I was quite shocked to find out she had been given immunity in — by the Justice Department in the Hillary Clinton email case."

The FBI/DOJ did not investigate subjects with classified information on computers

The DOJ and FBI did not investigate Mills, Samuelson, or Clinton's lawyers for illegally having classified information on their computers. Comey said Mills was a "subject" of the investigation because of her computer. He said Mills and Samuelson had classified emails on their computers, but did not know if this was a crime without knowing the circumstances. Obviously, Comey had control over investigating the "circumstances" to determine if it was a crime.[xxix]

The FBI/DOJ permitted subjects of the investigation to attend Clinton's interview

The DOJ and FBI allowed Mills and Samuelson, both subjects of the investigation, to attend Clinton's interview. Comey said that he never heard of this before. McCarthy writes "Comey kept stressing that Mrs. Clinton's interview was 'voluntary' — contending that since she was not required to submit to it, she could impose any conditions on her agreement to do so. That is nonsense. The interview was voluntary on both sides. If Clinton declined to submit to an FBI interview unless Mills (or the similarly situated lawyer Heather Samuelson) was permitted to be present, the investigators could simply have handed her a grand-jury subpoena. They could then have politely directed her to a chamber where she would be compelled to answer questions — under oath and all by her lonesome, without any of her lawyer legion in attendance." McCarthy further explains that Comey "had to know that allowing Mills to be present at the interview could have jeopardized any eventual prosecution of Clinton. In such a prosecution, Mills would have been a key witness. But Clinton's lawyers would have claimed that the FBI let Mills sit in on Clinton's interview to help Mills get her story straight. They would have accused prosecutors of exploiting Mills, a former member of the Clinton legal team, to pry into Clinton's privileged strategic communications with her other lawyers."xxx

The Department of Justice's Inspector General (IG), Michael Horowitz, noted in a report that it was "inconsistent with typical investigative strategy" for the FBI to allow Mills to sit in during the agency's interview of Clinton during the email probe, given that classified information traveled through Mills' personal email account. "[T]here are serious potential ramifications when one witness attends another witness' interview."xxxi

The FBI/DOJ did not investigate or acquire evidence from Clinton's top aide

The FBI and DOJ did not acquire and examine Huma Abedin's personal computer and electronic devices during the investigation and did not investigate her as a subject. A DOJ Office of the Inspector General (OIG) report noted that Abedin was "the only State Department employee, besides Clinton, with an account on the clintonemail.com domain on Clinton's server." Witnesses interviewed by the OIG said that "there was a flaw in the culling process, which resulted in the exclusion of most of Abedin's clintonemail.com emails from the State Department production." The OIG's report noted that the FBI obtained from other sources classified email exchanges between Clinton and Abedin that were missing from the 30,490 emails turned over to the State Department by Clinton's attorneys.xxxii The FBI examined the 30,490 emails, but should have considered Abedin a subject of the investigation to find the missing emails between Clinton and Abedin.

On September 22, CNN reported federal prosecutors in the Southern District of New York (SDNY) were investigating Abedin's husband, Anthony Weiner, for sexting with a minor. Wiener, who does not have a security clearance, shared a computer with Abedin. Upon examining the computer, the FBI's New York Office discovered about 700,000 Clinton emails, including classified emails. To put this in context, Clinton's attorneys and aides reviewed more than 60,000 emails on Clinton's private server to determine the work-related and non-work-related emails. Clinton's attorneys and aides instructed the IT technician, Paul Combetta, to delete 33,000 emails that they assessed were not work-related even though they were under a preservation subpoena. This left 30,490 emails for the FBI to examine compared to 694,000 emails found on Weiner and Abedin's computer.

The FBI/DOJ did not investigate the theft of Clinton's emails by a foreign entity

Rep. Louie Gohmert, R-Texas, said a Chinese state-owned company located in Washington D.C. reportedly hacked former Secretary of State Hillary Clinton's email server, then inserted code that forwarded them a copy of virtually every email she sent or received after that. When the Intelligence Community Inspector General (ICIG) discovered this in 2015, they informed FBI agents, including Peter Strzok. Gohmert said there was no sign that Strzok and the FBI had taken any action when informed by the ICIG, and no indication that they even informed Clinton.

Strzok said in a May 2016 email "we know foreign actors obtained access" to some Clinton emails, including at least one "secret" message "via compromises of the private email accounts" of Clinton staffers.

The DOJ and FBI did not investigate emails between Clinton and President Obama

President Obama and Secretary Clinton exchanged emails over her private server. Andrew McCarthy writes that the DOJ and FBI never intended to indict Clinton because Obama would also be implicated:

"*Obama, using a pseudonymous email account, had repeatedly communicated with Secretary Clinton over her private, non-secure email account. These emails must have involved some classified information, given the nature of consultations between presidents and secretaries of state, the broad outlines of Obama's own executive order defining classified intelligence (see EO 13526, section 1.4), and the fact that the Obama administration adamantly refused to disclose the Clinton–Obama emails. If classified information was mishandled, it was necessarily mishandled on both ends of these email exchanges.*

If Clinton had been charged, Obama's culpable involvement would have been patent. In any prosecution of Clinton, the Clinton–Obama emails would have been in the spotlight. For the prosecution, they would be more proof of willful (or, if you prefer, grossly negligent) mishandling of intelligence. More significantly, for Clinton's defense, they would show that Obama was complicit in Clinton's conduct yet faced no criminal charges.

On March 4, just after the New York Times broke the news about Clinton's email practices [over her private server] at the State Department, John Podesta (a top Obama adviser and Clinton's campaign chairman) emailed Cheryl Mills (Clinton's confidant and top aide in the Obama State Department) to suggest that Clinton's "emails to and from potus" should be "held" — i.e., not disclosed — because "that's the heart of his exec privilege." At the time, the House committee investigating the Benghazi jihadist attack was pressing for production of Clinton's emails.

As his counselors grappled with how to address his own involvement in Clinton's misconduct, Obama deceptively told CBS News in a March 7 interview that he had found out about Clinton's use of personal email to conduct State Department business "the same time everybody else learned it through news reports." Perhaps he was confident that, because he had used an alias in communicating with Clinton, his emails to and from her — estimated to number around 20 — would remain undiscovered.

His and Clinton's advisers were not so confident. Right after the interview aired, Clinton campaign secretary Josh Scherwin emailed Jennifer Palmieri and other senior campaign staffers, stating: "Jen you probably have more on this but it looks like POTUS just said he found out HRC was using her personal email when he saw it on the news."

Scherwin's alert was forwarded to Mills. Shortly afterwards, an agitated Mills emailed Podesta: "We need to clean this up — he has emails from her — they do not say state.gov." (That is, Obama had emails from Clinton, which he had to know were from a private account since her address did not end in "@state.gov" as State Department emails do.)

So how did Obama and his helpers "clean this up"?

Obama had his email communications with Clinton sealed. He did this by invoking a dubious presidential-records privilege. The White House insisted that the matter had nothing to do with the contents of the emails, of course; rather, it was intended to vindicate the principle of confidentiality in presidential communications with close advisers. With the media content to play along, this had a twofold benefit: Obama was able (1) to sidestep disclosure without acknowledging that the emails contained classified information, and (2) to avoid using the term "executive privilege" — with all its dark Watergate connotations — even though that was precisely what he was invoking.

Note that claims of executive privilege must yield to demands for disclosure of relevant evidence in criminal *prosecutions. But of course, that's not a problem if there will be no prosecution.*

All cleaned up: no indictment, meaning no prosecution, meaning no disclosure of Clinton–Obama emails. It all worked like a charm . . . except the part where Mrs. Clinton wins the presidency and the problem is never spoken of again."[xxxiii]

Comey never named a target or subject in the Clinton email investigation

In Senate testimony, the DOJ's Inspector General, Michael Horowitz, said "Nobody was listed as a subject of this [Clinton email] investigation at any point in time," adding this was "surprising" for a criminal probe. The fact that Comey did not name Clinton or anyone else as a subject makes perfect sense because the FBI did not use a grand jury, granted unnecessary immunity to the major witnesses, did not investigate the emails on Abedin's computer, obstructed justice, permitted false attorney-client privilege, etc. in order to protect everyone involved with Clinton's private server used for her State Department email communications. In this way, the DOJ and FBI obtained the silence of witnesses who could testify against Clinton.

Comey publicly called the investigation a "matter" to help Clinton's campaign

Comey publicly called the FBI's email investigation a "matter," coinciding with the Clinton campaign's mischaracterization. Lynch ordered Comey to do this.

Summary

Comey, Lynch, McCabe, Strzok and the other conspirators conducted a sham investigation aimed at protecting Hillary

Clinton from indictment. In doing so, the DOJ and FBI violated their own investigation standards and protocols, and even committed felonies. For example, the FBI and DOJ:

- did not convene a grand jury in order to impede their investigation (e.g., a grand jury can compel testimony, issue subpoenas) and assure Clinton would not be indicted by a grand jury
- granted unnecessary immunity to witnesses who perjured themselves
- allowed Clinton's aides to use a false attorney-client privilege and to represent Clinton as attorneys
- excluded emails from President Obama and Huma Abedin from the investigation
- Ignored felonies such as perjury and obstruction of justice
- conspired with defense attorneys to hide obstruction of justice by Clinton's attorneys and top aides

3. The FBI and DOJ Planned the Wrongful Exoneration of Clinton

"The most sacred of the duties of a government [is] to do equal and impartial justice to all its citizens." --Thomas Jefferson

Comey drafted an exoneration statement two months before the investigation ended

President Obama publicly stated on April 10, 2016, that Clinton showed "carelessness" in her email system, but said she "would never intentionally put America in any kind of jeopardy." He said that some classified information is "basically stuff that you could get in open-source" and "I continue to believe that she has not jeopardized America's national security."

On May 2, 2016, Comey emailed a draft statement exonerating Hillary Clinton in the email investigation requesting comments. He sent it to McCabe, general counsel James Baker, and chief of staff and senior counselor James Rybicki, and they forwarded it to additional people, including Strzok. The draft reflected all of the points President Obama made three weeks previously.

The Office of Special Counsel (OSC) began investigating whether Comey's actions in the Clinton email investigation violated the Hatch Act, which prohibits government employees from using their official position to influence an election. In the course of that investigation, OSC interviewed two FBI officials close to Comey: James Rybicki, Comey's Chief of Staff, and Trisha Anderson, the Principal Deputy General Counsel of National Security and Cyberlaw. The OSC attorneys questioned Rybicki and Anderson, about Comey's July 5, 2016, statement exonerating Secretary Clinton. Rybicki's answer indicates Comey had predetermined an exoneration outcome two months before the investigation's conclusion:

- OSC Question: And so at that point in time, whether it was April or early May, the team hadn't yet interviewed Secretary Clinton –
- Rybicki Answer: Correct.
- OSC Question: – but was there – I guess, **based on what you're saying, it sounds like there was an idea of where the outcome of the investigation was going to go**?
- Rybicki Answer: **Sure. There was a – right, there was – based on – [redacted section].**

Comey prepared the draft before 17 key witnesses, including Clinton, Cheryl Mills, Heather Samuelson, and Paul Combetta, were even interviewed, and before the DOJ entered into immunity agreements with Mills and Samuelson. In granting immunity, the DOJ agreed to a very limited review of Clinton's emails and to destroy their laptops after review. Comey stated "By her [Clinton's] account, there were about sixty thousand total emails on her personal server as of late 2014, when State asked for work emails. The secretary's personal lawyers reviewed those emails, producing about half of them and deleting the rest." Mills and Samuelson helped decide which Clinton emails were destroyed, totaling 30,000, before turning over the remaining 30,000 to the State Department. How could the FBI conclude "where the outcome of the investigation was going to go" without examining the remaining 30,000 emails or interviewing most of the key witnesses? The answer is that the FBI and DOJ planned from the beginning to exonerate Clinton. To accomplish this, they did not use a grand jury and hid evidence of Clinton wrongdoing in the sham investigation rather than search for it, and they drastically revised Comey's original draft exoneration statement, not based on new evidence, but to support their preordained conclusion.

The FBI reviewers made many significant changes in Comey's original draft statement by removing five separate references to terms like "grossly negligent" and to delete mention of evidence supporting felony and misdemeanor violations. As explained in the following examples, the only reason for the revisions to Comey's draft statement was to eliminate or obscure facts that did not support the exoneration decision.

The June 30, 2016 draft version stated "She [Clinton] also used her personal email extensively while outside the United States, including from the territory of sophisticated adversaries. That use included an email exchange with the President while Secretary Clinton was on the territory of such an adversary." This referred to Clinton's email correspondence with then-President Obama during a 2012 visit to Russia. Rybicki changed "President" to "senior government official." The change itself was problematic because the media would try to identify the "senior government official," so the final version simply stated "She also used her personal e-mail extensively while outside the United States, including sending and receiving work-related e-mails in the territory of sophisticated adversaries." **(The purpose of the changes was to hide the fact that Clinton and Obama unlawfully exchanged classified emails over Clinton's unsecure system, and that Obama lied on CBS news by saying that he only learned about Clinton's private email server when it had been reported in the news.)**

The original draft stated "There is evidence to support a conclusion that Secretary Clinton, and others, used the email server in a manner that was grossly negligent with respect to the handling of classified information." "Gross negligence" is the statutory term in Section 793(f) of the federal penal code making mishandling of classified information a felony. Peter Strzok changed "grossly negligent" to "extremely careless." **(The purpose of Strzok's change was obviously to disconnect**

Clinton's mishandling of classified information from the word "gross negligence" in the applicable federal penal code.)

The original draft stated "Although there is evidence of potential violations of the statute proscribing gross negligence in the handling of classified information and of the statute proscribing misdemeanor mishandling, my judgment is that no reasonable prosecutor would bring such a case." **(The purpose of replacing references to "gross negligence" and "misdemeanor mishandling" with the generic "potential violations of the statutes" is to cast doubt on Clinton's culpability.)**

The original statement concluded that it was "reasonably likely" that Clinton's nonsecure private server was accessed or hacked by hostile actors, though there was no evidence to prove it. The reviewers changed "reasonably likely" to the much weaker "possible." This is very deceptive, if not an outright lie, because, as described in the last chapter, the Intelligence Community Inspector General (ICIG) told FBI agents, including Peter Strzok, in 2015 that a foreign entity gained access to virtually all of Clinton's emails, but the FBI reportedly did not investigate. Strzok said in a May 2016 email "we know foreign actors obtained access" to some Clinton emails, including at least one "secret" message "via compromises of the private email accounts" of Clinton staffers. **(The purpose of the revision was to deceptively downplay the possibility that Clinton's server was hacked.)**

One edit that concerned Senator Ron Johnson was a decision to delete from Comey's original draft a reference to the FBI working on a joint assessment with the intelligence community about possible national security damage from the classified information that passed through Clinton's non-secure email servers. Johnson wants to know whether other intelligence agencies had assessments of damage that differed or were more negative than that of the FBI. **(The purpose of the revision** was to deceptively downplay the possibility that Clinton's server was hacked.)

Loretta Lynch secretly met with Bill Clinton five days before Hillary's interview

Lynch improperly held a secret meeting with Bill Clinton on June 27, 2016 in Lynch's parked plane at Sky Harbor International Airport in Phoenix, Arizona. This was five days before Hillary Clinton's interview with the FBI.

Clinton and Lynch's planes were on an out-of-the-way tarmac, where their security details arranged for both their planes to be parked. The fact that the FBI said "No photos. No pictures. No cellphones." of Lynch and Bill Clinton on the tarmac indicates Lynch obviously knew it was wrong and was trying to keep the meeting secret.xxxiv However, Christopher Sign, an Arizona reporter received a tip about Clinton and Lynch meeting in Lynch's plane from two sources. Sign asked Lynch about it at a news conference. Lynch told Sign that she and the former president only discussed grandchildren, and some golf Clinton played in Phoenix.

Considering the many obstruction of justice measures she oversaw to exonerate Clinton as summarized in the previous chapter, it is highly plausible that Lynch gave advice to Bill Clinton on how Hillary should best answer the FBI's questions in her imminent interview in order to support the preordained decision not to indict her due to lack of intent. Lynch did not recuse herself after the improper secret meeting.

Comey improperly made and announced the decision to exonerate Clinton

The Attorney General is responsible for prosecutorial decisions, not the FBI. The FBI interviewed Clinton on July 2, and Comey held a press conference on July 5 to recommend against indicting Clinton due to lack of intent. In his May 3, 2017 testimony before the Senate judiciary committee, Comey said the Lynch–Clinton tarmac meeting was the "capper" among "a number of things" that had caused him to determine that Department of Justice leadership "could not credibly complete the investigation and decline prosecution without grievous damage to the American people's confidence in the justice system."

After the tarmac meeting, Loretta Lynch said she would accept whatever recommendations career prosecutors and the FBI director made about whether to bring charges in the case. However, Page and Strzok texts on July 1, 2016, after the tarmac meeting, indicate Lynch already knew the FBI planned to exonerate Hillary Clinton:

- Strzok – Holy cow....nyt breaking Apuozzo, Lync [sic] will accept whatever rec and career prosecutors make. No political appointee input.
- Strzok – Lynch. Timing not great, but whatever. Wonder if that's why the coordination language added.
- Page – No way. This is a purposeful leak following the airplane snafu.
- Strzok – Timing looks like hell. Will appear to be choreographed. All major news networks literally leading with "AG to accept FBI D's recommendation."
- Page – Yeah, that is awful timing. Nothing we can do about it.
- Strzok – What I meant was, did DOJ tell us yesterday they were doing this, so D added that language.
- Strzok – Yep. I told Bill the same thing. Delaying just makes it worse.
- Page – And yes. I think we had some warning of it. I know they sent some statement to rybicki, bc he called andy.
- Page – And yeah, **it's a real profile in couragw [sic], since she knows no charges will be brought.**

The OSC attorneys questioned Trisha Anderson, the FBI's Principal Deputy General Counsel of National Security and Cyberlaw, about Comey's July 5, 2016, statement exonerating Secretary Clinton. Anderson indicated that Comey intended to make a public statement about Clinton's exoneration since early May 2016:

- OSC Question: **When did you first learn that Director Comey was planning to make some kind of public statement about the outcome of the Clinton email investigation?**
- Anderson's answer: The idea, I'm not entirely sure exactly when the idea of the public statement um first emerged. Um it was, I just, I can't put a precise timeframe on it um but [redaction]. And then **I believe it was in early May of 2016 that the Director himself wrote a draft of that statement.**

According to Lisa Page's text on July 1st, Lynch knew no charges would be brought. Comey had planned a public announcement to exonerate Clinton two months before the investigation ended. Although it was the DOJ's responsibility, Comey made the exoneration announcement on July 5 under the ruse of protecting the credibility of the FBI and Justice Department. Contrary to Lisa Page's text, Comey said DOJ officials "do not know what I am about to say."

Rod Rosenstein wrote in his letter of May 9, 2017 that Comey "was wrong to usurp the Attorney General's authority on July 5, 2016, and announce his conclusion that the case should be closed without prosecution. It is not the function of the Director to make such an announcement."

The DOJ's Office of Inspector General (OIG) issued a report on June 14, 2018 titled "A Review of Various Actions by the Federal Bureau of Investigation and Department of Justice in Advance of the 2016 Election." The OIG's report sharply criticizes Comey for his public statements about the Clinton email case, including his July 5, 2016 public announcement that he wouldn't recommend any charges, and then his October 2016 decision to tell Congress about the new Clinton emails found. The OIG concluded that Comey "usurped the authority of the Attorney General," "chose to deviate" from established procedures, and engaged "in his own subjective, ad hoc decisionmaking."xxxv

The FBI interviewed Clinton on July 2, and Comey wrongfully held a press conference on July 5 to recommend against indicting Clinton due to lack of intent. As described below, Comey made false statements, omitted incriminating material evidence, excluded applicable law, and failed to make recommendations for other subjects of the investigation.

Comey falsely stated no evidence of intentional email deletion

Comey: Comey said "we found no evidence that any of the additional work-related e-mails were intentionally deleted in an effort to conceal them."

Comments: In fact, strong evidence indicates Clinton's aides, lawyers, and a vendor worked together in March 2015 to delete more than 30,000 emails under subpoena. The Department of Justice (DOJ) obstructed justice by agreeing to terms requested by Mills and Samuelson's attorney, Beth Wilkinson, in two letters dated June 10, 2016 after the DOJ learned Combetta deleted the emails. The DOJ agreement restricted the FBI review of Clinton email archives to those dated between June 1, 2014, and Feb. 1, 2015. The letters also "memorialized" the FBI's agreement allowing the Clinton aides to destroy their records and laptops. Congressional leaders questioned "why the FBI would enter into such a limited evidentiary scope of review with respect to the laptops." The congressmen wrote "These limitations would necessarily have excluded, for example, any emails from Cheryl Mills to Paul

Combetta in late 2014 or early 2015 directing the destruction or concealment of federal records." and "Similarly, these limitations would have excluded any email sent or received by Secretary Clinton if it was not sent or received by one of the four email addresses listed."[xxxvi]

Also, Mills and Samuelson received legal protection for their destruction of emails in a "transactional immunity" agreement.[xxxvii] McCarthy wrote "Mills and Samuelson were given immunity because Justice did not want to commence a grand-jury investigation, which would have empowered investigators to compel production of the laptops by simply issuing subpoenas. Justice did not want to use the grand jury because doing so would have signaled that the case was headed toward indictment. The Obama Justice Department was never going to indict Hillary Clinton, and was determined not to damage her presidential campaign by taking steps suggestive of a possible indictment."[xxxviii] The DOJ and FBI also took other measures as described previously to obstruct the investigation into deletion of emails. Comey had drafted an exoneration letter several months prior to his press conference, and before the FBI had interviewed 17 witnesses or granted this immunity.

Comey falsely stated no evidence of intentional misconduct in providing emails

Comey: Clinton's lawyers and aides "relied on header information and used search terms to try to find all work-related e-mails among the reportedly more than 60,000 total e-mails.... It is highly likely their search terms missed some work-related e-mails" "It could also be that some of the additional work-related e-mails we recovered were among those deleted as "personal" by Secretary Clinton's lawyers when they reviewed and sorted her e-mails for production in 2014." "we believe our investigation has been sufficient to give us reasonable confidence there was no intentional misconduct in connection with that sorting effort."

Comments: Comey falsely stated no intentional misconduct. Clinton illegally sent her emails, including top-secret SAP intelligence, to her lawyers and aides' computers, so they could determine personal versus work-related ones. She should have sent all emails to the State Department. As McCarthy notes "there is no lawyer exception to the federal criminal law that prohibits the transmission of classified information to unauthorized persons."[xxxix] Coffin wrote "her e-mails were at no time during her tenure in office subject to the Federal Records Act. Setting up a shadow e-mail server to conduct all official business as secretary of state is an action plainly undertaken for the purpose of evading federal-records laws. And Clinton was successful at that, avoiding congressional and citizen demands for review of her record during her term in office."[xl] McCarthy also notes that "The classified information on Mills' private laptop was excused, according to Comey's testimony, because it merely duplicated (for purposes of sorting through e-mails) what was on Clinton's server — a rationalization that, even if true, is not a defense to recklessly storing classified information on a non-secure computer."[xli]

Comey failed to address felony violations of other investigation subjects

Comey: Comey did not make recommendations for other subjects of the investigation: Abedin, Mills, Samuelson, Pagliano, Combetta, and Bentel.

Comments: All of these subjects either helped Clinton set up a personal server in violation of the Espionage Act (section 793 of the federal penal code) and/or had government records, including classified emails, on their personal computers in violation of the Espionage Act, or were involved in the destruction of emails under subpoena, or, in the case of Bentel, knowingly ignored the violation. Combetta, Mills, and Samuelson perjured themselves in the FBI interviews. For example, Peter Strzok interviewed top Clinton aides Huma

Abedin and Cheryl Mills. Strzok's notes said Mills and Samuelson denied knowing about Clinton's private server, but Strzok knew this was a lie because he had e-mails in which they discussed Clinton's server.

Comey failed to consider felony violation of other applicable laws

Comey: Comey did not address the federal embezzlement statute (Section 641 of Title 18, U.S. Code) that states that someone who "without authority . . .conveys or disposes of any record . . . of the United States or of any department or agency thereof" commits a criminal offense.

Comments: This statute, applicable to Clinton and her employees, covers all government records, not just classified records, and carries a penalty of up to ten years' imprisonment for each instance of theft. McCarthy states that this statute is "very easy to prove" and that Clinton "took these government records with her: She didn't tell anyone she had them, and she converted them to her own use — preventing the government from complying with lawful Freedom of Information Act disclosure demands, congressional inquiries, and government-disclosure obligations in judicial proceedings, as well as undermining the State Department's reliance on the completeness of its recordkeeping in performing its crucial functions."[xlii]

Comey presented very strong evidence and then falsely said no case to indict

Comey: "Although we did not find clear evidence that Secretary Clinton or her colleagues intended to violate laws governing the handling of classified information, there is evidence that they were extremely careless in their handling of very sensitive, highly classified information.... There is evidence to support a conclusion that any reasonable person in Secretary

Clinton's position, or in the position of those government employees with whom she was corresponding about these matters, should have known that an unclassified system was no place for that conversation...., our judgment is that no reasonable prosecutor would bring such a case... we are expressing to Justice our view that no charges are appropriate in this case."

On May 3, 2017, Comey testified before the Senate Judiciary Committee that declining to bring charges against Hillary Clinton for mishandling classified information was the right call because proof of intent was lacking.

Comments: Coffin writes "Comey found all of the factual predicates for this statute satisfied... Gross negligence and 'extreme carelessness' are interchangeable terms, something Comey obviously knows. The result of that extreme carelessness was to substantially raise the risk of exposing our national secrets to foreign powers. Yet he found no violation of 18 U.S.C. § 793(f). Why? According to Comey, all the past cases in which similar transgressions were prosecuted involved 'some combination of clearly intentional or willful mishandling of classified information or vast quantities of information exposed in such a way to support an inference of intentional misconduct or indications of disloyalty to the United States or an obstruction of justice.' One could seriously debate whether that standard could be met here. But even if it couldn't, Comey simply ignored — or rewrote — the plain language of § 793(f), which does not require any showing of criminal intent. There is a reason that Congress did not require a showing of intent in this provision of the Espionage Act: to protect against even inadvertent disclosure or risk of disclosure of protected information where the perpetrator demonstrated gross disregard for the national security. How Comey could conclude that 'no reasonable prosecutor' could make this case is inexplicable in light of his own words."[xliii]

McCarthy said that Comey's conclusion was "an example of how divorcing an inquiry from its context leads to indefensible results. Comey found that Hillary Clinton quite plainly mishandled classified information and exposed the United States to a heightened risk of national-security harm. But he forgot to explain the reason she did so — to keep her business, both public and private, beyond the reach of public scrutiny. She did all of this to avoid congressional oversight, FOIA requests, and accountability to the public. Comey's decision simply ensures that she was successful in avoiding that accountability."[xliv]   Jedd Babbin, a former deputy undersecretary of defense, wrote that "Hillary Clinton established a private, non-government email system for her and her aides to use with the obvious intent of preventing anyone from knowing what she did that would violate laws against public corruption (such as her dealings with foreign governments to benefit the Clinton Foundation)."[xlv]

McCarthy wrote that Comey, along with President Obama and Lynch's DOJ, claimed "there was insufficient proof of criminal intent to charge Clinton with mishandling classified information. They would have you believe that because Clinton was not motivated by a desire to harm national security she cannot have intended to violate the classified-information laws. It is sleight-of-hand.... While Clinton may not have been motivated to harm our national security, she was precisely motivated to conceal the corrupt interplay of the State Department and the Clinton Foundation. That was the real objective of the home-brew server system... and, critically, it perfectly explains why she deleted and attempted to destroy 33,000 e-mails."[xlvi] "The greatest shortcomings of Comey's public comments, though, were in his conclusion that 'no reasonable prosecutor' would bring a case for mishandling of classified information. Comey himself made the case for such a prosecution."[xlvii]

Comey lied about the FBI's review of Clinton emails on the Abedin/Weiner computer

Comey exonerated Clinton at his July 5, 2016 press conference. On September 22, CNN reported federal prosecutors in the Southern District of New York (SDNY) were investigating Abedin's husband, Anthony Weiner, for sexting with a minor. The FBI's New York Office discovered hundreds of thousands of Clinton emails on Anthony Weiner's laptop. William Sweeney, the head of the FBI's New York office, immediately informed McCabe and two FBI Executive Assistant Directors (EAD) on September 28, 2016 about the Clinton emails. One of the FBI EAD's told the OIG that there "was no doubt in my mind when we finished that conversation that [McCabe] understood the, the gravity of what the find was."

Sperry writes "McCabe told Horowitz [the OIG interviewer] that he didn't remember Sweeney briefing him about the Weiner laptop, but personal notes he took during the teleconference indicate he was briefed. Sweeney also updated McCabe in a direct call later that afternoon in which he noted there were potentially 347,000 relevant emails, and that the count was climbing. McCabe was fired earlier this year [2018] and referred to the U.S. Attorney's office in Washington, D.C., for possible criminal investigation into allegations he made false statements to federal agents working for Horowitz."[xlviii]

Strzok texted Page on September 28: "Got called up to Andy's earlier...hundreds of thousands of emails turned over by Weiner's atty to sdny, includes a ton of material from spouse. Sending team up tomorrow to review ... this will never end."

Comey tried to dissimulate his early knowledge of the Wiener/Abedin computer. He wrote in his book *A Higher Loyalty* that McCabe told him "in passing" about the emails on the Abedin/Weiner computer in early October. Comey told the OIG interviewer that McCabe informed him in early October, but allowed that it might have been late September.

Sidney Powell, a former federal prosecutor, debunks Comey's dissimulation writing "There was a flurry of activity at Headquarters. Strzok-Page texts show that Strzok, McCabe and Priestap discussed the Weiner laptop among themselves shortly after the "bomb" dropped in the video conference that day [September 28]. In fact, Priestap and Strzok were waiting outside McCabe's office to discuss it while McCabe was with Comey. There were also two calls between Comey and McCabe that evening... Remarkably, McCabe, Comey, Priestap, Strzok, and then Mary McCord at DOJ have little recollection of much of this at all. It just kind of 'fell off the radar.'" xlix

The FBI did nothing significant about the emails from the time McCabe was informed on September 28 until October 27. On October 27, McCabe, who was in London, sent an email requesting Comey to meet with the Clinton email investigation team. Comey met that day and asked the team how long it would take to review the hundreds of thousands of emails. The team said it would take many weeks, so there was no chance the review could be completed before the November 8 election. That same day Strzok and another FBI agent drafted "the first cut" of the letter notifying Congress of the decision to reopen the Clinton email investigation. After comments and revisions, James Rybicki forwarded the final draft to Comey.

On October 28, Comey sent the letter to Congress stating, "In connection with an unrelated case, the FBI has learned of the existence of emails that appear to be pertinent to the investigation... I agreed that the FBI should take appropriate investigative steps designed to allow investigators to review these emails to determine whether they contain classified information, as well as to assess their importance to our investigation."

Comey and McCabe ignored the Clinton emails on the Abedin/Wiener computer until the SDNY filed a complaint about their lack of action. Comey was also worried that FBI agents at the New York office would leak the information about the emails before the election. Rep. Devin Nunes said that in late September 2016, "good FBI agents" came to him and told him they'd found the Weiner laptop with Huma Abedin's emails with Secretary Clinton.

The OIG report states, "Additional discussions took place on October 3 and 4, 2016. However, after October 4, we found no evidence that anyone associated with the Midyear [Clinton email] investigation, including the entire leadership team at FBI Headquarters, took any action on the Weiner laptop issue until the week of October 24, and then did so only after SDNY raised concerns about the lack of action, prompting SDNY to contact the Office of the Deputy Attorney General (ODAG) on October 21 to raise concerns about the lack of action."[l]

Sperry reported that

> *During the October time frame, McCabe called Sweeney in New York and chewed him out about leaks coming out of his office. On Oct. 26, then-Attorney General Loretta Lynch was so worried about the leaks, she called McCabe and Sweeney and angrily warned them to fix them. Sweeney confirmed in an interview with the inspector general that they got "ripped by the AG on leaks." McCabe said he never heard the attorney general "use more forceful language."*[li]

Comey said one reason he felt it necessary to disclose the new batch of Clinton emails in late October was because he was concerned the information would leak out anyway. Stephanopoulos asked if he was "dealing with a rogue element of FBI agents and former FBI agents up in New York," and Comey said he knew there "appeared to be leaks about criminal investigation of the Clintons coming out of New York," and he "commissioned an investigation to find out" where the leaks were coming from. "I don't know what the investigation found," he added. The New York investigators have "a different culture" than the counterintelligence team in Washington, and "there'd been enough up there that I thought there was a pretty reasonable likelihood that it would leak."[lii] [liii]

Sidney Powell writes:

> The New York agents described it as the "entire file" of all Hillary Clinton emails from 2006 until 2016, including the BlackBerry messages that Comey himself had referred to as "the golden emails."

> As early as October 3, the Weiner case agent was "agitated" over the sound of "crickets" from headquarters and the "inaccurate" statements of Director Comey regarding the number of emails they possessed. He felt compelled to push the issue in New York, all the way up to U.S. Attorney Preet Bharara.

> The case agent himself recognized that the FBI had 10 times the number of Clinton emails that the director had reported on the record, and they had the significant BlackBerry messages as well. He could not believe someone in New York had not called him to get the hard drive.

> Extremely concerned, the case agent went to the U.S. attorneys for the Southern District of New York. An assistant United States attorney told the inspector general the agent believed "somebody was not acting appropriately, somebody was trying to bury this." The attorneys were concerned the agent might "act out."

> "Act out" means blow the whistle.

> United States Attorney Bharara was so sufficiently aware of the deafening silence from Washington that he instructed his chief counsel to document everything his office had done — "with a hundred percent accuracy." "Things seemed unusual" to him, and he wanted a record of their actions, including their recovery of more than 700,000 emails.

Bharara instructed his deputy to call the Justice Department directly in case "something had fallen through the cracks." That call made it impossible for the FBI and DOJ to continue to keep this "trove" buried. The same day, October 21, Agent Strzok wrote to Lisa Page: Toscas at DOJ was "now aware NY has hrc-huma emails via weiner invest[igation]."

Finally, five days later, on October 26, the New York case agent was able to talk directly to the mid-year agents. ("Mid-year" is the name the FBI gave the investigation.) The case agent reported again: "Based on the number of emails, we could have every email that Huma and Hillary ever sent each other."[liv]

Paul Sperry writes:

Once George Toscas, the highest-ranking Justice Department official directly involved in the Clinton email investigation, found out about the delay, he prodded headquarters to initiate a search and to inform Congress about the discovery.

By Oct. 21, Strzok had gotten the word. "Toscas now aware NY has hrc-huma emails," he texted McCabe's counsel, Lisa Page, who responded, "whatever."

Four days later, Page told Strzok - with whom she was having an affair - about the murmurs she was hearing from brass about having to tell Congress about the new emails. "F them," Strzok responded, apparently referring to oversight committee leaders on the Hill.

The next day, Oct. 26, the New York agent finally was able to brief Strzok's team directly about what he had found on the laptop. On Oct. 27, Comey gave the green light to seek a search warrant.

"This decision resulted not from the discovery of dramatic new information about the Weiner laptop, but rather as a result of inquiries from the Weiner case agent and prosecutors from the U.S. Attorney's Office [in New York]," Horowitz said in his recently released [OIG] report on the Clinton investigation.

Former prosecutors say that politics is the only explanation for why FBI brass dragged their feet for a month after the New York office alerted them about the Clinton emails.

The OIG report cited suspicions that the [FBI's] inaction "was a politically motivated attempt to bury information that could negatively impact the chances of Hillary Clinton in the election."

He [the IG] noted that on Nov. 3, after Comey notified Congress of the search, Strzok created a suspiciously inaccurate "Weiner timeline" and circulated it among the FBI leadership.

The odd document, written after the fact, made it seem as if New York hadn't fully processed the laptop until Oct. 19 and had neglected to fill headquarters in on details about what had been found until Oct. 21. In fact, New York finished processing on Oct. 4 and first began reporting back details to top FBI executives as early as Sept. 28.[lv]

Comey was literally between a rock and a hard spot after delaying one month in acting on the newly found Clinton emails. He would be accused of influencing the election if he publicly reopened the Clinton email investigation 11 days before the election to review the new emails. He would be accused of hiding new evidence in the Clinton email investigation if the New York FBI agents leaked the information to the media shortly before the election. Either way, the newly found Clinton emails would influence the election. When Comey expressed his concern about reopening the investigation, Loretta Lynch asked him

"Would they feel better if it leaked on November the 4th?" Of course, Comey, McCabe and Strzok only have themselves to blame for the situation because they should have examined Abedin's computer and electronic devices during the Clinton email investigation that ended July 5.

Comey wrote in his book *A Higher Loyalty,* that he reopened the investigation to help Clinton: "Assuming, as nearly everyone did, that Hillary Clinton would be elected president of the United States in less than two weeks, what would happen to the FBI, the Justice Department or her own presidency if it later was revealed, after the fact, that she still was the subject of an FBI investigation?"

Comey sent a letter to Congress on November 6, 2016, two days before the election, stating:

> *I write to supplement my October 28, 2016 letter that notified you the FBI would be taking additional investigative steps with respect to former Secretary of State Clinton's use of a personal email server. Since my letter, the FBI investigative team has been working around the clock to process and review a large volume of emails from a device obtained in connection with an unrelated criminal investigation. During that process, we reviewed all of the communications that were to or from Hillary Clinton while she was Secretary of State.*

> *Based on our review, we have not changed our conclusions that we expressed in July with respect to Secretary Clinton.*

Page 388 of the OIG report provides Strzok's statement that the process was greatly speeded up by eliminating duplicate emails:

> *Midyear agents obtained a copy of the Weiner laptop from NYO immediately after the search warrant was signed on October 30.*

The laptop was taken directly to Quantico where the FBI's Operational Technology Division (OTD) began processing the laptop. The Lead Analyst told us that given the volume of emails on the laptop and the difficulty with de-duplicating the emails that "at least for the first few days, the scale of what we're doing seem[ed] really, really big."

Strzok told us that OTD was able "to do some amazing things" to "rapidly de-duplicate" the emails on the laptop, which significantly lowered the number of emails that the Midyear team would have to individually review. Strzok stated that only after that technological breakthrough did he begin to think it was "possible we might wrap up before the election." (pg 388)

Page 389 of the OIG report states that duplicate emails could not be eliminated, which directly contradicts Strzok's statement on page 388:

The FBI determined that Abedin forwarded two of the confirmed classified emails to Weiner. The FBI reviewed 6,827 emails that were either to or from Clinton and assessed 3,077 of those emails to be "potentially work-related."

The FBI analysis of the review noted that "[b]ecause metadata was largely absent, the emails could not be completely, automatically de-duplicated or evaluated against prior emails recovered during the investigation" and therefore the FBI could not determine how many of the potentially work-related emails were duplicative of emails previously obtained in the Midyear investigation.

Comey falsely certified to Congress that the FBI had "reviewed all of the communications" discovered on a personal laptop used by Clinton aide, Huma Abedin, and her husband, Anthony Weiner. Comey testified to Congress that "thanks to the wizardry of our technology," the FBI was able to eliminate the vast majority of messages as "duplicates" of emails they'd previously seen. Tireless agents, he claimed, then worked "night after night after night" to scrutinize the remaining material.

In fact, only 3,077 of the 350,000 emails and 344,000 Blackberry communications were directly reviewed for classified or incriminating information. Three FBI officials completed that work in a single 12-hour spurt the day before Comey again cleared Clinton of criminal charges.[lvi]

Paul Sperry writes:

Although the FBI's New York office first pointed headquarters to the large new volume of evidence on Sept. 28, 2016, supervising agent Peter Strzok, who was fired on Aug. 10 for sending anti-Trump texts and other misconduct, did not try to obtain a warrant to search the huge cache of emails until Oct. 30, 2016. Violating department policy, he edited the warrant affidavit on his home email account, bypassing the FBI system for recording such government business. He also began drafting a second exoneration statement before conducting the search.

The search warrant was so limited in scope that it excluded more than half the emails New York agents considered relevant to the case. The cache of Clinton-Abedin communications dated back to 2007. But the warrant to search the laptop excluded any messages exchanged before or after Clinton's 2009-2013 tenure as secretary of state, key early periods when Clinton initially set up her unauthorized private server and later periods when she deleted thousands of emails sought by investigators.

Far from investigating and clearing Abedin and Weiner, the FBI did not interview them, according to other FBI sources who say Comey closed the case prematurely. The machine was not authorized for classified material, and Weiner did not have classified security clearance to receive such information, which he did on at least two occasions through his Yahoo! email account.[lvii]

Comey said that the Abedin/Wiener laptop contained never-before-reviewed emails from Clinton's Blackberry domain that predated her move to a private server (referred to as "golden emails). Comey explained that the timing of these emails was critically important because they could have included incriminating evidence about the decision to start using the private email system:

> *And what they told me was, "We have found, for reasons we can't explain, hundreds of thousands of Hillary Clinton's emails on Anthony Weiner's laptop. And something much more important than that. Thousands of emails from Hillary Clinton's Blackberry domain."*

> *She used a Blackberry for the first three months or so of her tenure as secretary of State before setting up the personal server in the basement. And the reason that matters so much is, if there was gonna be a smoking gun, where Hillary Clinton was told, "Don't do this," or, "This is improper," it's highly likely to be at the beginning.*

> *And we never found those emails. And so now they're telling me, "For reasons we can't explain, thousands of those Blackberry emails are on Anthony Weiner's laptop."*

The 694,000 emails found on the Abedin/Weiner laptop are more than 10 times the 60,000 emails that Clinton claimed existed. Comey, McCabe, Strzok and others did not analyze this critical evidence because their goal had always been to exonerate Clinton in the email investigation. Sidney Powell summarizes this very well:[lviii]

> *Shocker #1: Despite everyone's recognition of the importance of the "explosive" "bomb," and the "golden emails" on the Weiner laptop, the FBI never even sought to*

review the "golden" emails. FBI General Counsel Baker pushed hard to expand the application to include those, but Strzok and DOJ prosecutors shot it down.

Shocker #2: They deliberately ignored the emails between Huma Abedin and others — despite knowing she was a proxy for the Secretary and had lied to them in her interview.

Federal investigators knew people would email Abedin, and she would print things out for Clinton. Abedin admitted it was easier for her to print things from home in Brooklyn.

Logically then, it appears it was Abedin who deliberately stripped classified markings from emails to forward the information to Mrs. Clinton so she could then deny ever receiving anything marked classified. It's called "plausible deniability," and it was a deliberate and illegal scheme for handling classified information.

Shocker #3: Over analysts' objections, the FBI never reviewed the Weiner laptop to determine if it had been compromised by foreign agents despite finding that Huma Abedin had forwarded classified information to it. Those were flagrant violations of 18 U.S.C. §793.

There are important conclusions from these facts in the inspector general's report.

The Weiner laptop almost certainly contains the answers to the public's questions about all things Clinton — her scandals, the Clinton Foundation pay-to-play, obstruction of justice and also possible espionage act violations.

The FBI's claim to have reviewed all the relevant Clinton emails is obviously false.

The inspector general's report belies the FBI's claim to have left no stone unturned.

The Weiner laptop and content of all iCloud accounts must be immediately obtained and preserved by an independent counsel in whom the public can have confidence.

Justice requires both a full investigation of Mrs. Clinton's multiple potential crimes and of the efforts of agents of the FBI and the Department of Justice to cover it all up.

Multiple high-ranking officials including Barack Obama were emailing Mrs. Clinton directly or through Huma Abedin. The Weiner laptop and iCloud account had it all. It was the full archive they were supposedly searching for.

Who else among the high-powered elite are the FBI and DOJ protecting by their cover-up?

Clinton Email Investigation Conclusion

Lynch, Comey, McCabe, Strzok and the other conspirators conducted a sham investigation in order to exonerate Hillary Clinton. The key element of their exoneration plan was to not use a federal grand jury. The DOJ and FBI used the lack of grand jury subpoenas and search warrants as a fake excuse to grant many unnecessary immunity deals, and to accept defense attorneys' outrageous demands (e.g., limiting email examination to specific dates) in order to avoid finding evidence of criminality. Comey presented an abundance of evidence in his July 5 press conference that Clinton violated the Espionage Act, and then Comey concluded that "no reasonable prosecutor would bring such a case." Without a grand jury, Comey maintained control over the prosecutorial decision-making.

Based on the evidence Comey cited, a grand jury would have indicted Clinton.

The conspirators used the FBI and DOJ as a political weapon to assure Hillary Clinton was the Democratic candidate for president by wrongfully exonerating her. In doing so, they drastically changed the presidential election results because Bernie Sanders should have been the Democratic candidate. All Americans should be outraged by this corruption of the justice process.

4. The Clinton Foundation Investigation

The DOJ prevented Clinton Foundation investigators from accessing Clinton's emails

Devlin Barrett reported in The Wall Street Journal that FBI agents on the Clinton Foundation case in the SDNY office requested to review the emails on Mills' and Samuelson's nongovernment laptop computers acquired in the Clinton email investigation. Prosecutors at the EDNY refused the request citing the immunity deals.[lix]

McCarthy explained that the immunity agreements in the email investigation "should not, in the main, be binding on the Clinton Foundation investigation. Of course, the immunity grants to Mills and Samuelson must be honored even though they should never have been given in the first place. But those agreements only protect Mills and Samuelson. They would not prevent evidence found on the computers and retained by the FBI from being used against Hillary Clinton or any other possible conspirator.... As I have detailed, it was already clear that Lynch's Justice Department was stunningly derelict in hamstringing the bureau's e-mails investigation. But now that we know *the FBI was simultaneously investigating the Clinton Foundation yet being denied access to the Clinton e-mails*, the dereliction appears unconscionable."

An FBI official with a conflict of interest impeded FBI agents' Clinton Foundation investigation

After the EDNY rejected their request, the FBI agents requested permission to ask federal prosecutors in SDNY. FBI Deputy Director Andrew McCabe refused, saying they could not "go prosecutor-shopping."[lx] McCarthy notes that McCabe is "the official whose wife's Virginia state senate campaign was infused with $675,000 in cash and in-kind contributions by political committees controlled by Governor Terry McAuliffe, a notorious

Clinton fixer and former Clinton Foundation board member.... Here, however, is the real outrage: Beneath all this noise, Loretta Lynch's Justice Department is blocking the FBI from examining Clinton e-mails in connection with its investigation of the Clinton Foundation — an investigation that is every bit as serious. Were it not for the Clinton Foundation, there probably would not be a Clinton e-mail scandal. Mrs. Clinton's home-brew communications system was designed to conceal the degree to which the State Department was put in the service of Foundation donors who transformed the "dead broke" Clintons into hundred-millionaires."[lxi]

The DOJ inspector general (IG) published a report on Andrew McCabe's "lack of candor" and media leaks. The IG referred McCabe to the U.S. attorney's office for a possible false-statements prosecution. McCabe was ultimately fired for three ethics violations.

McCabe told the OIG that on August 12, 2016, he received a telephone call from Principal Associate Deputy Attorney General (PADAG), the DOJ's third-highest official, regarding the FBI's handling of the Clinton Foundation. McCabe said that the PADAG expressed concerns about FBI agents taking overt steps in the Clinton Foundation investigation during the presidential campaign. McCabe told us that the conversation was "very dramatic" and he never had a similar confrontation like [that] call with a high-level Department official in his entire FBI career.

McCarthy commented that "officials there [at the DOJ] considered the Clinton Foundation probe 'dormant' and were angry that the Bureau [FBI] was still "chasing" it. ... Obama Justice Department officials, figuring they were only a few days from succeeding in their quest to become Clinton Justice Department officials, decided to try to disappear the Clinton Foundation investigation, too."[lxii]

McCabe admitted that the Clinton Foundation investigation was validly predicated, but it was shut down anyway.

5. Origin and Evolution of the Russia Probe

Introduction

Hillary Clinton, the DNC, and the Obama administration began creating the false Trump/Russia collusion story in 2015 and continued adding false evidence throughout 2016. In January 2016, a Ukrainian-American DNC consultant, Alexandra Chalupa, told a senior DNC official that, when it came to Trump's campaign, "I felt there was a Russia connection." The DNC said that it had been building robust research books on Trump and his ties to Russia long before Chalupa began sounding alarms.

Beginning in the last quarter of 2015, European intelligence agencies began surveilling the Trump campaign. In 2015, the FBI hired contractors (thought to be working for the DNC and Fusion GPS) to illegally search the raw FISA 702 data containing incidental collection of US citizens' communications with surveilled foreign agents. These contractors were able to illegally spy on U.S. citizens using 702 database searches. Susan Rice and others unmasked the names of Trump campaign members caught in the incidental FISA surveillance collection of foreign nationals. Admiral Mike Rogers, the NSA director, stopped these illegal 702 searches in April 2016.

The DNC servers were hacked by the Russians in 2015 using a malware denoted as APT29 (Cozy Bear). Even though the FBI informed them in September 2015 of the malware, the DNC never did anything about it. The DNC discovered they were hacked again in April 2016, and they hired CrowdStrike, a cybersecurity firm. CrowdStrike found APT29 on the computer network, and also a newly placed Russian malware denoted as APT28 (Fancy Bear).

The DNC and Hillary Clinton's campaign plotted to blame the hack on the Trump campaign coordinating with Russia to harm Clinton. They hired Glenn Simpson of Fusion GPS, Nellie Ohr, the wife of a high-level DOJ official, and Christopher Steele, a former British spy to create a document containing false evidence of Trump/Russia hacking collusion. The document was known as the Steele dossier. Simpson and Steele provided the dossier to the FBI, the DOJ, the State Department, and the media.

Someone, most likely a CIA person such as John Brennan, enlisted the help of former and perhaps current UK intelligence officers to use London-based covert agents to entrap people in the Trump campaign beginning as early as December 2015 to create false evidence of Russian collusion.

In March 6, 2016, Carter Page and George Papadopoulos joined the Trump campaign team as unpaid advisers. Trump announced publicly on March 21 that Papadopoulos and Page were advisers on his team. Page had worked as an FBI informant, and he successfully obtained evidence to convict a Russian spy. In March, the FBI interviewed Page to finalize his role in the Russian spy case.

On March 14, a covert agent with intelligence links in the U.K. began an entrapment operation on Trump team member, George Papadopoulos. The timing before the public hiring announcement of Papadopoulos suggests that the FBI or CIA may have found out about Papadopoulos through illegal surveillance of Trump's campaign team. A second covert agent joined in May, and in June, a third UK based covert agent began working to entrap a second American citizen in Trump's campaign team. On July 31, 2016, Peter Strzok of the FBI initiated the Trump/Russia collusion investigation, known as "Crossfire Hurricane," based on the Steele dossier and the entrapments. The Obama administration spied on the Republican candidate's team without probable cause prior to the initiation of the Crossfire Hurricane investigation.

Although, the covert agents failed to create real collusion, Fusion GPS, John Brennan, James Comey, and James Clapper succeeded in convincing the mainstream media and many members of Congress to promote the Trump/Russia collusion narrative.

Devin Nunes, the chairman of the United States House Permanent Select Committee on Intelligence, said his review of FBI and Justice Department "electronic communication" documents shows no intelligence was used to begin the investigation into possible collusion between the Trump campaign and Russia during the 2016 election.

Andrew McCarthy writes

"there was no criminal predicate to justify an investigation of any Trump-campaign official. So, the FBI did not open a criminal investigation. Instead, the bureau opened a counterintelligence investigation and hoped that evidence of crimes committed by Trump officials would emerge. But it is an abuse of power to use counterintelligence powers, including spying and electronic surveillance, to conduct what is actually a criminal investigation... With the blessing of the Obama White House, they took the powers that enable our government to spy on foreign adversaries and used them to spy on Americans — Americans who just happened to be their political adversaries.

...opening up a counterintelligence investigation against Russia is not the same thing as opening up a counterintelligence investigation against the Trump campaign. Even if Putin did want Trump to win, and even if Trump-campaign advisers did have contacts with Kremlin-tied figures, there is no evidence of participation by the Trump campaign in Russia's espionage.

That is the proof that would have been needed to justify investigating Americans. Under federal law, to establish

that an American is acting as an agent of a foreign power,
the government must show that the American is
purposefully engaging in clandestine activities on behalf of
a foreign power, and that it is probable that these activities
violate federal criminal law. (See FISA, Title 50, U.S. Code,
Section 1801(b)(2), further explained in the last six
paragraphs of my Dec. 17 column.)

But of course, if the FBI had had that kind of evidence,
they would not have had to open a counterintelligence
investigation. They would not have had to use the Clinton
campaign's opposition research — the Steele dossier — to
get FISA-court warrants. They would instead have opened
a criminal investigation, just as they did on Clinton when
there was evidence that she committed felonies.

To the contrary, the bureau opened a
counterintelligence investigation in the absence of any (a)
incriminating evidence, or (b) evidence implicating the
Trump campaign in Russian espionage. At the height of the
2016 presidential race, the FBI collaborated with the CIA
to probe an American political campaign. They used
foreign-intelligence surveillance and informants.

That's your crossfire hurricane."[lxiii]

Conspirators in the UK and US jointly worked to subvert the 2016 Presidential Election

Donald Trump appalled the politicians and intelligence services in Europe because he called for friendlier relations with Russia and criticized NATO, and because he sometimes displayed a quick temper. A former head of the UK's Secret Intelligence Service (SIS), commonly known as MI6, Sir John Sawers, encapsulated the extreme anxiety when he said of Trump's election win that he feared a nuclear clash between the US and China or the US and Russia, which would cause "widespread devastation." He later said in 2017 that America led by Donald Trump is the greatest menace facing the world today.

The "Special Relationship" between the UK and the US is described as unparalleled cooperation among major powers. John Brennan worked many years at the CIA and, as the CIA Director, he has a very close and influential relationship with current and former UK intelligence personnel. Covert agents based in London tried to entrap Trump campaign team members. Did Brennan use the fear of a Trump presidency and the special relationship to convince former and current European intelligence people to help create the false Trump/Russia collusion story? Doing so would have concealed Brennan's own role.

European intelligence began in 2015 to look for collusion as described in The Guardian:[lxiv]

> *GCHQ [a UK intelligence agency] first became aware in late 2015 of suspicious "interactions" between figures connected to Trump and known or suspected Russian agents, a source close to UK intelligence said. This intelligence was passed to the US as part of a routine exchange of information, they added.*
>
> *Over the next six months, until summer 2016, a number of western agencies shared further information on contacts between Trump's inner circle and Russians, sources said.*

All of the "evidence" that the FBI used to justify the Russia probe emanated from Britain. Peter Strzok, the head of the Trump/Russia collusion investigation, texted on December 10, 2016 that he was "managing (for the case) a ton of people in various divisions and multiple agencies and foreign governments."

The head of GCHQ at the time, Robert Hannigan, came to the U.S. in the summer of 2016 to personally give Brennan highly sensitive information about Trump/Russia collusion. Hannigan should have provided the information to his U.S. counterpart, the NSA director, Mike Rogers, but did not. This begs the question: Was Brennan directing and coordinating the overseas covert operations against the Trump campaign? Hannigan abruptly quit after Donald Trump won the election.

In September 2018, President Trump ordered the DOJ and Office of the Director of National Intelligence to initiate the "immediate declassification" of selective portions of the Foreign Intelligence Surveillance Act application on former Trump foreign policy aide Carter Page and "all FBI reports of interviews" prepared in connection with the FISA applications, and notes of FBI interviews with Bruce Ohr, the DOJ official who met numerous times with Christopher Steele. Shortly after the announcement, the president delayed the declassification because two foreign allies pleaded with him not to declassify documents related to the Russia investigation. Did the UK request the president not declassify the documents because it would reveal their role in using covert agents based in London to entrap Trump campaign team members?

Did Hannigan or any other British government officials participate in the covert agent operations on Trump campaign members or work with the CIA and/or FBI to spy on American citizens? An affirmative answer would mean that the British government interfered in the 2016 US presidential election to help Hillary Clinton win.

The CIA Director, Gina Haspel, was the CIA's London Chief of Station (COS) at that time, so all UK intelligence information should have been passed directly to her, including any information on the covert agents. (Section A4 of the Appendix has examples of interview topics for Gina Haspel to find out if she has knowledge of the Steele dossier creation and the London covert agent entrapment operations.)

Much of the evidence for the Trump/Russia collusion narrative emanated from the UK. The

US/UK collusion to fabricate evidence resulted in the Trump/Russia investigation and, in fact, did affect the US presidential election. Millions of people did not vote for Trump because of the false story. President Trump should request UK government participation in an investigation. (Section A1 of the Appendix describes intelligence services' links to the London covert agent entrapment operations and the Steele dossier)

The conspirators set up many innocent people to achieve their malevolent goal of harming Donald Trump

Peter Strzok headed the Trump/Russia investigation and he was the liaison between the FBI and Brennan. The US and UK co-conspirators and Fusion GPS vilely set up innocent people to create false evidence of a non-existent crime or to hide the truth. Strzok texted to FBI counsel Lisa Page on December 28, 2015 "You get all our oconus lures approved?" OCONUS is an acronym for Outside of the Continental United States. This likely refers to the covert agents the FBI and former/current U.K. intelligence officers used to entrap people on the Trump campaign team.

A summary of evidence is presented below on how the conspirators set up or attempted to set up the following people: Sergei Millian, Carter Page, George Papadopoulos, Paul Manafort, Lieutenant General Michael Flynn, Donald Trump, Jr., Michael Cohen, Aleksej Gubarev, Seva Kaptsugovich, Sam Clovis, Jeff Sessions, Roger Stone and Michael Caputo, Reince Priebus, Stephen Miller, Boris Epshteyn, the Trump campaign, and President Trump. I used public information to identify these people, so the conspirators may have set up other people not listed.

The setups included:

- Entrapment to create false evidence of Russian collusion using covert agents
- Entrapment to create evidence of a crime
- False allegations in the Steele dossier
- Dissemination of false information to the media and Congress
- Unnecessary Recusal (Jeff Sessions)

The James Bond author, Ian Fleming had been a British intelligence officer. Fleming said: "Once is happenstance. Twice is coincidence. Three times is enemy action." These many setups are not coincidence – they are enemy action.

Hillary Clinton, the DNC, James Comey, Loretta Lynch, Glenn Simpson, Bruce Ohr, Peter Strzok, Andrew McCabe and many others betrayed the United States by criminally conspiring with foreign nationals to elect Hillary Clinton president through criminal acts.

Chapters 6 through 21 describe how the conspirators set up people to harm Donald Trump.

6. Sergei Millian – The Most Influential Person in America

Sergei Millian – the Source of the Major Allegations in Steele's Dossier

Sergei Millian is ground zero of the false allegations that Carter Page and Paul Manafort coordinated with Russia to hack the DNC servers, steal the DNC emails, and publish them on WikiLeaks in order to help Trump win the presidential election.

Steele attributes the major allegations in the dossier to Sources D and E, which he describes as "an ethnic Russian close associate of Republican US presidential candidate Donald TRUMP." News reports identified both of these sources as Sergei Millian. Glenn Simpson testified that Steele's research discovered that Millian had connections to Trump. Steele used Millian to create false allegations for the dossier.

Millian's background explains why he was such an easy prey for Steele, and why it is impossible for him to have any of the information attributed to him in the dossier. Millian was born Siarhei Kukuts in a tiny poverty-stricken village in Belarus. He is not Russian. He graduated from Minsk State Linguistic University as a 'military interpreter. He studied at a Belarus university to be a military translator. Afterwards he enrolled at the Presidential Academy of Management, majoring in law, and around 2001 he won a grant to go to the US, participating in an international education programs sponsored by Marriott International Inc. Eventually he obtained U.S. citizenship. He changed his name from Siarhei Kukuts to Sergei Millian.

In 2006, he founded the Russian-American Chamber of Commerce (RACC), which assists US firms looking to do business in Russia, and the Millian Group, Inc., a real estate, translation and business consulting business both in Atlanta,

Georgia. Millian activated his real estate license when he formed Millian Group, and he moved to New York in 2010.

Glenn Simpson testified before Congress that Millian "came up in connection with Chris' [Steele] work as one of the people around Trump who had a Russian background." Simpson said Millian organized a 2007 trip for Trump organization representatives to promote the billionaire's vodka brand in Russia and referred to the Russian-American Chamber as a "shadowy kind of trade group." "Russians are known to use chambers of commerce and trade groups for intelligence operations," Simpson said. Simpson suggested that Millian was working with Michael Cohen.

Steele found the perfect dupe in Millian to use as the principal source for the dossier. Millian is an incessant and convincing liar, an opportunist, and a self-promoter bragging about non-existent accomplishments and connections. Steele used Millian in several ways:

- Highlighting Millian's false boasts of connections to Donald Trump and the Trump organization.
- Taking advantage of Millian's very strong con-artist capabilities by paying him to set up people associated with the Trump campaign (Note: The opportunistic Millian may well have only focused on the money while being oblivious to the setup)
- Feeding Millian false information (e.g., the golden showers) that he then repeats to another person.

Millian's False Associations with the Trump Organization

Millian is a very effective communicator and comes across as highly intelligent, charming, and convincing as he lies and deceives.

Even Simpson noted Millian's lies when he testified that "In one resume he said he was from Belarus and he went to Minsk State, and then in another he was from Moscow and went to Moscow State. In one he said he worked for the Belarusian Foreign Ministry; in the other, he said he worked for the Russian Foreign Ministry."

Millian told ABC News that he met Trump in Florida in 2008 at a race track, but the Wall Street Journal notes that Millian told a Russian news outlet that he met Trump in Moscow in 2007 at the Millionaire Fair when Trump was there to promote his brand of vodka.

Simpson testified that Millian organized a trip for Trump representatives to promote the billionaire's vodka brand in Russia.

Steele wrote in the dossier that Source D (Millian) is "a close associate of TRUMP who had organized and managed his recent trips to Moscow."

Millian boasted "Our common acquaintances engaged in the organization of his [Trump's] trip to Russia in the "Millionaire Fair" in 2007. Then Trump invited me as the head of the Russian-American Chamber of Commerce (RACC) on horse races "Gulf Stream" in Miami. In an April 2016 interview with Russian news agency RIA Novosti, Millian, who was introduced as the president of the Russian-American Chamber of Commerce, contradicted his earlier statement with a blatant lie saying that he developed a lasting acquaintance with Trump while organizing the developer's trip to Russia for the Millionaire Fair in 2007. Millian's statement that he organized Trump's trip is absurd because he had not met Trump prior to the 2007 Moscow trip (he once stated that he first met Trump in 2008), and Millian had minimal financial assets, including a very tiny business he founded in 2006.

In his constant self-promotion, Millian frequently posts photos of himself with well-known people or at significant events along with a deceptive or false story about it. For example, he posted a 2008 photo of himself with Trump during a marketing meeting to help bring attention to the Trump-branded development in Hollywood, Florida. Millian probably charmed his way into the photo with Trump by saying he was the president of the Russian-American Chamber of Commerce and worked with wealthy Russians to buy real estate in Florida.

Millian made many claims stemming from that Florida photo meeting with Trump. In appearances on the Russian news agency RIA, Millian boasted that he brokered deals for Trump Hollywood, a Florida condo project and that he has an exclusive deal to market Trump properties to Russians, and that the "level of business (investment) amounted to hundreds of millions of dollars." Millian bragged of assisting Trump in "studying the Moscow market" for the potential real estate investments. "Later," Millian said, "we met at his office in New York, where he introduced me to his right-hand man—Michael Cohen. He is Trump's main lawyer, all contracts go through him. Subsequently, a contract was signed with me to promote one of their real estate projects in Russia and the CIS. You can say I was their exclusive broker."

Millian told ABC News that he helped broker a real estate deal involving Trump and Jorge Perez, the billionaire CEO of The Related Companies. But Related Companies told ABC that it has no record of paying Millian for brokerage services.

Millian's Russian-American Chamber of Commerce said in 2009 that it had signed formal agreements with The Trump Organization to service Russian real estate clients, but the Trump Organization denied that Trump had any such relationship.

Cohen said "I've never met the guy," and there is no record of any signed agreement with Millian. Alan Garten, executive vice president and general counsel of the Trump Organization said that "Sergei Millian does not work for the Trump

Organization, is not affiliated with the Trump Organization, has no connections with the Trump Organization" and "we don't have an agreement with him. Nobody knows who he is."

During the 2016 election, Millian gave many positive interviews on his relationship with Trump, especially in the Russian domestic press. In an interview with the Russian state news service RIA Novosti on April 13, 2016, Millian gave a glowing account of his relationship to Trump and Trump's character. RIA Novosti is widely read on the web and social media and the basis for state TV news. Asked how often he met with Trump, Millian replied that he had just seen him a few days prior to the interview. He said by contrast to his TV persona, Trump came across as more paternal and more business-like in person. While Trump himself doesn't drink, he offered Millian a glass of Kristall champagne. "He knew that Russians like to have a drink sometimes. Let's put it this way: he knows the culture of other countries," said Millian. The interviewer asked Millian many questions about what Trump would do as president. For example, questions about sanctions, and the differences between Obama and Trump. Millian answered them very convincingly, as if he and Trump were good friends.

After Trump was elected, Millian used photos and interviews to boost his claims of an association with Trump. Millian attended several black-tie events at Trump's inauguration and posted the photos. He posted a photo of himself with a Trump Inauguration sign in the background. He told the Russian news agency RIA that he had been in touch with the Trump Organization as late as April 2016.

After being outed as a Steele source, Millian backtracked. Contrary to what he told RIA, Millian told Business Insider in an email last year that the last time he worked on a Trump-brand project was "in Florida around 2008."

Examples of other Millian lies include:

- The Russian-American Chamber of Commerce (RACC) has more than 200 sponsors and clients including "The Coca-Cola Company Delta Air Lines, Inc American Airlines Smith, Gambrell & Russell, LLP Delloite Gazprombank Arnall Golden Gregory LLP InterContinental Hotels Group, Rosneft The Related Group the Trump Organization etc." When asked, the International Hotel Group, The Related Group, the Trump Organization, and Delta Airlines denied this.
- A January 2011 biography states "Mr. Millian specializes in representing foreign investors, Russian oligarchs and pied-à-terre lifestyle individuals. Mr. Millian serves as President of the Russian American Chamber of Commerce in the USA, and has worked as exclusive selling broker for projects with Donald Trump and Jorge Perez."
- "His extensive government and business connections will also provide equally important diplomatic access for the Atlanta chamber [RACC] as it seeks to build business ties in Moscow and beyond." Millian is not Russian and the RACC is tiny with no known significant Russian government or business connections.
- In February 2018, ABC News reported that Millian posted a photo of himself on Twitter addressing what appears to be a Harvard Business School event with the caption, "Speaker at Harvard University." Harvard said Millian was not a speaker there, and the Harvard photo was geo-tagged in New York.

Millian presents himself as the president of the Russian-American Chamber of Commerce, the president, CEO, and equity partner at Millian Group Inc., and the vice president of the World Chinese Merchants Union Association. He boasts of offices in Atlanta, New York, Azerbaijan, Belarus, Bulgaria, China, Jordan and Russia. When one examines the public information on his companies, it is like pulling back the curtain shrouding the Wizard of Oz:

81

- The Millian Group's Atlanta "headquarters" office address is shared with 11 companies, such as Bliss Weddings & Events of ATL with revenues of $142,000; Clean By Design Cs LLC (office cleaning services) with revenues of $68,000.
- Sergei Millian is the only licensed broker at the Millian Group
- The Atlanta-based Millian Group's revenues, before expenses, are currently estimated to be $38,000 per employee.
- The 2011 tax return shows RACC revenues of $38,048, expenses of $24,606 for excess revenues of $13,442. The net assets increased from $921 at the beginning of the year to $14,363 at year end. Millian works 40 hours/week for the RACC, and his CFO, based in Atlanta, works 10 hours/week for the RACC. Neither receives compensation or health benefits.
- The Financial Times (FT) investigated Millian and the RACC and found that most of the board members are obscure entities and nearly half of their telephone numbers went unanswered.

Millian's January 6, 2011 biography states "In 2010, Mr. Millian established International Business Development Center on New York's Wall Street at the Russian American Chamber to assist the Russian entrepreneurs in entering the US market with maximum speed and minimal risk and expenses." A FT reporter found no trace of the Chamber of Commerce [RACC] at the Wall Street address listed on its website. The 2011 tax return listed the RACC address as Millian's apartment

The address of the Millian Group's New York office is his apartment. The Millian Group and the RACC have the same phone number.

Steele Set up Millian to be the Source of False Information

Millian constantly and convincingly lies to create the illusion that he is a successful businessman with significant influential connections, including close connections to Donald Trump and his associates, and to influential Russian government officials. Millian obviously has no qualms about lying to make money. Christopher Steele and Glenn Simpson found the perfect "useful idiot" in Sergei Millian to be the major source of the Steele dossier allegations.

Steele used intermediaries with Millian instead of dealing directly with him.

- The Wall Street Journal, citing an unnamed source, reported that Millian didn't tell Steele directly, "Rather, his statements about the Trump-Russia relationship were relayed by at least one third party to the British ex-spy who prepared the dossier."
- ABC News reported that Millian "may have unwittingly" described Trump's alleged sexual romps in a conversation with a person who was reporting to Steele. Millian's name was also listed as a source in a copy of the dossier that was provided to the FBI.
- Michael Isikoff, an old friend of Glenn Simpson, wrote that Millian spoke with a "collector" who was working for Steele to gather information for the Trump project

Millian denies having provided information to Christopher Steele, however he did not deny that his comments may have been passed to Steele by an associate.

Steele paid the dossier sources. His intermediaries paid Millian since Steele did not directly deal with him. Steele likely used the same method to trick Millian into making false statements that the UK covert agents used on Papadopoulos. For example, one intermediary would tell Millian that Putin had compromising information on Trump, and then a second intermediary would get Millian to repeat the allegation, which Steele would then include in the dossier. Steele said in the dossier that Millian, an ethnic Russian, spoke in confidence to a *compatriot* in late July 2016. Millian, as president of the Russian-American Chamber of Commerce, had many Russian acquaintances, so Steele could have easily paid an ethnic Russian to set Millian up.

Steele describes Source D (Millian) as "a close associate of TRUMP who had organized and managed his recent trips to Moscow." Source D appears in Steele's first dossier report dated 6/20/16. Steele very likely began preparations with Millian and the intermediaries at least a month prior to the first report.

Steele numbered the reports in his dossier. For example, report 2016/094 is dated July 19, 2016 and report 2016/097 is dated July 30, 2016.

On June 12, 2016, Julian Assange said that WikiLeaks has obtained and will publish a batch of Clinton emails, which it did starting July 22, 2016. On June 14, CrowdStrike posted its findings that Russian government hackers accessed the DNC servers and stole opposition research.

Steele's report denoted as 2016/095 is titled "RUSSIA/US PRESIDENTIAL ELECTION: FURTHER INDICATIONS OF EXTENSIVE CONSPIRACY BETWEEN TRUMP'S CAMPAIGN TEAM AND THE KREMLIN." The report is undated but based on report numbers is probably between July 19 and July 30. Millian is Source E. This report contains the claim that Trump colluded with Putin to steal and publish the DNC emails to hurt Clinton in the election. It states:

"Speaking in confidence to a compatriot in late July 2016, Source E [Millian], an ethnic Russian close associate of Republican US presidential candidate Donald TRUMP, admitted that there was a well-developed conspiracy of co-operation between them

and the Russian leadership. This was managed on the TRUMP side by the Republican candidate's campaign manager, Paul MANAFORT, who was using foreign policy advisor, Carter PAGE, and others as intermediaries. The two sides had a mutual interest in defeating Democratic presidential candidate Hillary CLINTON, whom President PUTIN apparently both hated and feared.

Inter alia, Source E, acknowledged that the Russian regime had been behind the recent leak of embarrassing e-mail messages, emanating from the Democratic National Committee (DNC), to the WikiLeaks platform. The reason for using WikiLeaks was 'plausible deniability' and the operation had been conducted with the full knowledge and support of TRUMP and senior members of his campaign team.....

In the wider context of TRUMP campaign/Kremlin co-operation, Source E claimed that the intelligence network being used against CLINTON comprised three elements. Firstly, there were agents/facilitators within the Democratic Party structure itself; secondly Russian émigré and associated cyber-operators based in the US; and thirdly, state-sponsored cyber operatives working in Russia. All three elements had played an important role to date."

Steele's next report (number 2016/097 and dated July 30), cited the Russian émigré figure close to Trump's campaign team (Millian) saying that the

"Kremlin [is] concerned that political fallout from DNC e-mail hacking operation is spiralling out of control." "The émigré associate of TRUMP opined that the Kremlin wanted the situation to calm but for 'plausible deniability' to be maintained concerning its

(extensive) pro-TRUMP and anti-CLINTON operations."

The above statements in bold that Steele attributes to Millian are the genesis of the story and the sole "evidence" that <u>the Trump campaign coordinated with the Russian government to steal the emails from the DNC servers and post them on WikiLeaks to harm Hillary Clinton in the presidential election</u>. Millian's allegations were recited thousands of times by the media, was harped on by Hillary Clinton, her campaign, and the Obama administration throughout the 2016 election campaign, was used to obtain a warrant to surveille the Trump campaign team and to prepare the Intelligence Community Assessment, was the focus of multiple congressional investigations, and was the origin of the Trump/Russia counterintelligence investigation that morphed into Mueller's Special Counsel investigation. For this reason, Millian has undoubtedly been the most influential person in the United States for the past two years. The Debbie Wasserman Schultz/DNC and Hillary Clinton's plot to blame the Trump campaign for coordinating the DNC hack with Russia worked unbelievably well. Even though Mueller's indictment of 12 Russian intelligence officers contains incontrovertible evidence that the Trump campaign was not involved at all with Russia's DNC hack, the Clinton/DNC hoax continues unabated with the Special Counsel investigation.

Millian, as Source D and E, provided most of the major allegations in Steele's dossier. For example, Millian alleges:

- "According to Source D [Millian], where s/he had been present, TRUMP's {perverted} conduct in Moscow included hiring the presidential suite of the Ritz Carlton Hotel, where he knew President and Mrs. OBAMA {whom he hated} had stayed on one of their official trips to Moscow, and defiling the bed where they had slept by employing a number of prostitutes to perform a 'golden showers' {urination} show in front of him. ..... The Moscow Ritz Carlton episode involving TRUMP reported above was confirmed by Source E [Millian] redacted name, who said that s/he and several of the staff were aware of it at the time and subsequently. S/he believed it had happened in 2013." (Note: Millian was not in Moscow in 2013 when Trump was there)

- Russian diplomatic staff in key U.S. cities were using the émigré 'pension' distribution system to reward relevant assets. The U.S. Russian émigré community was involved in the hacking operations and tens of thousands of dollars were used to pay them. (Note: It is a preposterous claim that a billionaire and the Russian government would use diplomats and émigré pensions to pay U.S. located "cyber operators" a tiny amount of money for a secret hacking operation when such a complex system involving the Russian émigré community would be highly susceptible to leaks. The thus far two-year Trump/Russia investigation found no indication of émigré pension payments to hackers. This claim also contradicts a subsequent Steele report claiming the principal hackers were 1) a millionaire, Aleksei Gubarov, and 2) a convicted pedophile, Seva Kapsugovich, in a remote Soviet prison with no access to the internet. Mueller's indictment of 12 Russian intelligence officers in the DNC hack irrefutably proves this allegation is false.)

- Trump was relaxed about the negative media on the Russian election interference because it deflected media and Democrats attention away from Trump's business dealings in China that involved large bribes and kickbacks. (Note: A ridiculous Millian lie because 1) no negative news on any Trump business dealings in China has appeared during the two-year Trump/Russia investigation, and 2) Millian has no knowledge of any Trump business dealings because he has zero connection with Donald Trump and his associations.)

- Source D said that Russian intelligence provided to Trump over several years on his opponents, including Clinton, had been very helpful. Source D was a close associate of Trump who arranged and managed Trump's recent trips to Moscow. (Note: Millian has no inside knowledge of any activities related to Trump or Putin, and he did not arrange any trips for Trump.)
- Much of the intelligence flow from the Trump team to Russia concerned the activities of business oligarchs and their families' activities and assets in the U.S. with which Putin seemed preoccupied. (Note: Millian has no inside knowledge of any activities related to Trump or Putin. Trump would not have any "intelligence" of Russian oligarchs' families and assets in the U.S.)

Oleg Deripaska, Bruce Ohr, and Christopher Steele

Oleg Deripaska, a Russian billionaire, is very close to Putin. Deripaska is a longtime business associate of Paul Manafort, Trump's campaign chairman. Deripaska is angry at Manafort for stealing $19 million from him.

The State Department revoked Deripaska's visa in 2006 because of concerns about his ties to Russian organized crime. Putin publicly complained in 2008 about the State Department's action against his friend. Deripaska and Sergei Lavrov, the Russian foreign minister, hired a lobbyist named Adam Waldman to help with Deripaska's visa issue, including meetings with U.S. policymakers. Deripaska also used Christopher Steele in 2016 to help with his U.S. visa during the same time that Steele was preparing the dossier for Clinton's campaign.

Bruce Ohr was the Associate Deputy Attorney General until January 2018. He reported to Sally Yates and then to Rod Rosenstein. Ohr's wife, Nellie Ohr, worked for Glenn Simpson at Fusion GPS to help with the Steele dossier. Bruce and Nellie Ohr, Christopher Steele, and Glenn Simpson were all close friends as evidenced by their email communications. Steele emailed Bruce Ohr frequently and Ohr always quickly replied. Whenever Steele requested that Ohr phone him or meet with him, Ohr promptly did so. Whenever Steele asked Ohr to do something, Ohr expeditiously complied.

Bruce Ohr and Steele's email communications during 2016 concerned the Deripaska visa and Steele's dossier. The emails that the DOJ provided to Congress began on January 12, 2016. Following are examples (note: Steele refers to Deripaska as 'OD' or 'OVD' in the emails):

On January 12, 2016, Steele sent Ohr a New Year's greeting. Steele brought up the case of Russian aluminum magnate Oleg Deripaska (referred to in various emails as both OD and OVD), who was at the time seeking a visa to attend an Asia-Pacific Economic Cooperation meeting in the United States.

Steele also asked Ohr when he might be coming to London, or somewhere in Europe, "as I would be keen to meet up here and talk business." Ohr replied warmly the same day and said he would likely travel to Europe, but not the U.K., at least twice in February.

Steele emailed again on Feb. 8 to alert Ohr that "our old friend OD apparently has been granted another official [emphasis in original] visa to come to the US later this month." Steele wrote, "As far as I'm concerned, this is good news all round although as before, it would be helpful if you could monitor it and let me know if any complications arise." Ohr replied that he knew about Deripaska's visa, and "to the extent I can I will keep an eye on the situation." Steele again asked to meet anytime Ohr was in the U.K. or Western Europe.

Steele wrote again on Feb. 21 in an email headlined "Re: OVD - Visit To The US." Steele told Ohr he had talked to Waldman and to Paul Hauser, who was Deripaska's London lawyer. Steele reported that there would be a U.S. government meeting on Deripaska that week — "an inter-agency meeting on him this week which I guess you will be attending." Steele said he was "circulating some recent sensitive Orbis reporting" on Deripaska that suggested Deripaska was not a "tool" of the Kremlin. Steele said he would send the reporting to a name that is redacted in the email, "as he has asked, for legal reasons I understand, for all such reporting be filtered through him (to you at DoJ and others)."

Deripaska's rehabilitation was a good thing, Steele wrote: "We reckon therefore that the forthcoming OVD contact represents a good opportunity for the USG." Ohr responded by saying, "Thanks Chris! This is extremely interesting. I hope we can follow up in the next few weeks as you suggest."

The St. Petersburg International Economic Forum is a major annual Russian business event drawing more than 10,000 people from over 120 different countries, including many political and business leaders. President Putin attends and speaks at the forum. Deripaska met with Millian in June 2016 at the forum as documented in a photo of them together on Millian's Facebook page. What are the odds that out of 10,000 people at the forum, a very unsuccessful small business owner, Millian, meets with one of the most powerful people in Russia, who is angry at Trump's campaign manager and working with Steele on a visa issue? To paraphrase Ian Fleming, this was an "enemy action," not a coincidence. Steele obviously set Millian up by somehow getting him to attend the forum so that Deripaska and Steele's Russian intermediaries could meet with him. Steele likely had one person feed Millian false information and a second person (the "collector") would get the witless Millian to regurgitate it. This is the same method that Steele's British colleagues used on George Papadopoulos.

Two days after the forum ended, Steele completed a dossier memo based on information from a "collector" intermediary. The memo said that Russia recorded Trump with prostitutes in a Ritz-Carlton hotel room performing "golden showers" and Russia used this "kompromot" to blackmail Trump. A later memo would blame Paul Manafort, who stole $19 million from Deripaska, for managing a "well-developed conspiracy" between the Trump campaign and Russia to steal the DNC emails and publish them on WikiLeaks. Deripaska very likely worked with Steele on Millian's set up in order to get his U.S. visa and to get revenge on Manafort. Steele and Simpson probably told Deripaska that his help would be viewed very favorably in a Clinton presidency.

Steele simply describes a source of many dossier allegations as "an ethnic Russian associate" of Trump, which is the same description Steele used for Millian as Source D and E. It would also describe Boris Epshteyn, a Trump adviser who Millian tried to get set up. One of the allegations attributed to this source is:

- In report 2016/102 dated August 10, 2016, this source alleges that "the aim of leaking the DNC e-mails to WikiLeaks during the Democratic Convention had been to swing supporters of Bernie SANDERS away from Hillary CLINTON and across to TRUMP.... This objective had been conceived and promoted, inter alia, by TRUMP's foreign policy adviser Carter PAGE who had discussed it directly with the ethnic Russian associate."

As described in Chapter 7, Page was anything but a cunning influential person in Trump's campaign. He was brought onto the campaign team because Trump needed to demonstrate to the media that he had foreign policy advisors, and Page's only contribution had been to attend some campaign meetings and rallies. It is preposterous to allege that Carter Page, who had a tiny business run on a shoestring budget, was influential in the Trump campaign. As previously described, Millian's allegation that Manafort and Page coordinated a sophisticated DNC hack and email theft with Russia was physically impossible due to the timing, and also disproved by evidence in Mueller's indictment of 12 Russian intelligence officers.

It is truly incredible that Ohr, the fourth highest DOJ official, granted Steele instant access and dutifully fulfilled Steele's every request. For example, Steele requested to work with Mueller's Special Counsel investigation, and Ohr tried unsuccessfully to help with this.

In 2009, Deripaska hired Adam Waldman, an American lawyer, for "legal advice on issues involving his U.S. visa as well as commercial transactions" at a retainer of $40,000 a month. In 2010, Waldman additionally registered as an agent for Russian foreign minister Sergei Lavrov, "gathering information and providing advice and analysis as it relates to the U.S. policy towards the visa status of Oleg Deripaska." Lavrov's intercession evidences Deripaska's influence in the Russian government. Deripaska has paid Waldman at least $2.36 million thus far. As the following emails show, Steele worked with Waldman and Ohr on Deripaska's visa.

- In a January 12, 2016 email, Steele told Ohr "I heard from Adam WALDMAN yesterday that OD is applying for another official US visa ice [sic] APEC business at the end of February."
- Steele told Ohr in a February 8 email "our old friend OD apparently has been granted another official visa to come to the US later this month.... As far as I'm concerned, this is good news all round although as before, it would be helpful if you could monitor it and let me know if any complications arise." Ohr replied that he knew about Deripaska's visa, and "to the extent I can I will keep an eye on the situation."

Why would Ohr intervene to help lift State Department sanctions on a Russian citizen at the request of a British citizen running a small private investigation business? The only plausible answer is that Bruce and Nellie Ohr, Glenn Simpson, and Christopher Steele needed Deripaska's help to set up Sergei Millian as a primary Steele dossier source. Deripaska helped them as a quid pro quo (aka bribe) because they helped him obtain his U.S. visa.

Steele and Simpson were working with a top Democratic senator to undermine President Trump in March 2017. Sen. Mark Warner is the ranking Democratic member of the Senate Intelligence Committee, which is investigating the Trump/Russia collusion story. In the following texts with Waldman, Warner sought to meet secretly with Steele:

- On March 16, 2017, Waldman texted Warner "Chris Steele asked me to call you."
- "We have so much to discuss u need to be careful but we can help our country," Warner wrote to Waldman on March 22.
- "I'm in," Waldman replied.

Warner also asked Waldman to help set up an interview with Deripaska.

Other messages suggested that Warner sought to keep other members of the Senate Intelligence Committee in the dark about the back channel to Steele.

- "Ok but I wud (sic) like to do prelim call u me and him no one else before letter just so we have to trail to start want to discuss scope first before letter no leaks," he wrote.
- And on March 30, he texted: "We want to do this right private in London don't want to send letter yet cuz if we can't get agreement wud rather not have paper trail."

These emails add further strong evidence that Deripaska was a key source in the Sergei Millian dossier allegations.

A bizarre claim by a woman in Thailand adds further strong evidence that Deripaska helped Steele with the dossier. Anastasia Vashukevich (aka Nastya Rybka) is from Belarus. She is a prostitute currently in a prison in Pattaya, Thailand for plying her trade without a permit. Vashukevich, using the name

Nastya Rybka, posted an Instagram photo with her and Deripaska together.[lxv]

Vashukevich (aka Nastya Rybka) is an instructor for a course titled "Training: Hunting for the Oligarch." The advertisement says that Nastya Rybka will conduct an exclusive outreach training for girls from 18 to 23 years old. The training will include "How and where to meet people from Forbes, How can you satisfy a man who is tempted by a woman's attention in bed and probably uncover his sexual potential, find his fetishes and hidden sexual desires; How to tear down the roof of the oligarch, make his life fascinating...Best pupils will receive a bonus: the opportunity to meet Oleg Deripaska, Mikhail Prokhorov and Roman Abramovich on January 2 at a closed event and try to seduce them. The training will take place in Thailand. After the training, homework will be given, carried out under the supervision of trainers, to prepare for the meeting with billionaires. There is a Schengen visa for the meeting. The cost of training is 20 thousand rubles (about $300)."

CNN reported that "she [Vashukevich] witnessed meetings between the Russian billionaire and three Americans who she refused to name. He [Deripaska] claims they discussed plans to effect the U.S. elections but she wouldn't give any further information because she fears she could be deported back to Russia." Vashukevich told the Associated Press that she had turned over audio recordings to Russian oligarch Oleg Deripaska, whose conversations about election interference she claimed to have taped. She has said she provided "escort" services to Deripaska.

A young prostitute in Thailand would not have the necessary knowledge to make up a story that Deripaska discussed plans to affect the U.S. elections with three English-speaking foreigners. This is strong evidence.

The FBI did not Try to Verify Any Dossier Allegations

Sergei Millian is ground zero of the false story that Trump colluded with Putin to steal and publish DNC emails through a hack in order to hurt Clinton in the election. Comey testified that Peter Strzok was responsible to verify the allegations in Steele's dossier. Millian's name is shown as a source on the FBI's dossier copy. Strzok could have easily determined that Millian is a lying con-artist who had absolutely zero Trump connections whatsoever to find out this type of information. Millian is an American citizen residing in the U.S., so Strzok could have easily: 1) traced Millian's allegations back to Steele's intermediaries and to Steele himself, 2) discovered the many lies such as Millian arranging Trump's trip, 3) found that Manafort and Page could not have coordinated the DNC hack with Russia because of the timeline. Strzok could have easily investigated any U.S. located sources such as the ethnic Russian associate of Trump. Comey testified that the dossier is salacious and unverified, so Strzok obviously did not even attempt to verify any allegations because Millian's allegations would have been easy to investigate and disprove.

Rossotrudichestvo is a Russian agency that promotes the Russian image through international development assistance, education, science, culture and language. The Financial Times reported that the FBI investigated Millian in 2011 because he organized a trip to Rossotrudichestvo in Moscow for 50 American entrepreneurs. FBI agents questioned some of the participants over whether they were recruited by Russian intelligence. One entrepreneur told the Financial Times that an FBI agent said the bureau suspected that the trip organizers, which included Millian, were Russian spies. Strzok therefore had much knowledge about Millian because of this counterintelligence investigation.

Comey testified that the FBI included the dossier allegations in the FISA applications because Steele was considered reliable due to his past work with the FBI. The facts however clearly prove that Comey conspired with Strzok, Ohr, Lynch, Steele and many others to help Hillary Clinton become president by harming Donald Trump with the false collusion story:

Comey was guilty of perjury because he and others in the DOJ and FBI knew that Steele told Bruce Ohr that he was "desperate that Donald Trump not get elected and was passionate about him not being president." Comey also knew that Hillary Clinton and the DNC financed Steele's dossier.

The DOJ, Comey, and Strzok did not attempt to verify anything because they knew the allegations were false and many could be easily disproved. Strzok texted FBI counsel Lisa Page on May 19, 2017 that "There's no big there there." Lisa Page later testified Strzok's text meant that there was no significant evidence of Trump Russia collusion.

On March 18, 2017, two days before Comey testified before Congress, Steele wrote to Ohr, "Hi! Just wondering if you had any news? Obviously, we're a bit apprehensive given scheduled appearance at Congress on Monday. Hoping that important firewalls will hold. Many thanks."

McCabe testified that the dossier was needed to obtain the FISA surveillance warrant on Carter Page, so they knowingly used the false dossier allegations to obtain the warrant. The Page surveillance warrant allowed the DOJ and FBI to spy on the entire Trump campaign team and certain people in the Trump administration due to the "two-hop rule" for FISA warrants.[lxvi]

Steele tricked Millian into repeating lies told to him by Steele's "intermediaries." This destroys the credibility of any allegation in Steele's dossier, so nothing in the dossier should be believed. The lies attributed to Millian comprise the major allegations in the dossier. Essentially Steele and Simpson created the provably false lies used by the FBI to start the Trump/Russia collusion investigation.

Some people suspect that Millian is a Russian spy. I believe this to be a low probability scenario because of Millian's character and history – he fits the profile of a useful idiot much better than a spy. Regardless of whether Millian was a spy or not, Hillary Clinton and her paid contractors coordinated with Russian and British nationals to create and publish false information on her presidential opponent in order to win the election and harm Donald Trump through a criminally unjust investigation.

Steele uses Millian to entrap Trump campaign members

As described above, Millian very publicly touted his connections to Trump during the 2016 election campaign, most probably because Simpson's intermediaries paid him to do so. Millian gave many interviews in the U.S. and Russia. In June 2016, Millian posted on Facebook a photo of himself with the Russian oligarch Oleg Deripaska, a longtime business associate of Trump's campaign chairman Paul Manafort. Simpson told ABC News that they should talk to Millian. Simpson and Steele's objective in this public promotion was to add credibility to Millian's association with Trump in order to increase the likelihood that Millian could successfully gain access to certain members of Trump's campaign team and set them up.

Millian set up or tried to set up the following people at the behest of Steele's intermediaries:

- George Papadopoulos
- Michael Cohen
- Jared Kushner
- Boris Esphteyn

Millian tried to set up Papadopoulos twice. He approached Papadopoulos over LinkedIn "out of the blue" during the summer of 2016 to propose that he and Papadopoulos "form an energy-related business that would be financed by influential Russian billionaires." Although Papadopoulos declined, Millian and he became friends. After Trump won the election, Millian offered Papadopoulos $30,000 per month "while he worked inside the Trump administration." Millian did not have the financial resources or connections to do this, so Steele obviously had his intermediaries pay Millian to make these entrapment offers.

Millian was in regular touch with George Papadopoulos in 2016. Papadopoulos tried unsuccessfully to schedule a meeting with Millian and Boris Epshteyn, a Trump campaign advisor, in September 2016. A Steele intermediary probably paid Millian to schedule this meeting. Millian was not a member of the Trump campaign team, so he had no reason to meet with Epshteyn, who is a successful political strategist, investment banker, and attorney. Epshteyn is a Russian-American, who was born in Moscow. Steele's dossier refers to one source as an ethnic Russian associate of Trump. Simpson and Steele likely wanted Millian to meet with Epshteyn to set him up in a manner similar to the Donald Trump Jr. setup meeting with Russians offering dirt on Clinton.

Millian sent emails to Michael Cohen on November 2, 2016 requesting that Donald Trump speak at a business event in either New York or Switzerland. He also spoke with Cohen by phone two or three weeks prior to the email exchange. Millian did not have the financial resources or connections to do this, so Steele obviously had his intermediaries pay Millian to make these entrapment offers. Cohen said he never met Millian, and he told Millian to "cease contacting me."

Steele probably had Millian keep trying to entrap Cohen to add credibility to the dossier claim that Cohen became Trump's manager of Russian collusion after Manafort left the campaign. This explanation is bolstered by Simpson's testimony:

"As further time went on, we found [Millian] was connected to Michael Cohen, the president's lawyer," Simpson told the House committee. "Michael Cohen was very adamant that he didn't actually have a connection to Sergi, even though he was one of only like 100 people who followed Sergi on Twitter. And they — we had Twitter messages back and forth between the two of them just — we just pulled them off of Twitter."

Simpson is referring to an August 2016 twitter exchange about polls of Trump vs Clinton. Steele most likely got Millian to tweet Cohen about the polls in order to get Cohen to engage with Millian and have a public twitter record as "evidence" of their connection.

Millian put Jared Kushner on copy of emails sent to Michael Cohen as an obvious attempt to implicate Kushner.

Millian Sought Protection

According to his father, Millian sought protection from the U.S. government for his safety when his name was revealed as Source D and Source E in Steele's dossier. The U.S. refused to provide protection.

7. The Carter Page Setup

Carter Page's Background

Page frequently talks favorably about Russia and is critical of US foreign policy toward Russia, and Russian sanctions. His background provides insight into his views. Page said he was inspired by the summit meetings as a teenager between Reagan and Gorbachev negotiating arms control treaties to decrease nuclear weapons. Page said "I thought this is the beginning of a new era and something that's of the highest significance and importance for the future of both of our respective countries and also the world, just given the threat. I was very motivated by that and it was something that really inspired me." At the summit, several Naval Officers flanked Reagan, which also inspired him. Page majored in political science, graduated from Annapolis in 1993, and served five years in the Navy. He received master degrees from Georgetown University and New York University, and a PhD from the University of London. Page said he joined the campaign because Trump's viewpoint on Russia was similar to his.

Page began working for Merrill Lynch in 2000 and was in their Moscow office from 2004 to 2007. Upon leaving in 2008, he founded Global Energy Capital with two partners in New York.

Page Helps the FBI Catch a Russian Spy

The FBI informed Page in 2013 that a Russian national working at a Russian bank in Manhattan might be a spy trying to recruit him. FBI special agent Gregory Monaghan described how Russian agents tried to take advantage of Page and said Page was a guileless victim, who was only "interested in business opportunities in Russia."

Page fully cooperated with the FBI upon learning that he had been duped by Russian agents. He is referred to as an FBI undercover employee ("UCE-1") in the indictment. Working with the FBI, Page provided a Russian spy with binders containing industry analysis that the spy had requested. The binders contained hidden recording devices so when the spy brought the binders to the secure spy facility the FBI recorded their conversations. The FBI arrested Evgeny Buryakov, a Russian banker, in January 2015 based on the recorded conversation evidence and Page's witness testimony. Buryakov pled guilty in March 11, 2016. The FBI and federal prosecutors had a final meeting with Page on this case in March 2016. In May 2016, the court sentenced Buryakov to 30 months in prison for conspiring to work for Russian intelligence.

It is very important to note that Peter Strzok headed the investigation for the FBI, and Assistant Attorney General John Carlin headed it for the DOJ's National Security Division, so they both had knowledge of Page's help to successfully prosecute the Russian spy.

Carter Page Commencement Speaker Setup

James Clapper admitted that there was foreign and domestic surveillance of Trump in 2015 and 2016. Since 2015, the FBI permitted contractors (thought to be the DNC and Fusion GPS associates) to illegally search raw FISA 702 data containing incidental collection of American communications with surveilled foreign agents. The query would illegally allow the contractor to search for a specific American (e.g., Michael Flynn) to see their incidental conversations with foreign persons under surveillance without a warrant. In late 2015, the British intelligence agency, GCHQ, and other European intelligence agencies began surveillance of suspicious "interactions" between Trump associates and known or suspected Russian agents, which they passed on to U.S. counterparts.

The DNC had been doing research on Trump and his ties to Russia since 2015 and received Ukrainian research help in 2016. In March 2016, Trump was increasingly seen as the probable Republican candidate as he racked up many primary wins. Despite all of the efforts, the conspirators could not find credible evidence of Trump/Russian collusion. On top of that, Rogers shut down the illegal 702 FISA queries on April 18, so contractors such as the DNC could no longer search for American members of Trump's team this way. As a result, the conspirators plotted ways to create false evidence of Trump/Russia collusion.

Carter Page joined the Trump campaign team as unpaid volunteer foreign policy adviser on March 6, 2016 because he said Donald Trump's position on Russia was similar to his. The conspirators desperately needed a Trump campaign team member to go to Russia so that they could create false evidence of the Trump campaign's collusion with Russia. Page was a vulnerable target because he criticized US policy on Russia, he boasted of nonexistent accomplishments and government contacts in Russia, and he routinely travelled to Russia for his business.

The New Economic School of Moscow (NES) is a private graduate school of economics dependent on private funding. Its faculty is composed of economists with PhDs from the world's leading universities. NES has a history of exceptionally distinguished commencement speakers. For example, President Obama in 2009, the former Mexican president, Ernesto Zedillo, in 2013, and the world-famous economist, Branko Milanovic, in 2018. High level Russian government officials attend the commencement ceremonies.

Carter Page is remarkably undistinguished and somewhat offbeat, yet in April 2016, one month after he joined the Trump campaign, the NES extended an invitation for him to be its commencement speaker in July. Although very intelligent, Page at times expounds peculiar theories, is a poor communicator, and leads a mediocre career.

Examples of Page's "scholarly" endeavors are:

- Page wrote articles for the Global Policy Journal, an academic publication based at the U.K.'s Durham University. In February 2015, he wrote a bizarre article titled: "New Slaves, Global Edition: Russia, Iran and the Segregation of the World Economy." In it, he argued that the US National Security Strategy, which included aggressive sanctions on Russia over its actions in Ukraine, paralleled an 1850 publication on how to produce the ideal slave.

- Page submitted a book manuscript on Russian relations in Central Asia for publication by the academic press. The editor said "I would never have seen him playing a role or being seen as an intermediary between the Russian government and a political candidate... He struck me just as someone who had developed some strange academic views ... and wanted to have them published...I just came to see him as a kook."

- Page's British academic supervisors at the University of London failed his doctoral thesis twice, an unusual move. In a report they described his work as "verbose" and "vague." Page responded by angrily accusing his examiners of "anti-Russian bias".

- In 1998 Page spent three months working for the Eurasia Group, a strategy consulting firm. Its founder, Ian Bremmer, described Page as his "most wackadoodle alumnus" with vehemently pro-Kremlin views.

On March 2, 2016, more than one hundred GOP foreign policy leaders signed an open letter declaring that "We are unable to support a party ticket with Mr. Trump at its head." The well-known foreign policy advisors joined other candidates' teams. Trump faced criticism for the lack of foreign policy advisors on his team, so he met with the Washington Post editors on March 21 to announce five little-known foreign policy advisers, including Page.

In April, when NES invited Page to be their commencement speaker, Trump was not yet the GOP candidate and polls showed him behind Clinton by double digits in a presidential match-up. With a history of highly exceptional commencement speakers, the only credible explanation for why the NES invited the unknown Page in April 2016 to be their commencement speaker is that the conspirators arranged for it.

In April 2016 Clinton and the DNC hired Fusion GPS to create false evidence of the Trump campaign's collusion with Russia to influence the election. Fusion GPS would turn the eccentric Navy veteran Carter Page from a hero in helping the FBI successfully prosecute a Russian spy into a cunning traitor working with Russia to elect Trump president by stealing the DNC emails and publishing them on WikiLeaks. Page's visit to Moscow for the commencement speech is the very basis of Fusion GPS's false evidence, and the excuse used by the DOJ and FBI to spy on Carter Page and launch a counterintelligence investigation on Trump/Russia collusion. The New York Times reported in April 2017 that "current and former law enforcement and intelligence officials" said the investigation was triggered by Carter Page's trip to Moscow.

The conspirators set Page up through: 1) Steele dossier allegations, and 2) Spying on Page.

Steele Dossier Allegations Against Page

The DNC was developing the Trump/Russia collusion story since 2015. The FBI told the DNC in September 2015 that hackers had "compromised at least one computer." On April 28, 2016, the DNC IT staff detected access to the DNC network by unauthorized users, and their cybersecurity vendor, CrowdStrike, said it was Russia. Clinton and the DNC seized upon the email theft as an opportunity to greatly increase the impact of their collusion story by blaming the theft on Trump campaign collusion with Russia. The DNC and Clinton campaign hired Fusion GPS in April to provide false evidence that the Trump campaign worked with Russian officials to hack the DNC servers, steal the emails, and post them on WikiLeaks. Fusion GPS hired a former UK MI6 spy, Christopher Steele, to create the false evidence. Steele documented this misinformation in a series of reports called the "Steele Dossier."

Steele's dossier consisted of individual numbered reports. Report 2016/09, no date, is titled "<u>Russia/US Presidential Election: Further Indications of Extensive Conspiracy Between Trump's Campaign Team and the Kremlin</u>." Some of its allegations include:

- "Speaking in confidence to a compatriot in late July 2016, Source E, an ethnic Russian close associate of Republican US presidential candidate Donald TRUMP, admitted that there was a well-developed conspiracy of co-operation between them and the Russian leadership. This was **managed on the TRUMP side by the Republican candidate's campaign manager, Paul MANAFORT, who is using foreign policy adviser Carter PAGE, and others as intermediaries**. The two sides had a mutual interest in defeating presidential candidate Hillary CLINTON, whom president PUTIN apparently both hated and feared.
- "Inter alia, Source E, acknowledged that the Russian regime had been behind the recent leak of embarrassing e-mail messages, emanating from the Democratic National Committee (DNC), to the WikiLeaks platform. The reason for using WikiLeaks was "plausible deniability" and the operation had been conducted with the full knowledge and support of TRUMP and senior members of his campaign team. In return the TRUMP team had agreed to sideline Russian intervention in

Ukraine as a campaign issue and to raise US/NATO defence commitments in the Baltics and Eastern Europe to deflect attention away from Ukraine, a priority for PUTIN who needed to cauterise the subject."

- "TRUMP's team using moles within the DNC and hackers in the US as well as outside in Russia."

Report 2016/09, dated July 30, 2016, is titled "Kremlin Concern that Political Fallout from DNC Hacking Affair Spiralling Out of Control." Two allegations are:

- "Kremlin concerned that political fallout from DNC e-mail hacking operation is spiralling out of control."
- "the émigré associate of TRUMP opined that the Kremlin wanted the situation to calm down for "plausible deniability" to be maintained concerning the extensive pro-TRUMP and anti-CLINTON operations."

Report 2016/100, dated August 5, 2016, is titled "Growing Backlash in Kremlin to DNC Hacking and Trump Support Operations"

- "Premier MEDVEDEV's office furious over DNC hacking and associated anti-Russian publicity.
- "Speaking in early August 2016, two well-placed and established Kremlin sources outlined the divisions and backlash in Moscow arising from the leaking of Democratic National Committee (DNC) e-mails and the wider pro-TRUMP operation being conducted."

These allegations are patently false because of the timeline. Carter Page joined the campaign on March 6, and Manafort joined on March 28, both as unpaid volunteers. It was physically impossible for Manafort and Page to plot and coordinate with Russian intelligence agencies to arrange a complex hack of the DNC servers and steal emails in April, days after they joined Trump's team. Such a complex hack would take months of planning. Evidence in a Robert Mueller indictment indicates that a Russian spear phishing campaign to steal logon credentials was already in progress when Page and Manafort joined the team. Both were unpaid volunteers at that time with Manafort focused on getting Trump delegates, and with Page playing no role in the campaign other than attending some meetings. Page and Manafort have never even met to this day. Steele attributes these absurd allegations to Source E, Sergei Millian.

At the invitation of the New Economic School of Moscow in April, Page traveled to Moscow and gave a speech on foreign policy on July 7, 2016 and delivered the school's commencement address the following day. Steele incorporated the trip, which was public knowledge, into his dossier. Report 2016/134, dated 10/18/2016, is titled "<u>Further Details of Kremlin Liaison with Trump Campaign,</u>" and alleges that Page met with Igor Sechin in a secret meeting on either July 7 or 8.

> Sechin "was so keen to lift personal and corporate western sanctions imposed on the company (Rosneft) that he offered Page/Trump's associates the brokerage of up to a 19 percent (privatized) stake in Rosneft in return. PAGE had expressed interest and confirmed that were TRUMP elected US president, then sanctions on Russia would be lifted." Page clearly implied he was speaking with Trump's authority.

Igor Sechin is the head of Rosneft, the giant Russian state oil company, is a close Putin ally, and is "widely believed to be Russia's second-most powerful person."

Another Steele report stated that Page had "conceived and promoted" the idea that the DNC emails to WikiLeaks should be leaked during the Democratic convention, "to swing supporters of Bernie Sanders away from Hilary Clinton and across from Trump."

Steele's allegations paint a picture of the cunning and influential Carter Page, a key person in Trump's campaign, conspiring with Russia to hack the DNC and publish the stolen emails and negotiating with Russia's second most powerful person. Page's background shows the absurdity of the allegations.

- Page's former boss at Merrill Lynch, Sergei Aleksashenko, said he was "without any special talents or accomplishments," someone who was "a gray spot." His business website states Page was an advisor on key transactions for Gazprom, the giant Russian natural gas company, but Aleksashenko says "No one let him into Gazprom. He didn't go shake [Gazprom chief Alexey] Miller's hand. He made sure there were cars, hotels and meetings for investors in London." Another of Page's colleagues from Merrill Lynch confirmed that Page's role was simply arranging meetings between Gazprom and Western investors.[lxvii]
- Page is the only employee of his company, Global Energy Capital. He "rents a windowless room... by the hour. Other tenants include the National Shingles Foundation and a wedding-band company called Star Talent Inc."
- Page had a minimal role in the Trump campaign. An administration official who worked with the campaign said "Page had no badge, and never signed a non-disclosure agreement — two requirements of anyone working with the campaign in an official capacity. He also wasn't on the campaign's payroll and did not have a campaign email account."

It is a preposterous to claim Russia's second most powerful person would ever meet with Page, much less offer him a multi-million-dollar commission on a Rosneft transaction. It is equally absurd to claim Sechin would believe that Page spoke for Trump on anything, much less spoke for Trump in agreeing to lift sanctions.

Steele's false allegation that Page met with Sechin is of no benefit to the FBI's investigation because there is no prohibition meeting with a sanctioned individual.

Steele used public information in his dossier. Rosneft's plan to sell a 19 percent stake in the company, and Page's commencement speech in Moscow were publicly known before the dossier was created.

Spying on Page

Page was a patriotic hero in helping the DOJ and FBI to successfully prosecute a Russian spy, who pled guilty in March 2016. The conspirators in the DOJ and FBI then used Page as an unknowing dupe to spy on him and the Trump campaign.

Shortly after Trump's March 21 announcement, James Comey, Andrew McCabe, and Loretta Lynch met to discuss the news of Page joining the Trump campaign and how he may be "compromised" by the Russians, according to a declassified memo. In the "late spring" of 2016, Comey held an unusual briefing concerning Page, and the alleged risk he posed, with the Obama administration's highest-ranking national-security officials, who, in addition to Lynch, included National Security Adviser Susan Rice, CIA Director John Brennan, and National Intelligence Director James Clapper.

In June, the DOJ and FBI submitted an application for a FISA warrant to surveille specified Trump campaign members as alleged Russian agents. The FISA court turned down the application, which is very rare.

In a decision most likely approved by Loretta Lynch, the FBI assigned a covert agent named Stefan Halper to the Trump campaign (refer to Appendix for additional information on Halper). On April 18, 2016, Admiral Rogers shut down the illegal practice of the FBI using contractors to query on the FISA database (referred to as 702 queries). On April 30, Peter Strzok texted to Lisa Page:

"So now we've switched from the Patriot Act to a wire carrying current (redacted)".

Following is the most likely meaning of this text:

> The Patriot Act encompasses the Foreign Intelligence Surveillance Act (FISA), Section 702. When a foreigner is under FISA surveillance, their incidental communications with Americans is collected and maintained in a government database. A 702 query can identify communications of an American who communicated with a foreigner under surveillance. Strzok appears to be telling Page that wired informants now need to be used since 702 queries on US citizens were stopped by Admiral Rogers. Rogers stopped the widespread 702 queries because constitutional rights were abused.

Halper's first publicly known covert agent activity occurred in May 2016 when he sent an invitation to Stephen Miller, a high-level Trump campaign adviser, to attend a Cambridge University campaign-themed conference at which Halper's colleague, Sir Richard Dearlove, was one of the speakers. Dearlove was formerly head of the British Secret Intelligence Service, known as MI6. Miller did not attend the event. Halper's action predates the July 31st start of the FBI investigation by more than two months. In late May or early June, a graduate assistant for Halper sent Page an invitation to attend the Cambridge conference held four days after Page's speaking engagement in Moscow. **(Note: this invitation by an FBI covert agent is two months before Strzok initiated the investigation).** It was an all-expense paid invitation even though Page was not a speaker. There was no public news of Page's trip to Moscow until Corey Lewandowski approved it in late June. Page met with

Halper during the London visit, and would continue to meet and communicate with him until September 2017.

Some people defend the FBI's use of Halper. For example:

- Legal experts cited by the media say Halper's work was most likely part of a legitimate counterintelligence operation targeted at Russia's election interference campaign and not any kind of political attack on Trump. Congressman Trey Gowdy said "the FBI did exactly what my fellow citizens would want them to do when they got the information they got."
- Rep. Adam Schiff and other Democrats on the House Intelligence Committee falsely stated in their 10-page memo defending the Obama Justice Department's monitoring of Page: "The FBI interviewed Page multiple times about his Russian intelligence contacts, including in March 2016. The FBI's concern about and knowledge of Page's activities therefore long predate the FBI's receipt of Steele's information."

These defenses are wrong. Halper was not acting as a spy to uncover any Russian election influence. The FBI was instead using Halper to set up Papadopoulos and Page in order to create false evidence of Trump/Russia collusion. As previously described, Halper tried to get Papadopoulos to talk about emails after the covert agents Mifsud and Downer completed their entrapment operation.

Contrary to Schiff's false claim, there was no probable cause to spy on Carter Page because he helped the FBI and DOJ from 2013 through March 2016 to convict a Russian spy. Peter Strzok and John Carlin headed this investigation, so they knew Carter Page very well and how he fulfilled his patriotic duty to help them. Strzok and Carlin submitted an application for a FISA warrant to surveille Page as a suspected Russian agent. They used Steele's dossier allegations as evidence in the application and deceived the FISA court by not stating the dossier was funded by Clinton and the DNC. The FISA application also cited as additional evidence a news article written by Yahoo News reporter Michael Isikoff in September 2016. Steele provided Isikoff with the information in the article. McCabe testified "that no surveillance warrant would have been sought from the FISC without the Steele dossier information." The FISA court approved the warrant on October 19.

The FBI and DOJ met shortly after Page joined the Trump campaign to discuss how he may be "compromised" by the Russians, and in the "late spring" of 2016, Comey briefed the Obama administration's highest-ranking national-security official on the risk that Page posed. In actuality, they did not believe Page to be a threat. They feigned concern to justify spying on and investigating the Trump campaign without probable cause. The FBI was obviously not truly concerned about Steele's allegation that Page colluded with Russia to influence the election, because the FBI waited until March 2017 to question Page – five months after the election!

At the same time the FBI and DOJ were exonerating Clinton, they were seeking to surveil Trump and his campaign team on the pretext that they were Russian agents. McCarthy said "an application to wiretap the presidential candidate of the opposition party, and some of his associates, during the heat of the presidential campaign, based on the allegation that the candidate and his associates were acting as Russian agents – it seems to me that there is less than zero chance that could have happened without consultation between the Justice Department and the White House... FISA national-security investigations are not like criminal investigations. They are more like covert intelligence operations – which presidents personally sign off on."

In September 2016, Page quit as a member of Trump's campaign team. The FISA warrant was requested and approved in October 2016, and then renewed three times through September 2017. A FISA warrant approval ends in 90 days, so must be renewed to continue monitoring the subject. Each renewal requires new evidence.

The conspirators used Page's visit to Russia in multiple ways: a) in Steele's dossier allegations, b) as a pretext for the FBI to use Halper as a covert agent, c) to justify a FISA warrant to spy on Americans, d) in widely disseminated media stories about Trump's collusion with Russia, e) for the Clinton campaign to use against Trump, f) to brief members of Congress, and g) ultimately to authorize a Special Counsel. The false evidence of Trump/Russian collusion would have been profoundly weaker if Page had not visited Russia.

The fact that the FBI and Stefan Halper continued to surveille Page for one year after he quit the Trump campaign implies that they did in fact continue to collect new evidence needed to justify each renewal. The objective of the surveillance was to gather evidence for the Trump/Russia collusion investigation, so what could the FBI collect since Page was not associated with Trump during the entire FISA surveillance period? The answer is that the Page surveillance warrant allowed the DOJ and FBI to spy on the entire Trump campaign team due to the "two-hop rule" for FISA warrants.[lxviii] After Trump was inaugurated president, did the FBI and/or the Mueller team surveille anyone in the Trump administration using the Page FISA warrants, including the warrant approved by Rosenstein?

Page Setup Conclusion

Carter Page was a patriotic veteran who helped the FBI convict a Russian spy. He volunteered as an unpaid campaign adviser because Trump advocated better relations with Russia. The vile Comey, Strzok, Lynch and the other conspirators set him up as a villain who colluded with Russia to help Trump win the presidency. Page said his "huge nightmare" started in September 2016, when Yahoo News posted an article written by

Simpson's friend, Michael Isikoff, who used Steele's false dossier allegations to reveal Page was under federal investigation for his ties to Russian government officials. The article falsely alleged that Page discussed with senior Russian officials the potential removal of economic sanctions if Trump became president.

Page said the FBI ruined his life. His business was hurt by the false accusations, and his girlfriend broke up with him due to the press reports about him. Interestingly, Page's girlfriend was British and left him in "late 2016." One must wonder if the girlfriend was a covert agent, who left Page after the surveillance warrant was approved.

8. The George Papadopoulos Setup

Introduction

George Papadopoulos was an inexperienced young man who joined the Trump campaign as an unpaid Foreign Policy Adviser on March 6, 2016. Prior to that, the bulk of his experience was as an unpaid intern at the Hudson Institute. Papadopoulos is from Chicago, and lived there when Ben Carson announced on December 8, 2015 that Papadopoulos was on his National Security and Foreign Policy Advisory Committee. Papadopoulos worked on Carson's team for only six weeks.

The conspirators used at least seven covert agents for Papadopoulos: Joseph Mifsud, Alexander Downer, Stefan Halper, Azra Turk, Charles Tawil, David Ha'ivri, and Sergei Millian. Mifsud, Downer, Turk, and Halper are located in London, Tawil in Washington D.C., Ha'ivri in Israel, and Millian in New York. As will be explained in the summary of this section, the evidence is inconclusive as to whether Papadopoulos was an innocent dupe or a covert agent himself.

The conspirators began their first set up of Papadopoulos at the London Centre of International Law and Practice (LCILP), which offers training courses in international law in a short time frame. "The LCILP training, delivered by experts and renowned practitioners, emphasises the practical application of international law as a field inseparable from its geopolitical and global economic context."

Some media stories describe LCILP in very negative terms. In reality, LCILP's training events are run by very influential and distinguished people. For example, two LCILP directors, Arvinder Sambei and Martin Polaine, are speakers at LCILP anti-corruption forums. Sambei and Polaine were both Senior

Crown Prosecutors. Sambei was previously an attorney for the FBI in the UK.

In February 2016, Papadopoulos moved to London to become the Director of the Centre for International Energy and Natural Resources Law & Security at the London Centre of International Law and Practice (LCILP), where he only worked two months until April 2016. His appointment to that position was ludicrous because he had no qualifications for it. For example, Papadopoulos attended LCILP's "1st Annual Conference on Energy Arbitration and Dispute Resolution in the Middle East and Africa" held in London from March 7 to 9 in 2016. The International Court of Arbitration announced that it was pleased to be one of 21 prominent global organizations lending their support to LCILP, STLP and their conference. The conference's "Session Chairs" included the former Senior Vice President of the American Arbitration Association, the Editor in Chief of the Arab Bankers Association, and the Former Legal Director & Member of Executive Committee of Royal Dutch Shell Plc.

Papadopoulos was way out of his league at that conference, so obviously LCILP did not hire him as a director for his knowledge or experience. It was a ruse so Papadopoulos could interact with covert agents located in London.

The Joseph Mifsud Setup of Papadopoulos

Joseph Mifsud, a well-known academic, was the director of the London Academy of Diplomacy. He became the Director of International Strategy at LCILP in November 2015. Mifsud was a UK covert agent who set a trap for Papadopoulos. He met Papadopoulos in Italy at an LCILP luncheon on March 14. Mifsud told Papadopoulos that he had substantial connections with Russian government officials. Knowing that Trump advocated better relations with Russia, Papadopoulos thought these Russian connections could increase his importance as a policy advisor to the campaign, so he pursued meeting with Mifsud. As subsequent events would show, the real reason LCILP hired the unqualified Papadopoulos in a prestigious position was to arrange this "chance" meeting with Mifsud without raising suspicion. (The Appendix section A2 has additional information on Mifsud, and section A2 has a detailed timeline on George Papadopoulos.)

On March 24, 2016, Papadopoulos met with Mifsud, and a lady named Olga Polonskaya in a London cafe. Mifsud introduced Polonskaya as Putin's niece with high-profile ties to the Russian government. Polonskaya is a 30-year-old Russian from St. Petersburg and the former manager of a wine distribution company. Putin has no niece. Polonskaya was a student at Link Campus University in Rome (LINK). Mifsud has been associated with the LINK since he helped found it in 1999 and he is LINK's Dean of the Bachelor of Arts degree program in political sciences and international relations and a visiting professor. Polonskaya was in London discussing a possible internship with Mifsud, a friend of hers, the morning before the meeting with Papadopoulos. Polonskaya told her brother that she understood only about half of the discussion with Papadopoulos "Because my English was bad."

One Papadopoulos email to Trump campaign officials said that the woman had offered "to arrange a meeting between us and the Russian leadership to discuss U.S.-Russia ties under President Trump." After Papadopoulos asked for help arranging a trip to Moscow, Polonskaya/Vinogradova said in an April email "I have already alerted my personal links to our conversation and your request." "As mentioned we are all very excited by the possibility of a good relationship with Mr. Trump. The Russian Federation would love to welcome him once his candidature would be officially announced," she added.

Polonskaya's email was clearly written by someone with excellent English. For example, the proper use of the word "candidature" is too sophisticated for a non-native speaker without an excellent command of English.

Papadopoulos continued corresponding with Vinogradova throughout the spring of 2016, including multiple efforts to arrange a meeting in Russia between the Trump campaign and government connections that Vinogradova purported to have.

The media portrayed Mifsud as a shadowy professor suspected of being a Russian spy. This characterization is completely false. Mifsud has associations with high level western intelligence officials through his academic endeavors but does not have publicly known associations with any significant Russian government officials. (Refer to section A2 of the Appendix for more details about Mifsud.) Mifsud was very well known in his academic and diplomatic circles, including with Russian academicians and diplomats. For example, he knows Dr. Ivan Timofeev who is the Director of Programs for a Russian non-profit academic and diplomatic think tank. Dr. Timofeev is an author and co-author of more than 80 publications.

On April 18, 2016, Mifsud introduced Papadopoulos by email to Timofeev, who Mifsud said had connections to the Russian Ministry of Foreign Affairs. Mifsud made the email introduction one day before he appeared on a panel with Timofeev at the Valdai Discussion Club think tank event in Russia. Over the next several weeks, Papadopoulos and Timofeev had multiple conversations over Skype and email about setting "the groundwork" for a "potential" meeting between the Trump campaign and Russian government official.

Between March and September 2016, Papadopoulos made at least six requests to campaign officials for Trump or representatives of his campaign to meet in Russia with Russian politicians. In May, campaign chairman Paul Manafort forwarded one such request to his deputy Rick Gates, saying "We need someone to communicate that [Trump] is not doing these trips."

On April 26, 2016, Mifsud told Papadopoulos at a breakfast meeting that high-level Russian government officials said "They [the Russians] have dirt on her." Mifsud's purpose in communicating this information was so Papadopoulos would repeat it to another covert agent, Alexander Downer, in order to fabricate false evidence that the Trump campaign was colluding with Russia to steal emails.

The Alexander Downer Setup of Papadopoulos

Alexander Downer was the Australian High Commissioner to the United Kingdom from 2014 to 2018 (Refer to Appendix for more information). Mifsud, the director of the prestigious London Academy of Diplomacy, undoubtedly knows Downer. Downer has very close ties to UK intelligence. He was on the advisory board of a private UK intelligence firm, Hakluyt & Company (now called Holdingham), from 2008 to 2014, and attended corporate meetings through 2015. Hakluyt, founded by former MI6 officials, has close associations with Sir Richard Dearlove and Stefan Halper, both of whom Downer knows well. Downer was the Australian Minister for Foreign Affairs from 1996 to 2007, during which time the Australian Secret Intelligence Service (ASIS) reported to him. Downer has been friends with the Clintons for many years. He arranged a $25 million Australian donation to the Clinton Foundation in 2006, jointly signing the Memorandum of Understanding with Bill Clinton.

At Downer's request, Papadopoulos met with him at a London bar on May 10 and told Downer that Mifsud said the Russians have damaging information on Clinton. As required by the Five Eyes Agreement with the U.S., Downer should have reported the information to Australian intelligence (ASIS) and they would communicate the information to US intelligence. As the former head of ASIS, Downer knew the protocol, but ignored it and relayed what Papadopoulos told him to Elizabeth Dibble at the U.S. Embassy in London. Dibble previously served as a principal deputy assistant secretary in Hillary Clinton's State Department. This is one of multiple publicly known times that the State Department participated in the conspiracy to create the false Trump/Russia collusion story.

The State Department must have given Downer's information to the FBI because within hours of opening the Trump/Russia investigation on July 31, Strzok flew to London to interview Downer. The New York Times, citing anonymous sources, wrote that the FBI opened the investigation because of the Papadopoulos information.

Some accounts say that Papadopoulos told Downer the Russians have dirt on Clinton in the form of emails, but Downer disputes that. Downer stated in an Australian interview "He [Papadopoulos] didn't say dirt, he said material that could be damaging to her. He didn't say what it was." Downer noted "Nothing he said in that conversation indicated Trump himself had been conspiring with the Russians to collect information on Hillary Clinton." Joseph Mifsud vigorously denied that he said anything about Clinton emails to Papadopoulos.

Footnote 5 of Rep. Adam Schiff's memorandum responding to Devin Nunes on Foreign Intelligence Surveillance Act abuse verifies that the FBI only knew that the Russians had damaging information on Clinton, as Downer had said, but nothing about emails. Margot Cleveland says "Papadopoulos merely stated that 'Russians might use material that they have on Hillary Clinton in the lead-up to the election, which may be damaging.' That statement cannot possibly justify opening a counterintelligence investigation on a presidential campaign. Half the world expected that at the time."[lxix]

The Stefan Halper and Azra Turk Setup of Papadopoulos

In a September 2, 2016 email, the FBI covert agent, Stefan Halper offered Papadopoulos $3,000 to write a policy paper on issues related to Turkey, Cyprus, Israel and the Leviathan natural gas field. Halper also offered to pay for Papadopoulos's flight and a three-night stay in London. Papadopoulos accepted the proposal, flew to England, and met with Halper. He delivered the paper electronically Oct. 2 and received payment.[lxx]

While in London, Papadopoulos had dinner multiple times with Halper and a Turkish woman described as his assistant. Sources familiar with Papadopoulos's version of their meetings said Halper randomly asked Papadopoulos whether he knew about Democratic National Committee emails that had been hacked and leaked by Russians. Papadopoulos strongly denied the allegation. Halper grew agitated and pressed Papadopoulos on the topic. Halper's assistant, who is named Azra Turk, brought up Russians and emails over drinks with Papadopoulos. Turk also flirted heavily with Papadopoulos and attempted to meet him in Chicago, where he lived. Halper and Turk were unsuccessfully trying to entrap Papadopoulos to fabricate evidence of Trump collusion with Russia.[lxxi]

The Sergei Millian Setup of Papadopoulos

Sergei Millian was the source of the major allegations in Steele's dossier. Millian was also a dupe that Steele used to set up other people. As described above in Chapter 6, Millian tried to set Papadopoulos up twice.

- Millian approached Papadopoulos over LinkedIn "out of the blue" during the summer of 2016 to propose that he and Papadopoulos "form an energy-related business that would be financed by influential Russian billionaires."
- After the election, Millian offered to pay Papadopoulos $30,000 per month "while he worked inside the Trump

administration" as a consultant to hunt for business opportunities with wealthy Russian clients.

Millian could not have afforded to pay Papadopoulos, so the conspirators obviously deployed him in this plot to entrap Papadopoulos. Of all the Trump advisers, why would Steele target Papadopoulos? The answer is that Steele knew that the British conspirators were setting Papadopoulos up to fabricate "evidence" of Trump collusion with Russia. The FBI informant, Halper, was very good friends of the former MI6 head, Sir Richard Dearlove. Dearlove and Halper direct the Cambridge Security Initiative (CSi), a non-profit intelligence consulting group. Steele and his business partner, Chris Burrows, worked for Dearlove at MI6 as intelligence officers, and they met with Dearlove during the dossier preparation process to discuss it and obtain advice. Halper and Dearlove are also friends of the covert agent, Alexander Downer. Steele paid his sources, so it is highly likely that Steele paid Millian to befriend Papadopoulos to gather information (e.g., Mifsud conversations) for the dossier, and entrap Papadopoulos with a monetary offer to work with wealthy Russians while employed in the Trump administration.

The Israeli Setup of Papadopoulos

After the election, Papadopoulos told a Greek reporter that he had "a blank check" for any job he wanted in the Trump administration because of his services to the campaign. "Everyone knows I helped him [get] elected, now I want to help him with the presidency," Papadopoulos boasted in a text message.

Papadopoulos did not get a job in the Trump administration. The Chicago-Tribune reported that "he became a frequent guest on Mykonos, the Greek island that's a paradise for the well-heeled. During the late spring and into the summer, locals said he was a regular if discreet visitor at the island's poshest clubs. He judged a beauty contest — watching impassively as bikini-clad contestants marched by — and onlookers at the clubs described him as partying hard and spending freely. By midsummer, Papadopoulos was telling people on Mykonos that he had grown disenchanted with the United States and planned to settle permanently in Greece."[lxxii]

In July 2017, Charles Tawil, an Israeli-American living in Washington D.C., went to meet Papadopoulos in Mykonos. At Tawil's invitation, Papadopoulos went to Israel where Tawil gave him $10,000 during a meeting in an Israeli hotel room in July 2017 for a purported business deal. On July 27, Papadopoulos returned to the U.S. and waiting FBI agents arrested him at the Dulles airport.[lxxiii]

As Ian Fleming would say, the $10,000 Tawil gave to Papadopoulos was an "enemy action," not a coincidence. The evidence strongly suggests that Mueller tried to entrap Papadopoulos. A person bringing more than $10,000 into the U.S. must file a report declaring the funds to U.S. Customs and Border Protection (CBP). The prosecutors had the FBI waiting at the airport to arrest Papadopoulos, but they had no warrant for him and no indictment or criminal complaint. This implies that the prosecutors assumed the FBI would arrest Papadopoulos for bringing $10,000 and not declaring it. Papadopoulos left the $10,000 in Greece, so the prosecutors filed a complaint the morning after the arrest.

The story on why Tawil gave Papadopoulos $10,000 does not add up. David Ha'ivri said that he introduced Tawil and Papadopoulos "at my own initiative" to facilitate a business deal involving an oil and gas project in the Aegean and Mediterranean seas. Ha'ivri said that Tawil "is a part time consultant for companies that operate in Africa and Middle East." He believed when he introduced Tawil to Papadopoulos that the former Trump aide had "good connections" in the Eastern Mediterranean and Middle East.[lxxiv]

Ha'ivri is a religious activist, Zionist leader, writer, and speaker, who is a settler on the West Bank. He has no background in putting together business deals. Ha'ivri's explained the $10,000 to TheDCNF:[lxxv]

"Ha'ivri said he was not aware of a payment from Tawil to Papadopoulos. But he said Tawil succeeded in getting a consulting contract with a petroleum and gas infrastructure company. That company agreed to give a retainer of $10,000 a month. The retainer would go firstly to cover [George's] needs as he said that he had financial problems. This first job was to help preparing bidding document to Exxon Mobil for their project in Cyprus and help negotiating a subcontracting deal there."

Ha'ivri said "the deal quickly fell apart, blaming Papadopoulos' 'immaturity.' After that the whole story fell apart. Charles left back to Washington and the story was over."

Ha'ivri explanation is preposterous and contradictory:

- Ha'ivri first said he did not know about the $10,000, and then he explained it in detail.
- Tawil gave Papadopoulos $10,000 in July for assistance in preparing a bid for a major Exxon Mobil project, then in only a few days Papadopoulos made the deal fall apart because of 'immaturity.'
- Ha'ivri said that Tawil gave Papadopoulos his whole first month retainer because Papadopoulos had financial problems. A retainer is a fee paid in advance to someone, especially an attorney, in order to secure their services when required. Papadopoulos was unemployed, so it is unbelievable that Tawil would give a complete stranger a very large $10,000 gift out of the goodness of his heart.

Ha'ivri's claim that he believed Papadopoulos had "good connections" in the Eastern Mediterranean and Middle East is false. Papadopoulos's major career accomplishment was working for the Trump campaign for 8 months as an unpaid adviser, and he was not offered a job in the Trump administration afterwards. Papadopoulos did not work after the election, opting instead to spend much of his time partying in Greece. Ha'ivri sent Tawil over to Greece to meet with Papadopoulos rather than wait a very short time for him to return to Chicago. The fact that Ha'ivri knew that Papadopoulos, a complete stranger, was vacationing on the Greek island of Mykonos further supports that Ha'ivri and Tawill were setting Papadopoulos up for entrapment.

An internet search found a Charles Tawil in Washington D.C., who is a consultant for Gestomar. Bloomberg did not have information about Gestomar. Companies named Gestomar are located in Spain, Portugal, Switzerland, and Morocco, but none are related to the oil and gas energy market.

A Charles Tawil had been a CIA and FBI intelligence asset according to a WikiLeaks 2006 document, but it is unknown if it is the same person who met with Papadopoulos.

Another Israeli was slightly involved in the Downer set up meeting. Erika Thompson was a counselor to Downer and served in Australia's London embassy. Papadopoulos knew an Israeli embassy official in London named Christian Cantor, who introduced Papadopoulos to Erika Thompson. Thompson told Papadopoulos that Downer wanted to meet with him, and they scheduled the meeting at the bar, which Thompson also attended.

Papadopoulos's wife said he "pled guilty because [Mueller's prosecutors] threatened to charge him with being an Israeli agent." If, as evidence suggests, Mueller did use Tawil to entrap Papadopoulos, his threat to charge him as an Israeli spy to get him to plead guilty is an outrageous abuse of power.

Mifsud's Connections to Western Intelligence Services

Although Mifsud's Russian connections are only academic and diplomatic, he has a strong association with Western intelligence at LAD and LINK. Claire Smith was a member of the UK's Joint Intelligence Committee (JIC), a supervisory body overseeing all UK intelligence agencies. The JIC is part of the Cabinet Office and reports directly to the Prime Minister. She was also an eight-year member of the UK Cabinet Office Security Vetting Appeals Panel, which oversees the vetting process for UK intelligence placement. Smith and Mifsud were involved with an international security training program for high level Italian military officers that was organized by LINK and LAD in 2012. Claire Smith was a visiting professor at LAD from 2013-2014. Charles Crawford, a former MI6 officer, and Robert Whalley, former UK Director for Counter Terrorism and Intelligence at the Home Office and the Cabinet Office, also taught there.

Mifsud and associates worked with Vincenzo Scotti, a former Italian Minister, to obtain approval to open a University of Malta branch in Rome. It was the first foreign university authorized to operate in Italy. The name was changed to LINK Campus University. Scotti is the President. Link Campus is a private university, accredited by Italy's education ministry, with six Italian politicians on its governing body, including two former foreign ministers. One of the university's courses is a MA degree in Intelligence and Security. LINK runs the Consortium for Research on Intelligence and Security Services (CRISS). CRISS is an Italian consortium of Defense and Technology sector companies specializing in the high tech, security and intelligence sectors. CRISS operates in five main areas: Territorial Security, Intelligence, Security Devices, Systems and Infrastructures, Training and Support Systems. LINK also offers anti-drug trafficking studies.

LINK has trained intelligence and police personnel from the West for years. In 2004 the CIA arranged a conference on terrorism there. David Ignatius of the Washington Post wrote about the conference saying "'New Frontiers of Intelligence Analysis' brought together officials from intelligence and police agencies of nearly 30 countries."

The FBI has trained students at Link since 2010. In September 2016, or two months after the FBI opened its Russia investigation, the FBI's legal attaché working out of the U.S. Embassy in Rome sent Special Agent Preston Ackerman to conduct a seminar at Link.

Mifsud's Reward?

Mifsud told his staff in 2015 that the LAD would close in 2016 because of financial losses. This was very bad news for Mifsud's career because LAD was not only his main income stream, but also his reputation as the director of the prestigious LAD spawned influential contacts and income-producing requests to teach at seminars and universities, hold conferences, speak at events, and consult.

After his covert Papadopoulos entrapment operation, however, Mifsud's career blossomed. Influential people in Saudi Arabia and Italy were behind his rapidly rising career trajectory.

Mifsud's two significant Saudi connections are Nawaf Obaid and Majed Garoub

- Nawaf Obaid was a "visiting fellow" at the LAD. He is a counselor to both Prince Mohammad bin Nawaf, Saudi ambassador to the United Kingdom, and Prince Turki Al Faisa. Turki al-Faisal ran the Saudi foreign intelligence service for almost a quarter of a century, from 1977 until 2001. Turki al-Faisal has been a friend of Bill Clinton since their college days at Georgetown University and a very large donor to the Clinton Foundation.
- Majed Garoub is pictured in a photo with Papadopoulos at March LCILP event. Garoub owns a major Saudi law firm and he represents members of the royal house of

Saudi Arabia in sport and is a member of the Legal Committee at FIFA. Majed Garoub signed cooperation agreement with LCILP, at around the same time that Mifsud joined LCILP.

Mifsud's two significant Italian connections are Vincenzo Scotti and Gianni Pittella:

- Vincenzo Scotti, a former Italian Minister, worked with Mifsud to obtain approval to open a University of Malta branch in Rome. It was the first foreign university authorized to operate in Italy. The name was changed to LINK Campus University. Scotti is the President.
- Gianni Pittella is a very influential Italian Member of the European Parliament (MEP) because he leads the second-largest power block of politicians. He was a Visiting Professor of the LAD, helping to develop programs there, and a close friend of Mifsud's, even bringing Mifsud campaigning with him. Pittella is on a LINK steering committee with Scotti. Pittella, who called Donald Trump a 'virus,' said "I have taken the unprecedented step of endorsing and campaigning for Hillary Clinton because the risk of Donald Trump is too high." He spoke at the 2016 Democratic National Convention in Philadelphia. Pittella told Time magazine. "I believe it is in the interest of the European Union and Italy to have Hillary Clinton in office. A Trump victory could be a disaster for the relationship between the U.S.A. and Italy."

On May 8, 2017, LINK and the Essam & Dalal Obaid Foundation (EDOF) signed a partnership agreement to establish the EDOF Centre for War and Peace Studies at LINK. The announcement stated that the "EDOF Centre will work closely with the various interdisciplinary academic departments at the Link Campus University as well as with international governments and organizations in order to support experts, academics, researchers, diplomats, governments, and civil society activists in their attempts to help countries in conflict, crisis and transition around the world." It said that Professor Joseph Mifsud will be appointed the Founding Director of the Centre for a period of three years. Mifsud was not qualified for the position. He received his PhD at Queen's University in Belfast in 1995, and his doctoral thesis was on educational reform. His work experience is unrelated to the Centre's mission.

On October 5, 2017, the Saudi King Salman visited Russia - the first ever state visit by a Saudi monarch. Mifsud was part of the Saudi delegation. (Refer to section A3 in the Appendix for more detailed information on 'Mifsud's Reward?'.)

The First FBI Interview of Papadopoulos

Strzok initiated the Trump/Russia investigation on July 31, 2016, and within hours he flew to London to interview Downer about his discussion with Papadopoulos about Mifsud's story on Russian 'dirt' on Clinton. The FBI learned about this when Downer gave the story to Elizabeth Dibble at the State Department, who got it forwarded to the FBI. After the initial sense of urgency, why did the FBI wait 6 months until January 27, 2017 to interview Papadopoulos.

Joseph Mifsud is Exposed in the Papadopoulos Indictment

On October 30, 2017, Mueller's court documents were unsealed and news media reported that "George Papadopoulos Pleads Guilty in Russia's Mueller Probe." The plea agreement referenced a "professor living in London," who the Washington Post identified as Joseph Mifsud.

November 1, 2017, Mifsud gives an interview to an Italian paper denying he had done anything wrong. He said "you know which is the only foundation I am member of? The Clinton Foundation. Between you and me, my thinking is left-leaning."

Stephan Roh, a millionaire Swiss-German lawyer, is a close Mifsud friend. Mifsud told Roh in January 2018 that that Vincenzo Scotti, the president of LINK, told Mifsud to go into hiding. Scotti, used to head of Italy's intelligence services. Mifsud had not been heard from until September.

In April 2018, the DNC filed a lawsuit against more than a dozen defendants, including Russia, WikiLeaks and the Trump campaign. In a September filing, the DNC said that "Mifsud is missing and may be deceased." A spokeswoman said "The DNC's counsel has attempted to serve Mifsud for months and has been unable to locate or contact him."

Roh called the allegation "nonsense." "I'm in a better mood today. I got it from really good sources. They say that he is alive, that he has another identity, and that he is staying somewhere, at a nice place," Stephan Roh told The Daily Caller News Foundation.[lxxvi]

After the Papadopoulos entrapment, Mifsud was given a highly prestigious position at LINK Campus, an Italian university involved in training western law enforcement, intelligence services and the military. Vincenzo Scotti, a former Italian minster, told Mifsud to go into hiding when his name was revealed after Mueller's indictment of Papadopoulos. Mifsud no longer receives an income from his LINK Campus University job or from his frequent conference speaker engagements. Mifsud was a very successful and well-known academic. Why would Mifsud give up everything he worked so hard for when Scotti told him to go into hiding after the media discovered he was linked to Papadopoulos in the Mueller indictment. The only plausible answer is that Mifsud was a covert agent trying to entrap Papadopoulos and a government(s) quickly gave him a new identity, a nice place to live, and an income in order to hide its involvement with Mifsud and the intelligence operation to influence the 2016 US presidential election to help Clinton win. Which government(s)? One must wonder if former Italian Minister, Vincenzo Scotti's call for Mifsud to go undercover or Saudi Arabia's sudden interest to help Mifsud's career provide any clues?

The Papadopoulos Enigma – Innocent Dupe or Covert Agent

George Papadopoulos moved from Chicago to London in February 2016 for a three-month job with LCILP and then returned to Chicago after the meetings with Mifsud and Downer. Two key questions arise from this curious major relocation of very short-term duration:

- Did the covert agents lure an innocent Papadopoulos to London with the very prestigious LCILP job offer in order to set him up? or
- Was Papadopoulos a paid covert agent (or "useful idiot" like Millian) who was working with Mifsud, Downer and others to fabricate evidence of Trump campaign collusion with Russia?

No public information exists on how Papadopoulos decided to join the Trump campaign, and how he managed to join. Carson's campaign manager, Barry Bennett, said that he would not have recommended Papadopoulos to the Trump campaign if he had been asked because he found him unimpressive. Did a conspirator convince Papadopoulos to join the Trump campaign team and help him get on the team?

Even curiouser, no public information exists on how the very unqualified and obscure Papadopoulos got the prestigious position at LCILP, and who offered him the position. Why would the conspirators offer him the position at LCILP if they did not know for certain that the Trump campaign would bring him onto the team because this was a mandatory requirement for fabricating collusion "evidence?"

Mifsud joined LCILP in November 2015, and Papadopoulos joined in February 2016. Mifsud was a covert agent trying to entrap Papadopoulos beginning with a "chance" meeting at an LCILP event. Papadopoulos first met Mifsud on March 14, only eight days after he joined the Trump campaign team. How could the conspirators know in November 2015 when the entrapment began (i.e., Mifsud joined LCILP) that Papadopoulos would join the Trump team in March 2016? This is not a coincidence.

One explanation is that Papadopoulos is a covert agent, so the conspirators would obviously know since they arranged this. On December 28, 2015, Peter Strzok texted the FBI attorney Lisa Page: "you get all your ocunus lures approved?" OCUNUS stands for Outside of the Continental United States. Was this regarding Mifsud and Papadopoulos?

Another explanation is that the FBI was surveilling an innocent Papadopoulos and the Trump campaign, so the FBI knew when he decided to join LCILP and when the Trump campaign decided to hire him.

The FBI first interviewed Papadopoulos on January 27, 2017. At that time, Papadopoulos had received only positive public recognition for his work on the Trump campaign, with no press reports of any wrongdoing. His lies to the FBI, however, definitely show an awareness of guilt on his part:

- He lied in saying "I wasn't even on the Trump team" when Mifsud told him the Russians had "dirt" on Clinton in the form of "thousands of emails."
- He lied saying Mifsud was "a nothing," and that he thought Mifsud was "just a guy talk[ing] up connections or something," while in fact, Papadopoulos thought Mifsud had high-level Russian connections.

One day after his second FBI interview on February 16, 2017, Papadopoulos deactivated his Facebook account, which contained information on an "overseas professor" with ties to high-level Russian officials. Six days later, he got a new cell phone number.

Did Papadopoulos lie and take these actions because he was guilty of being a covert agent or because of anxiety caused by FBI interviews in the context of increasing Trump/Russia collusion news?

Between March and September 2016, Papadopoulos made at least six requests to campaign officials for Trump or representatives of his campaign to meet in Russia with Russian politicians. Was Papadopoulos a covert agent trying to prompt a Russia trip to enable "collusion" stories similar to the Carter Page invitation to Moscow, or was an innocent Papadopoulos persistently trying to improve his status on the campaign team.

Strzok initiated the Trump/Russia investigation on July 31, 2016, and within hours he flew to London to interview Downer about his discussion with Papadopoulos about Mifsud's story on Russian 'dirt' on Clinton. The FBI knew Downer's story before Strzok's trip because Downer told Elizabeth Dibble at the State Department, who got it forwarded to the FBI. After the initial sense of urgency, why did the FBI wait 6 months until January 27, 2017 to interview Papadopoulos? A likely answer is that Strzok was part of his London co-conspirator's plot involving Papadopoulos.

The FBI interviewed Mifsud in Washington, D.C. on February 11, 2017. Mifsud was in Washington to speak at the large annual conference for Global Ties U.S., an organization that has been a partner of the U.S. State Department for over 50 years. Several State Department officials also spoke at the conference. The FBI had Downer's information about Mifsud since before July 2016, and this information was purportedly used as the factual predicate to initiate the Russia probe. This begs the question: why didn't the FBI arrest Mifsud as a Russian spy seeking to influence the election? A likely answer again is that Strzok was part of his London co-conspirator's plot involving Papadopoulos, and Mifsud may have been the OCUNUS lure that Strzok texted Page about.

If Papadopoulos was a covert agent, why did he not cooperate with Halper's and Millian's entrapment attempts? One possible scenario is that Papadopoulos was hired as a "useful idiot" to do certain defined tasks such as join the Trump team, go to London for the LCILP job, talk to Mifsud and Downer, and persistently pursue campaign trips to Russia. Papadopoulos might not have even realized how the conspirators were using him until events such as the Halper and Millian entrapment attempts and the FBI interviews.

Papadopoulos may be a weak link in the conspiracy, and the DOJ should definitely find out the details of his joining the Trump team and LCILP.

9. The Paul Manafort Setup

Paul Manafort was an expert in presidential campaigns. He worked on the Gerald Ford, Ronald Reagan, and George H.W. Bush campaigns. Manafort helped the pro-Russian Viktor Yanukovych win the Ukrainian presidency twice. Ukraine is a very corrupt country, and Manafort profited greatly while Yanukovych was president. Manafort lived a very lavish lifestyle, however, in February 2014, all of that changed when Yanukovych was overthrown and fled to Russia under Putin's protection. Manafort instantly lost his power and influence, and could not find new clients. As a result, his finances deteriorated, and the Russian billionaire oligarch, Oleg Deripaska, sued him for a $20 million debt. In addition to his financial problems, Manafort's family caught him having an affair. Manafort suffered an emotional breakdown in 2015, to the point of considering suicide, and he entered a rehabilitation clinic.

By March 15, 2016, Trump had 673 delegates and Ted Cruz had 411 delegates. If Trump did not reach the 1,237-majority delegate threshold in the state nominating contests, the delegates would pick their nominee in a contested convention. The Trump campaign lacked expert, experienced political operatives to help assure that the NeverTrump movement would not rig a contested convention against Trump (e.g., by changing the bylaws prior to the convention).

The desperate Manafort sensed an opportunity to regain power and money by helping the Trump campaign. Tom Barrack, a billionaire real estate investor, was a long-time mutual friend of Manafort and Trump. Manafort told Barrack "I really need to get to [Trump]," saying that he wanted to work for free as Trump's convention manager, helping him navigate what they expected would be a contentious affair." Both Barrack and Roger Stone recommended that Trump allow Manafort to join the campaign team as an unpaid volunteer, which he did on

March 28, 2016. Trump became the presumptive nominee on May 4, 2016, and he hired Manafort as his campaign chairman on May 19th.

As previously described in chapter 7 "The Carter Page Setup", Steele alleged in his dossier that Manafort used Page to coordinate with the Russians a hack of the DNC servers to steal the emails. The was literally impossible because Manafort and Page joined the Trump team as unpaid advisers mere days prior to the complex Russian hack that used the very sophisticated APT28 malware to steal the emails. The Russian spear phishing campaign to steal logon credentials was already in progress when Manafort and Page joined the team, and months of advance planning were needed for the hack.

10. The Michael Flynn Setup

Lieutenant General Michael Flynn is a 30-year decorated combat veteran. Flynn wrote a bestselling book that urged Americans to view Russia as an implacable enemy of the United States that must be checked. The Obama DOJ conducted two investigations to try and entrap General Flynn for criminal wrongdoing.

First, the FBI performed a counterintelligence investigation of Flynn for some period of time during 2016. Comey testified that "he authorized the closure of the CI [counterintelligence investigation] into General Flynn in late December 2016; however, the investigation was kept open due to the public discrepancy surrounding General Flynn's communications with Ambassador Kislyak." As Andrew McCarthy writes "a CI investigation on an American citizen proceeds on the suspicion that the citizen is an agent of a foreign power whose clandestine activities violate federal criminal law." The FBI viewed Flynn as a "criminal suspect" and "there are profound reasons to question the legitimacy of Flynn's treatment."[lxxvii]

Secondly, the DOJ's then–acting attorney general Sally Yates conducted a criminal investigation of Flynn in January 2017 based on the Logan Act. Flynn played a central role in the Trump transition and was designated as the incoming national-security adviser, it was Flynn's job to communicate with such foreign counterparts as Russian ambassador Sergey Kislyak. Flynn called Kislyak on December 29, 2016 as part of the Trump transition team, and just three weeks from formally becoming the new president's national-security adviser. His communications with Kislyak were just some of the many conversations Flynn was having with foreign officials.

McCarthy writes:[lxxviii]

"The call to Kislyak, of course, was intercepted. No doubt the calls of other American officials who have perfectly valid reasons to call Russian diplomats have been intercepted. It is the FBI's scrupulous practice to keep the identities of such interceptees confidential. So why single Flynn out for identification, and for investigation? FBI agents did not need to "grill" Flynn in order to learn about the call — they had a recording of the call."

"The Obama Justice Department and FBI investigated Flynn — including an ambush interview — on the theory that his discussions with Kislyak and other diplomats violated the Logan Act. Currently codified as Section 953 of the federal penal code, this statute purports to criminalize "any correspondence or intercourse" with agents of a foreign sovereign conducted "without authority of the United States" — an impossibly vague term that probably means permission from the executive branch. The Logan Act is patently unconstitutional, but no court has had the opportunity to invalidate it because, to borrow a phrase, no reasonable prosecutor would bring such a case. As our Dan McLaughlin has explained, the Act dates to 1799, a dark time for free-speech rights during the John Adams administration. Never in its 219-year history has it resulted in a single conviction; indeed, there have been only two indictments, the last one in 1852."

The "ambush interview" that McCarthy refers to occurred on January 24, 2017 when McCabe called Flynn and asked if two FBI agents could come over and ask him some questions. Flynn said 'yes,' not realizing that he was the FBI target in a criminal investigation. Peter Strzok and another FBI agent immediately went to Flynn's White House office to ask Flynn about what was said in his conversation with Kislyak. Flynn most likely chatted with them in an unguarded manner in this surprise, informal meeting. Flynn was a national security expert, so he certainly knew that his conversations with Kislyak were recorded. John

Dowd, President Trump's former attorney, wrote "Congress needs the FBI '302' report of the Flynn interview.... There are reports that Gen. Flynn referred to the FISA wiretap of Ambassador Sergey Kislyak conversation at the outset of the FBI interview. If those reports are true, his reference to the complete and accurate wiretap precludes any charge of false statement."

The House Intelligence Committee Russia report says Flynn "met alone with two FBI agents at the White House" following a call from McCabe to Flynn, at Comey's direction. Flynn did not have an attorney present at the impromptu meeting. The report states the committee "received conflicting testimony" from then-Deputy Attorney General Sally Yates, Comey, Principal Deputy Assistant Attorney General Mary McCord and McCabe about why the FBI interviewed Flynn as if he were a criminal suspect. It listed several possible reasons for the interview, including whether the FBI was investigating Flynn's "potentially misleading" statements to Vice President Pence, a possible violation of the Logan Act or to obtain more information about the Russia counterintelligence investigation.

Strzok and the other agent who questioned Flynn determined that Flynn did not lie to them. Shortly after the interview occurred, it was reported that the FBI had decided no action would be taken against Flynn. On March 2, Comey testified to a closed session of the House Intelligence Committee that, while Flynn may have had some honest failures of recollection during the interview, the agents who questioned him concluded that he did not lie.

Comey, on a book tour for "A Higher Loyalty," denies he ever made those statements. The Senate Judiciary Committee Chairman Charles Grassley sent a letter to Rosenstein and Wray to renew his request for a transcript of the Flynn-Kislyak telephone call which Justice denied last year. He also is seeking a copy of the agents' interview notes, or form 302. Grassley said "Contrary to his public statements during his current book tour denying any memory of those comments, then-Director Comey led us to believe during that briefing that the agents who interviewed Flynn did not believe he intentionally lied about his conversation with the Ambassador and that the Justice Department was unlikely to prosecute him for false statements made in that interview."

Flynn's call and discussion with Kislyak was perfectly proper and normal for an incoming national-security adviser. The FBI knew this because they recorded the conversation, so they did not have an intelligence need or any other reason to interview Flynn. The FBI had determined there was no corrupt quid pro quo in Flynn's discussion with Kislyak, and that Flynn did not make any assurances to Kislyak about withdrawing President Obama's sanctions.

Comey, McCabe, and Yates set up the informal FBI interview with Flynn as a perjury trap to find some discrepancy between the unsuspecting Flynn's interview statements and the recorded conversation with Kislyak. Typically, a lawyer for the National Security Council would be informed of such a meeting and be present for it. Comey, McCabe and Yates arranged the surprise meeting to avoid this, so that Flynn would more likely make an error of recollection in an informal chat. McCabe clearly states in his testimony that Strzok's interview with Flynn was a trap to catch him making a misstatement in comparison to the recorded transcript (i.e., "a false statement case"). A section of the House Intelligence Committee's final Russia report states:

> "Deputy Director McCabe confirmed the interviewing agent's initial impression and stated that the 'conundrum that we faced on their return from the interview is that although [the agents] didn't detect deception in the statements that he made in the interview ... the statements were inconsistent with our understanding of the conversation that he had actually had with the ambassador,'" the report states. McCabe then acknowledged that "the two people who interviewed

[Flynn] didn't think he was lying, [which] was not [a] great beginning of a false statement case."

When FBI agents conduct interviews of witnesses and subjects, they do not record the interviews. Instead, they enter their notes on the "form FD-302" and file this report for every interview.

Senate investigators suspect McCabe altered his 302 notes and requested Strzok to alter his 302 notes on General Flynn and have referred the matter to Inspector General Horowitz, who is investigating. McCabe and Comey cleared Sally Yates to use Peter Strzok's 302 summary report of the interrogation with General Flynn to brief White House Counsel and pressure Flynn's firing.

Sally Yates would deliver the final coup de grâce in the Flynn setup. On Jan. 26, two days after the interview, Yates met with the White House counsel, Don McGahn. Yate's objective was to precipitate General Flynn's firing by President Trump.

Yates told McGahn she was worried Flynn had not told the truth to his colleagues in the Trump administration, including Vice President Mike Pence, when Flynn, said he had not discussed sanctions with Kislyak. McGahn wrote that "Yates expressed two principal concerns during the meeting, 1) that Flynn may have made false representations to others in the administration regarding the content of the calls; and (2) that Flynn's potentially false statements could make him susceptible to foreign influence or blackmail because the Russians would know he had lied...Yates further indicated that on January 24, 2017, FBI agents had questioned Flynn about his contacts with Kislyak. Yates claimed that Flynn's statements to the FBI were similar to those she understood he had made to [press secretary Sean] Spicer and the vice president."

In 2012, Flynn became the head of the Pentagon's Defense Intelligence Agency. Clapper and the Undersecretary of Defense for Intelligence Michael Vickers fired Flynn in 2014. Flynn published an article in The New York Post entitled "The military fired me for calling our enemies radical jihadis." Comey, Yates, and McCabe knew that Flynn would reverse Obama's policies if he remained in the Trump administration.

McCabe should never have been involved in an investigation of Flynn. He should have recused himself because Flynn was a witness on the behalf of an FBI agent, Robyn Gritz, who filed an Equal Employment Opportunity Commission (EEOC) complaint against McCabe and her other FBI supervisors alleging sexual discrimination and hostile work environment.

> *Former Supervisory Special Agent Robyn Gritz worked 15 years for the FBI and was one its top intelligence analysts and terrorism experts. She was detailed to the CIA and worked closely with the Defense Intelligence Agency, which was led by General Michael Flynn.*

> *Throughout this time, her FBI bosses gave her excellent or outstanding performance reviews. But in 2012, she began working for Special Agent Andrew McCabe and his leadership team. It was then that she received her first negative performance rating and was subsequently forced to resign from the FBI.*

> *In 2013, she filed an Equal Employment Opportunity Commission (EEOC) complaint against her FBI supervisors alleging sexual discrimination and hostile work environment. Gritz described the retaliation from McCabe and others in the bureau as "vicious." One of her biggest supporters was Flynn, who then was the head of the Defense Intelligence Agency.*

> *In 2014, she amended her complaint by averring that she suffered "a hostile [work] environment, defamation of character through continued targeting by Andrew McCabe." The FBI's response claimed that she had become "underperforming, tardy to work, insubordinate, possibly mentally ill." In May 2014, Flynn wrote a letter praising*

her work, and in 2015, Flynn publicly supported Gritz on NPR.

Gritz's lawyer notified the EEOC that Flynn and other top officials would be witnesses on her behalf. McCabe was then required to submit an opposing sworn statement to EEOC investigators. He admitted under oath that the FBI had started an internal investigation into Gritz's personal conduct after learning that she "had filed or intended to file" a sex discrimination complaint against her supervisors. This was an unequivocal admission that the FBI had illegally retaliated against Gritz for exercising her protected right to file such a complaint. Two weeks after Gritz filed her EEOC complaint, McCabe had her investigated by the FBI's Office of Professional Responsibility for "time card irregularities." This constituted another illegal retaliatory act.[lxxix]

General Flynn resigned in February 2017 because of discrepancies in his answers versus the call transcripts. Yates, Comey, and McCabe achieved their objective of getting Flynn removed from the Trump administration with the perjury trap setup.

Mueller charged Flynn of "willfully and knowingly make materially false, fictitious, and fraudulent statements" in the Strzok interview about his conversations with Russian Ambassador Sergey Kislyak. Flynn pleaded guilty to one count of lying to FBI agents and agreed to be a cooperating witness as part of a plea to avoid a trial.

Steele also set up Flynn in the dossier by alleging that Moscow indirectly funded the trips of Michael Flynn and Carter Page to Moscow in order to achieve 3 objectives: 1) asking sympathetic U.S. action, 2) gathering intelligence, and 3) creating and disseminating compromising information.

11. The Donald Trump Jr. Setup

Bill Browder is the CEO and billionaire co-founder of Hermitage Capital Management, an investment fund that at one time was the largest foreign portfolio investor in Russia. Browder claimed the Russian government tortured and killed his tax accountant, Sergei Magnitsky, in prison in November 2009 because an investigation he conducted discovered a massive $230 million tax fraud by Russian government officials. The Russian government claims that Browder and Magnitsky committed the tax fraud, and that Magnitsky died of heart failure.

Browder successfully lobbied Congress to pass the Magnitsky Act in 2012. The Magnitsky Act is a U.S. law that blocks entry into the US and freezes the assets of specified Russian government officials and businessmen accused of human rights violations. Putin was very upset when it was passed and called it "a purely political, unfriendly act." Putin retaliated by imposing an adoption ban of Russian children by American families on December 28, 2012, three weeks after the Magnitsky Act was approved by the Senate.

The US DOJ investigated the $230 million scheme that Magnitsky uncovered for nearly four years. Prosecutors said the funds from the elaborate scheme had been laundered via shell companies and real-estate purchases. Prevezon Holdings Ltd. is a real-estate company incorporated in Cyprus. The US attorney in Manhattan accused Prevezon in September 2013 of receiving "at least $1,965,444 in proceeds from the $230 million fraud scheme" in early 2008 via wire transfers from at least two suspected shell companies through the Southern District of New York. In a civil forfeiture action, the DOJ accused Prevezon of being a front for laundering millions of dollars into New York City real estate. Natalia Veselnitskaya, a Russian attorney, worked on defending Prevezon. The case was settled out of court with Prevezon agreeing to pay $5.9 million while not admitting to any wrongdoing.

Simpson and Fusion GPS were hired by BakerHostetler in 2014, which represented Russian firm Prevezon through Veselnitskaya. Concurrent with her defense of Prevezon, Veselnitskaya represented the Russian owners of Prevezon, Pyotr Katsyv and his son Denis, in lobbying against the Magnitsky Act. In this effort, Simpson worked for Veselnitskaya to gather information to besmirch Bill Browder and Sergei Magnitsky.

Rinat Akhmetshin is Russian-American lobbyist with close ties to Glenn Simpson. He also has ties to Bill and Hillary Clinton. Akhmetshin worked on the Prevezon case and he hired Fusion GPS in 2016 to work on a campaign to repeal the Magnitsky Act. Clinton and the DNC hired Simpson's Fusion GPS in April 2016 to create Trump/Russia collusion misinformation.

Simpson was simultaneously helping the Russian government get Magnitsky Act sanctions reduced, and gather Russian misinformation on the Trump campaign. Simpson used his dual role in a cunning plot to entrap Donald Trump Jr. into the appearance of colluding with Russia to influence the election.

Aras Agalarov is an Azerbaijani billionaire oligarch with ties to Putin. He paid Donald Trump $20 million to host the 2013 Miss Universe pageant in Moscow. Emin Agalarov, the son of Aras Agalarov, is a popular singer. Emin performed during the pageant's worldwide broadcast. Putin awarded Aras Agalarov the Russian Order of Honor in 2013.

Donald Trump and Donald Trump Jr. became friends of the Agalarov family and Emin's British music promoter, Rob Goldstone, during the 2013 Miss Universe pageant. Goldstone works full-time for Emin.

Goldstone sent the following email to Trump Jr on June 3, 2016:

> "Emin just called and asked me to contact you with something very interesting.
>
> The Crown prosecutor of Russia met with his father Aras this morning and in their meeting offered to provide the Trump campaign with some official documents and information that would incriminate Hillary and her dealings with Russia and would be very useful to your father.
>
> This is obviously very high level and sensitive information but is part of Russia and its government's support for Mr. Trump — helped along by Aras and Emin.
>
> What do you think is the best way to handle this information and would you be able to speak to Emin about it directly?
>
> I can also send this info to your father via Rhona, but it is ultra sensitive so wanted to send to you first." (Note: Rhona Graff served as President Donald Trump's longtime secretary.)

Trump Jr., a politically naïve young businessman, replied "Seems we have some time and if it's what you say I love it." Six days later on June 9, 2016, a meeting took place in Trump Tower. Trump Jr. had Jared Kushner and Paul Manafort attend the meeting. Goldstone brought with him Veselnitskaya, Akhmetshin, Irakly "Ike" Kaveladze, and a translator.

All of the people at the meeting later testified before Congress. It is crystal clear based on the testimony that Simpson orchestrated the meeting to frame Trump Jr. by making it appear that he was colluding with Russia to get 'dirt' on Clinton.

Rob Goldstone's Testimony

The key to Simpson's trap for Trump Jr. is the wording of Rob Goldstone's email. Goldstone testified:

I received — I received the call from Emin that morning, and he asked me if I could contact the Trumps with something interesting and said that a well-connected Russian attorney had met with his father that morning in his father's office and had told him that they had some interesting information that could potentially be damaging regarding funding by Russians to the Democrats and to its candidate, Hillary Clinton.

Goldstone admitted that he "didn't quite understand what he (Emin) was asking and asked for more information. I asked if he could tell me a bit more about the attorney, as I felt I might be asked that. And he said that the attorney was well-connected."

He said that Emin told him that "all he knew was that there was some potentially damaging information re: Hillary, which could be of interest to the Trumps."

He admitted that when sending the email "I didn't know what I was really even talking about, because I had asked it to be elaborated on" and it wasn't.

During his testimony, Goldstone was asked about the part where he wrote about "very high level and sensitive information but is part of Russia and its government's support for Mr. Trump — helped along by Aras and Emin."

He responded that this section was just his own assumption from watching television and visiting Russia, and the email was not based on any actual knowledge of information originating with Russia:

Asked about the section of his email where he claims the purported Clinton information originated with Russia's nonexistent "Crown prosecutor," Goldstone claimed that his

British background led him to believe that former or current federal prosecutors are known as "crown prosecutors."

He stated: "I grew up in England, and when I studied journalism, we had to study a piece of law, a very small piece, but we were taught that all the equivalents of Federal prosecutors in this country were Crown prosecutors. I've always called them Crown. Russia hasn't had a crown since 1917."

Goldstone was asked to clarify a draft statement he sent to the committee stating, "I, therefore, used the strongest hyperbolic language in order to secure this request from Donald Trump Jr. based on the bare facts I was given." Goldstone responded that:

> *"my job was to get a meeting, and so I used my professional use of words to emphasize what my client had only given bare-bones information about, in order to get the attention of Mr. Trump Jr.*
>
> *I described it as a — that it appeared to me to have been a bait and switch of somebody who appeared to be lobbying for what I now understood to be the Magnitsky Act, and probably thought she wouldn't be able to get a meeting under that guise, and, therefore, had dangled the idea of having some damaging information on Hillary, which she may or may not have had, but it didn't appear to me as if anything had come out of it at the meeting."*

Veselnitskaya, in her written responses to the Judiciary Committee, verified that she was the well-connected Russian attorney who had met with Aras Agalarov to request the meeting with Trump Jr. Veselnitskaya wrote that her June 9 meeting at Trump Tower "was not a 'meeting with the Trump campaign.'" She said she expected it to be "a private meeting with Donald Trump, Jr.," who knows the son of Veselnitskaya's good friend in Russia. It was the good friend's son who helped to arrange the meeting, she said. Veselnitskaya told the Wall Street Journal that she approached Russian real estate magnate Aras Agalarov, whom she was representing, to help set up a meeting as part of her efforts opposing the Magnitsky Act.

Veselnitskaya wrote that she wanted Trump Jr. to inform Congress about "how terribly misled" they had been by William Browder, a man convicted of tax fraud in Russia. Veselnitskaya said she expected that Don Jr., as a businessman, "was sure to have some acquaintances among Congress people." After several years of lobbying for Magnitsky Act changes, Veselnitskaya knew that only Congress could enact any changes in the Magnitsky Act.

It is ludicrous to believe that Veselnitskaya on her own would select Trump Jr. as the best person to help with the Magnitsky Act. Simpson worked for Veselnitskaya to help repeal the Magnitsky Act, so he would be her guide in how to best accomplish this in the U.S. political system. The only plausible explanation is that Simpson convinced her to meet with Trump Jr. Simpson may have convinced her that Trump Jr. could help because of his good Congressional connections. Or Simpson could have convinced her in a more nefarious way, such as bribing her, asking Steele's friend, Oleg Deripaska to convince her, etc.

Veselnitskaya had to know that Trump Jr. would quickly end the meeting after discovering Goldstone lied about the Clinton information. This meeting was never about the Magnitsky Act. It was an obvious trap for Trump Jr.

Simpson's Plot to Frame Trump Jr.

Veselnitskaya, in her written testimony, said she does not know Christopher Steele, the "dossier" author, and she said she did not work with Fusion GPS, although she does know Glenn Simpson. She said she was not aware that Simpson had hired Christopher Steele to investigate Donald Trump's alleged ties to the Russian government.

Simpson used Donald Trump Jr.'s friendship with Rob Goldstone and Emin Agalarov in his setup. Simpson did that by convincing Veselnitskaya to ask her good friend, Aras Agalarov, to help her meet with Trump Jr. because he could help with repealing the Magnitsky Act. Simpson also convinced Veselnitskaya to tell Aras Agalarov the meeting was about damaging Russian information on Clinton so that Trump Jr. would accept the meeting.

Agalarov knew Putin despised the Magnitsky Act and strongly wanted the sanctions repealed and Veselnitskaya was a good friend, so he agreed to help. As a Russian, he probably considered "damaging information on Clinton" as only a positive for his friend, Donald Trump, in his campaign against Clinton.

The basic wording that Veselnitskaya gave to Aras Agalarov to use in Goldstone's email about dirt on Clinton had two objectives: 1) as a ruse to trick Trump Jr. into accepting the meeting, and 2) evidence that the Trump campaign was colluding with Russia to get compromising information on Clinton. Emin instructed Goldstone, his employee, to write the email.

Simpson's charter from Clinton and the DNC was to gather evidence of Trump/Russia collusion, and this meeting to set up Trump Jr. was a unique major opportunity to achieve that.

Coincidence or "Enemy Action?"

Simpson testified that he had dinner with Veselnitskaya both the day before and the day after her meeting at Trump Tower. He also saw her as part of a court case on the day of the meeting. Simpson testified that he never discussed the meeting with Veselnitskaya, and that he didn't know about the meeting until it was reported by the New York Times almost a year later. Simpson prepared the memo Veselnitskaya's used at the meeting.

Akhmetshin testified that he traveled by train from Washington to New York on the day of the meeting to attend an evening theater production with his friend, Ed Lieberman. Lieberman's late wife Evelyn previously served as Hillary Clinton's chief of staff when she was First Lady. Evelyn Lieberman also served as Bill Clinton's deputy chief of staff.

Akhmetshin said that he "knows" Hillary Clinton and has a personal relationship with her that dates back to the late-1990s. Akhmetshin also testified that he "knew some people who worked on" Clinton's 2016 presidential campaign.

Akhmetshin also described himself as a friend and colleague of Glenn Simpson. Akhmetshin said he met Simpson through Simpson's wife, whom he knew from her days as a reporter in Brussels. The day after the Trump Jr. meeting, Akhmetshin said he ended up at a "social" dinner in Washington, D.C., with Simpson, Simpson's wife, Veselnitskaya, and Ed Lieberman. Simpson's wife, Mary Jacoby, is from Arkansas, and she and her family are old friends of the Clintons.

Akhmetshin knows Senator McCain and his assistant David J. Kramer. He saw them at the Halifax security conference in 2016, but claimed he played no role in the contact where Sir Andrew Wood informed McCain and Kramer of Christopher Steele's dossier at that conference. Afterwards, Kramer got the dossier from Fusion GPS, and McCain gave it to the FBI.

In his testimony, Akhmetshin said he has known Simpson for more than a decade and has been a source for him when Simpson worked at The Wall Street Journal. Akhmetshin's testimony contained numerous sections that detail his past relationship with Fusion GPS and the company's co-founder, Glenn Simpson.

In December 2016 discussion, Ohr noted that Simpson said "Much of the collection about the Trump campaign ties to Russia comes from a former Russian intelligence officer (? not entirely clear) who lives in the U.S." Simpson was likely referring to his friend Akhmetshin. Sometimes Akhmetshin has bragged about being a former Soviet military intelligence officer and at other times he denied it. This is probably the reason Ohr put the question mark in "a former Russian intelligence officer (? not entirely clear) who lives in the U.S."

Lieberman and Akhmetshin are friends of Clinton. Simpson is working for Clinton, Akhmetshin and Veselnitskaya. It is not coincidence that they were all associated with a meeting that gave the appearance that Trump Jr. was colluding with Russians – it is "Enemy Action."

In sworn Senate testimony last year, Simpson claimed the meeting corroborated one of the key claims made in the reports filed by Fusion GPS contractor Steele: "Trump and his inner circle have accepted a regular flow of intelligence from the Kremlin, including on his Democratic and other political rivals." Simpson set up Trump Jr. to obtain false evidence, and then uses it to validate the false dossier allegations. This is similar to the Papadopoulos set up when the covert agent, Mifsud, told him that Russia has 'dirt' on Hillary Clinton.

Trump Jr. Setup Conclusions

Veselnitskaya, Simpson, and Akhmetshin all lied in their testimony.

Simpson's and Veselnitskaya's testimonies gave different accounts of when they met:

The Trump Jr. meeting was on June 9. Simpson testified that he met with Veselnitskaya for dinner and June 8 and 10, and met her in court on June 9.

Congress wrote and asked "Did you have contact with Glenn Simpson on June 8, 9, or 10, 2016? If so, please describe the contact." Veselnitskaya wrote in reply "No, there had been no contacts with him on specified dates."

Veselnitskaya lied. Anatoli Samochornov, the Russian translator who was present at the Trump Tower meeting, testified that he was present at several dinners between Simpson and Veselnitskaya, including around the date of the Trump Tower meeting. Samochornov also places Lieberman at one and likely two of those dinner meetings.

Simpson's claim that he did not know about Veselnitskaya's meeting with Trump Jr. until a year afterwards is not believable because:

- Simpson worked for both Veselnitskaya and Akhmetshin to repeal the Magnitsky Act, and Veselnitskaya purportedly believed that Trump Jr. could help with that.
- Simpson met with Veselnitskaya the day before, the day during and the day after the meeting.
- Veselnitskaya used the Magnitsky document that Simpson prepared for her in the meeting.

Akhmetshin attended a meeting at the campaign headquarters of Clinton's presidential challenger with Trump's son and other top Trump staffers, and he made the unbelievably claim that he did not tell Lieberman, a very good friend of the Clintons, about the meeting.

The meeting was only about the Magnitsky Act:

> Ike Kaveladze is the senior vice president at Crocus Group, the real estate development firm owned by Aras Agalarov. Kaveladze testified that he didn't see Goldstone's email claiming incriminating information on Clinton before the meeting. He says that Aras Agalarov contacted him on June 6, 2016 to tell him about it. He said Agalarov "asked me if I knew anything about (the) Magnitsky Act, and I said I did, and so he said the meeting is going to be about Magnitsky Act." Kaveladze flew from Los Angeles to attend the meeting.

Kaveladze says that he grew concerned about the suggestion the meeting would involve opposition information on Clinton. He said that his concerns were put to rest at lunch just before the Trump Tower meeting when Veselnitskaya gave him an 11-page synopsis of what she had planned to discuss at the meeting. It had only one sentence on public information about an American firm accused of evading Russian taxes and two of the company's leaders are major donors to Democratic candidates, including Clinton. The rest was about the Magnitsky Act.

Kaveladze's testimony supports that Veselnitskaya told Aras Agalarov that the meeting's true purpose was the Magnitsky Act – not damaging information on Clinton.

12. The Michael Cohen Setup

Steele needed a replacement to serve as Trump's Russia coordinator after Manafort and Page left the team, so he chose Trump's personal attorney, Michael Cohen, as the unsuspecting prey. Steele accuses Cohen of meeting with Russian government officials to discuss hiding Trump and Russia's payments to Romanian hackers for their work against the Clinton campaign. The evidence in Chapter 7 "The Carter Page Setup" proves it was impossible for Page and Manafort to have coordinated the hack with Russia due to the timeline. Therefore, Steele's allegation that Cohen replaced them as Trump's Russia coordinator is also false.

Steele's Cohen allegations are provably false based on the evidence. Following is an excerpt from Steele's 2016/136 report dated December 13, 2016, titled "US/Russia: Further details of secret dialogue between Trump campaign team, Kremlin, and associated hackers in Prague:"

> "[Name redacted] provided further details of these meeting/s and associated anti-CLINTON/Democratic Party operations. COHEN had been accompanied to Prague by 3 colleagues and the timing of the visit was either in the last week of August or the first week of September. One of their main Russian interlocutors was Oleg SOLODUKHIN operating under Rossotrudichestvo cover. According to [Name redacted], the agenda comprised questions of how deniable cash payments were to be made to hackers who had worked in Europe under Kremlin direction against the CLINTON campaign and various contingencies for covering up these operations and MOSCOW's secret liaison with the Trump team more generally."

> "[Name redacted] reported that over the period March to September 2016 a company called XBT/Webzilla and its

155

affiliates had been using botnets and porn traffic to transmit viruses, plant bugs, steal data, and conduct "altering operations" against the Democratic Party leadership. Entities linked to one Aleksei GUBAROV were involved and he and another hacking expert, both recruited under duress by the FSB, Seva KAPSUGOVICH were significant players in this operation. In Prague, COHEN agreed contingency plans for various scenarios to protect the [hacking] operation, but in particular what was to be done in the event that Hillary CLINTON won the presidency. It was important in this event that all cash payments owed were made quickly and discreetly and that cyber and other operators were stood down/able to go effectively to ground to cover their traces. (We reported earlier that the involvement of political operatives Paul MANAFORT and Carter PAGE in the secret TRUMP–Kremlin liaison had been exposed in the media in the run-up to Prague and that damage limitation of these also was discussed by COHEN with the Kremlin representatives)."

"In terms of practical measures to be taken, it was agreed by the two sides in Prague to stand down various "Romanian hackers..." "On payments IVANOV's associate said that the operatives involved had been paid by both TRUMP's team and the Kremlin, though their orders and ultimate loyalty lay with IVANOV, as head of the PA and thus ultimately responsible for the operation, and his designated successor/s after he was dismissed by president PUTIN in connection with the anti-CLINTON campaign in mid August."

This accusation is a good example of Steele's use of public information to create a fictitious meeting and fictitious meeting discussion that cannot be corroborated. For example, Rossotrudichestvo is a Russian agency that promotes the Russian image through international development assistance, education, science, culture and language. Rossotrudichestvo has offices in 80 nations, and it is public information that Oleg Solodukhin is the deputy head of its Prague office in the Czech Republic.

Steele and his sources made a huge mistake, however, in this allegation because if there was a Michael Cohen in Prague, it was not Trump's personal attorney. CNN's Jake Tapper reported "People tried to run that down and concluded it was a different Michael Cohen. It was a Michael Cohen with a passport from another country, same birth year, different birth date." Tapper tweeted on January 11, 2016 that "Government source confirms different Michael Cohen was in Prague."[lxxx] Michael Cohen testified under oath to Congress that he was never in Prague. Cohen never left the U.S. during the last week of August and first week of October and he provided proof with his passport and witnesses to his presence in New York and California. Cohen filed a defamation action against the BuzzFeed website for publishing the dossier with false information about him, but later dropped it because of a DOJ investigation into his business dealings.

The evidence in Mueller's indictment of 12 Russian intelligence officers irrefutably disproves Steele's allegations against Michael Cohen.

In addition to the dossier allegations, Steele also used Sergei Millian to set up Cohen as described in chapter 6 on Sergei Millian.

13. The Aleksej Gubarev Setup

Simpson hired Christopher Steele, a former MI6 official, to create documented evidence showing Trump and his campaign colluded with Russia to hack the DNC servers, steal the emails, and post them on WikiLeaks.

This dossier allegation states that Russia's Federal Security Service ("FSB") recruited Alexsei Gubarov (correct spelling Aleksej Gubarev), the owner of XBT/Webzilla, and Seva Kapsugovich (correct spelling Kaptsugovich) under duress as hackers that used botnets and porn traffic to transmit viruses, plant bugs, steal data, and conduct "altering operations" against the Democratic Party leadership.

A botnet is a group of computers/servers and devices infected with malware that a hacker remotely controls to send spam or phishing emails, deliver ransomware, spyware, or many other similar malicious acts. The botnet gives the hacker the capability to commit advertising fraud, steal online credentials (e.g. usernames, passwords, credit card details), lock a computer to get ransom. The hacker can also use a botnet to launch a Distributed Denial of Service (DDoS) attack that floods a website with so many requests for content that the server crashes (i.e., goes offline).

The allegation states Gubarev and Kaptsugovich are hacking experts who conducted an operation "over the period March to September 2016," in which "XBT/Webzilla and its affiliates had been using botnets and porn traffic to transmit viruses, plant bugs, steal data, and conduct 'altering operations' against the Democratic Party leadership." The reason for Steele and his source's selection of Gubarev as the fictitious hackers is puzzling. Gubarev's company, XBT/Webzilla, hosts websites and runs thousands of computer servers worldwide, so perhaps Steele thought the XBT/Webzilla servers could be linked and used as a botnet. Regardless of why Steele chose Gubarev and

Kaptsugovich, the assertion that botnets and porn traffic could steal the DNC emails is absurd for multiple reasons.

Steele and his source demonstrate their ignorance in alleging that botnets and porn traffic were used to steal the emails from the DNC servers because it is an impossibility. It is preposterous to allege porn traffic could do this. Botnets have the capability to use phishing emails and spam, steal online credentials, lock computers, or crash a website. However, a technology much more sophisticated than botnets was needed to steal emails from the DNC servers over a period of time – a technology called an Advanced Persistent Threat (APT). CrowdStrike found two APT's, APT28 (named Fancy Bear) and APT29 (Cozy Bear), on the DNC computer system.

Gubarev is a Russian-born tech entrepreneur and millionaire who emigrated to Cyprus in 2002. Kaptsugovich is a convicted pedophile imprisoned in a remote Russian gulag. Not only do they not have the capability to hack with an APT, it is ludicrous to allege that they worked together to hack the DNC.

The allegation, written a month after Hillary Clinton lost the election, states "COHEN agreed contingency plans for various scenarios to protect the [hacking] operation, but in particular what was to be done in the event that Hillary CLINTON won the presidency. It was important in this event that all cash payments owed were made quickly and discreetly and that cyber and other operators were stood down/able to go effectively to ground to cover their traces."

The whole allegation of Cohen's meeting in Prague and the hackers Gubarev and Kaptsugovich using botnets and porn traffic to steal DNC emails are provably false. Steele adds the statement "On payments IVANOV's associate said that the operatives involved had been paid by both TRUMP's team and the Kremlin" in order to implicate Trump's campaign in a felony.

Mueller indicted 12 officers of the Russian military intelligence service (GRU) for hacking the DNC computer system, stealing the emails, and publishing them on WikiLeaks. The evidence in the indictment proves beyond a doubt that the 12 GRU officers stole the emails using the APT28 malware. Julian Assange of WikiLeaks and the GRU were the only participants.

Mueller's evidence completely disproves Steele's allegations about Michael Cohen, the identity of the hackers, the payments, and everything else in this allegation. This allegation is yet another example of Steele simply inventing an absurd story and putting it in his dossier as a fact. Clinton and the DNC paid Simpson and Steele to make up evidence that Trump colluded with Russia and that is what they did. Steele is no "superspy" with sources close to Putin and his inner circle. Steele is a con artist, who, as he told Bruce Ohr, wanted to stop Trump from becoming president.

Comey and Strzok used the dossier to investigate and surveille Trump's campaign team. They did not attempt to verify the easily disprovable allegations that Cohen was in Prague, that Gubarev and Kaptsugovich were the DNC hackers, and that botnets and porn traffic could steal the DNC emails.

14. The Seva Kaptsugovich Setup

The dossier allegation quoted above in the "Aleksej Gubarev" states Gubarev and Kaptsugovich are hacking experts who conducted an operation "over the period March to September 2016," in which "XBT/Webzilla and its affiliates had been using botnets and porn traffic to transmit viruses, plant bugs, steal data, and conduct 'altering operations' against the Democratic Party leadership."

The allegation is impossible because Sevastyan (Seva) Kaptsugovich is a Russian pedophile convicted a second time on February 14, 2013, and sentenced to more than 18 years. Since 2013 he has been in remote penal colony 500 miles from Moscow. A human rights activist, Arthur Abashev, visited him on February 17, 2017 and stated that Kaptsugovich is in prison and "does not have access to the internet, a computer or a mobile phone."

Steele and his source likely chose Kaptsugovich as a fictitious hacker because he had posted porn on the internet, and the allegation states "porn traffic" was used in the attack against the Democratic Party. Also, Kaptsugovich had no means to find out about or dispute any allegation.

15. The Sam Clovis Setup

Carter Page said Stefan Halper asked to be introduced to Sam Clovis, the Trump campaign's national co-chairman. On July 16, 2016, Carter Page communicated to Clovis: "Professor Stef Halper spends part of the year in Virginia where he has a home in Falls Church; he's a big fan of yours having followed you on CNN and offered a range of possibilities regarding how he and the University might be able to help."

On August 29, 2016, Halper sent Clovis an email stating that he was a professor at Cambridge University, had met Carter Page at a Cambridge conference, and suggested that he and Clovis meet. When they met several days later, Halper offered to help the campaign by sharing research on foreign policy. Clovis later told a reporter "This is just my speculation — I have no knowledge. I think [Halper] was using his meeting with me to give him bona fides to talk to George Papadopoulos. He used Carter Page to get to me and he used me to get to George. George was the target. I think George was the target all along."[lxxxi]

Halper worked as an FBI covert agent to entrap Trump campaign team members, so, in addition to using Clovis as a connection to meet Papadopoulos, he may also have been trying to insinuate himself into the Trump campaign as a spy.

16. The Jeff Sessions Setup

Jeff Sessions recused himself from the Trump/Russia collusion investigation in early March citing the federal regulation 28 CFR Section 45.2 - Disqualification arising from personal or political relationship. The regulation states that disqualification is necessary only if there is a criminal investigation or prosecution as to which a prosecutor has a conflict of interest. Comey testified on March 20, 20917 that this was a counterintelligence investigation.

Andrew McCarthy said that Sessions did not need to recuse because the Russia investigation is not a criminal investigation. McCarthy added that "In the event the Russia counterintelligence probe turned up evidence of crimes that would warrant criminal investigations, Sessions — because of his prominent role in the Trump campaign — would likely have to recuse himself from those investigations, on a case-by-case basis (e.g., if criminal charges were brought against Michael Flynn, as ultimately happened)."[lxxxii]

Mollie Hemingway explained in a Federalist article how Comey and McCabe gamed Sessions so he would recuse.

> *In early March 2017, a Washington Post article based on a leak by "Justice Department officials" said Sessions' "previously undisclosed discussions [with Russians] could fuel new congressional calls for the appointment of a special counsel to investigate Russia's alleged role in the 2016 presidential election" and "He has so far resisted calls to recuse himself." At the end of the Post's article, the writers clarified that the "undisclosed discussion" occurred when Sessions was approached after a Heritage Foundation event by a small group of ambassadors, including the Russian ambassador.*

Comey testified "We also were aware of facts that I can't discuss in an open setting, that would make his [Sessions] continued engagement in a Russia-related investigation problematic and so we were—we were convinced and in fact, I think we had already heard that the career people [at the Justice Department] were recommending that he recuse himself, that he was not going to be in contact with Russia related matters much longer."

NBC News' Ken Dilanian reported "Comey confirmed that he had been talking about a story that NBC News and other outlets had already reported — about classified intelligence suggesting an undisclosed meeting between Sessions and the Russian ambassador to the U.S. in April 2016 at the Mayflower Hotel in Washington. That's according to two sources familiar with what Comey said." Hemingway said the meeting based on the "classified intelligence" was that both Kislyak, the Russian ambassador, and Sessions attended the same foreign policy address by candidate Trump and they both attended the same short VIP reception just before the event for ambassadors and senators and other important figures.[lxxxiii]

Sessions made the decision after meeting "with the relevant senior career Department officials to discuss whether I should recuse myself from any matters arising from the campaigns for President of the United States." These career officials may well have been complicit with Comey and McCabe to get Sessions to recuse. Sessions' recusal provided Rod Rosenstein and Robert Mueller carte blanche to search for unknown crimes without probable cause.

Andrew McCarthy wrote that the president could direct Sessions "to consider whether his recusal complies with the regulation that limits disqualification to criminal investigations as to which there is a conflict. To the extent it does not, he should amend the recusal to conform to the regulation."[lxxxiv]

Comey and McCabe used the leaks to the media to convince Sessions to recuse himself from the Russia probe. Jeff Sessions appears to be an honorable and trusting man. Unfortunately, Comey and McCabe took advantage of this, and gamed him into unnecessarily recusing from all aspects of the Russia investigation.

17. The Roger Stone and Michael Caputo Setup

In May 2016, Henry Greenberg, later identified as Henry Oknyasnky, reached out to a Russian immigrant business partner of Michael Caputo to request a meeting with Roger Stone. Caputo arranged the meeting, and Oknyasnky told Roger Stone he wanted Trump to pay $2 million for damaging information on Hillary Clinton. The Washington Post found out that Oknyasnky is a Russian national who has claimed to work as an FBI informant. Oknyasnky initially denied that a meeting took place in text messages with the Post, but he later did acknowledge one took place. He further said that the demand for money came not from himself but a Ukrainian friend he identified as Alexei, who claimed to have been fired from the Clinton Foundation.[lxxxv]

Stone and Caputo allege they were targeted in this setup by U.S. law enforcement during the 2016 campaign to entrap then-candidate Donald Trump. "Caputo said he now believes the Russian who met with Stone was an FBI informant because "the OSC (Office of Special Counsel) knew more about it than I did." He added that it was not until prosecutors informed him that Greenberg was Russian that he learned the man he had spoken with in 2016 was not a US citizen."[lxxxvi]

Simpson and Steele used other setups like this on George Papadopoulos and Donald Trump Jr. to support the dossier false allegation that Trump associates were colluding with Russia to get compromising information on Clinton. Simpson and Steele were most probably behind this also.

18. The Reince Priebus Setup

Andrew McCabe, with help from James Comey, set Reince Priebus up in February 2017 so it would appear that he and the White House were obstructing justice in the Trump/Russia collusion investigation. Comey already had begun writing memos to himself documenting his meetings with President Trump in a scheme to get a Special Counsel appointed based on the story that President Trump was obstructing justice.

McCabe asked to speak privately with White House chief of staff Reince Priebus following a February 2017 intelligence briefing. McCabe said he asked for the meeting to tell Priebus that "everything" in a New York Times story authored by Michael S. Schmidt, Mark Mazzetti, and Matt Apuzzo was "bullsh-t." McCabe was referring to a story headlined "Trump Campaign Aides Had Repeated Contacts With Russian Intelligence." The Times said it was sourced to four "current and former American officials."[lxxxvii]

Priebus told McCabe that he was "getting crushed" because the media was running the story non-stop. Preibus asked McCabe, "What am I supposed to do?" Priebus asked if the FBI could say publicly state what McCabe told him. McCabe said he'd have to find out, and later told Priebus that he couldn't do anything about it. Comey then called Priebus and said he believed the story to be inaccurate, but that the FBI could not "get into the position of making statements on every story."[lxxxviii]

One week later, CNN ran a story stating that "The FBI rejected a recent White House request to publicly knock down media reports about communications between Donald Trump's associates and Russians known to US intelligence during the 2016 presidential campaign, multiple US officials briefed on the matter tell CNN."[lxxxix] The CNN story said:

"The same White House official said that Priebus later reached out again to McCabe and to FBI Director James Comey asking for the FBI to at least talk to reporters on background to dispute the stories. A law enforcement official says McCabe didn't discuss aspects of the case but wouldn't say exactly what McCabe told Priebus.

Comey rejected the request for the FBI to comment on the stories, according to sources, because the alleged communications between Trump associates and Russians known to US intelligence are the subject of an ongoing investigation.

The White House did issue its own denial, with Priebus calling The New York Times story "complete garbage."

CNN has previously reported that there was constant communication between high-level advisers to then-candidate Trump, Russian officials and other Russians known to US intelligence during the summer of 2016.

The Trump administration's efforts to press Comey run contrary to Justice Department procedure memos issued in 2007 and 2009 that limit direct communications on pending investigations between the White House and the FBI."

The authors of the CNN news story included Evan Perez, who has extensive ties to Fusion GPS, and Jim Sciutto, a former Obama administration appointee with close ties to Obama administration officials.

Both Comey and McCabe are proven leakers to the press. McCabe or his legal counsel, Lisa Page, are probably the source of this CNN story that falsely alleges that Reince Priebus and the Trump administration tried to obstruct justice.

19. The Stephen Miller and Boris Epshteyn Setups

Stephen Miller

Stefan Halper's first publicly known covert agent activity occurred in May 2016 when he sent an invitation to Stephen Miller, a high-level Trump campaign adviser, to attend a Cambridge University campaign-themed conference at which Dearlove was one of the speakers. Miller did not attend the event. Halper's action to lure Miller to London predates the July 31st start of the FBI investigation by more than two months.

Boris Epshteyn

As detailed in chapter 6 on Sergei Millian, Millian attempted unsuccessfully to set up the Trump campaign adviser, Boris Epshteyn.

20. The Trump Campaign Setup

The conspirators attempted to hurt Donald Trump's candidacy throughout the 2016 presidential campaign by creating and broadly disseminating lies.

Simpson and Steele gave briefings to reporters about the dossier allegations. In September 2016, Steele met with The New York Times, The Washington Post, Yahoo News, The New Yorker and CNN. In October, he gave second briefings to The New York Times, The Washington Post and Yahoo News.

Simpson asked Steele to talk with Mother Jones reporter David Corn about the dossier allegations in the final days of the election. Corn's Oct. 31, 2016, story had the most detailed allegations of connections between the Trump campaign and Russia. Although Steele was forbidden by the FBI to make his allegation public, he did it anyway, and Bruce Ohr knew this. Ohr wrote "Glen asked Chris to speak to the Mother Jones reporter. It was Glen's Hail Mary attempt."

After Wikileaks posted thousands of DNC documents on July 22, 2016, Clinton's campaign manager, Robby Mook, said the Russian government was behind the release of DNC documents on WikiLeaks as a way to help Trump. Two days later, President Obama stated "What we do know is that the Russians hack our systems... What the motives were in terms of the leaks, all that - I can't say directly. What I do know is that Donald Trump has repeatedly expressed admiration for Vladimir Putin." Hillary Clinton harped on Russia hacking the DNC emails and Trump supporting Putin beginning in July 2016 in her speeches and ads, and in the debates with Trump.

When Steele provided his dossier allegations to British intelligence people such as the former head of MI6, Sir Richard Dearlove, did they then feed these allegations to John Brennan as intelligence? For example, the British spy head of QHHQ,

Robert Hannigan travelled to the U.S. in summer 2016 personally provide intelligence on Trump/Russia to Brennan, bypassing his U.S. counterpart, Mike Rogers of the NSA. Brennan pushed Comey to open a counterintelligence investigation of Trump/Russia collusion. Did Brennan cite phony British "intelligence" in his talks with Comey? House Intelligence Committee Chairman Devin Nunes said his review of FBI and Justice Department "electronic communication" documents show no intelligence was used to begin the investigation into possible collusion between the Trump campaign and Russia during the 2016 election.

Brennan persisted in getting the Trump/Russia collusion information publicly disseminated through the media and Congress.

In early August 2016, Brennan briefed Obama on Russian interference. He explained that Putin's explicit purpose is to aid Trump. The Washington Post reported on these meetings.

In late August, Brennan briefed congressional leaders on the same topic. The New York Times reported on these briefings.

Brennan briefed Harry Reid on August 25 in which "Brennan indicated that Russia's hackings appeared aimed at helping Mr. Trump win the November election." On August 27, Reid sent a letter to Comey expressing his "concern that the threat of the Russian government tampering in our presidential election is more extensive than widely known," and "evidence of a direct connection between the Russian government and Donald Trump's campaign continues to mount." Reid then alludes, without naming, former Trump campaign advisor Carter Page in his letter stating that this advisor "met with high-ranking sanctioned individuals while in Moscow in July, 2016, well after Trump became the presumptive Republican nominee." This last statement proves that Brennan provided the dossier allegations to Reid, because this information on Carter Page was unique to the dossier. On August 29, the New York Times reported on the letter. Brennan briefed Reid because he knew Reid would leak the briefing to the press. When Reid was asked if Brennan directly or indirectly had enlisted him to push information held by the intelligence community into the public realm, he told an interviewer, 'Why do you think he called me?'

On Oct. 30, Reid wrote another letter to Comey, criticizing him for reopening the Clinton email investigation, while sitting on "explosive information about close ties and coordination between Donald Trump, his top advisors, and the Russian government." The letter was reported on by all major news media on the same day.

Donald Trump lost an unknown millions of votes because of the false Trump/Russia collusion story that Hillary Clinton, the DNC, and her co-conspirators fabricated and disseminated.

21. The President Trump Setup

James Brennan, Loretta Lynch, James Clapper, Susan Rice left the government when Donald Trump became president. Comey and his co-conspirators knew:

- "There is no big there, there" as Strzok texted right after his interview for joining Mueller's team. Lisa Page affirmed this meant no substantial evidence existed of Trump/Russia collusion.
- Steele's dossier allegations were false. Comey and Strzok both knew Millian, the principal source of the dossier's most damaging allegations, was unreliable based on the FBI's 2011 counterintelligence investigation of Millian. Steele told Bruce Ohr that he wanted to stop Trump from being president so Steele was not reliable and his allegations could not be trusted.
- Clinton and the DNC paid for the dossier, and Strzok never tried to verify major allegations that were easily disprovable. Clinton's close allies, Sydney Blumenthal and Cody Shearer, provided misinformation to the FBI through the State Department.
- An FBI spy, Stefan Halper, tried to entrap and surveille four innocent members of Trump's campaign team, including two prior to the beginning of the counterintelligence investigation.

A FISA warrant was approved by the court using Steele's dossier allegations as evidence. The conspirators hid from the court in the application critical pertinent facts including: 1) the DNC and Clinton campaign funded the dossier, 2) the FBI never verified the allegations, nor checked the reliability of the sources, such as Millian, and 3) the author, Steele, was trying to prevent Trump from being elected president.

Comey and the conspirators remaining in the Trump administration knew that the FBI's Trump/Russia counterintelligence investigation would not be successful because there was no evidence of collusion. Strong circumstantial evidence indicates that they devised a plan to harm Trump's presidency, and possibly get him impeached, by getting a Special Counsel appointed.

On January 5, 2017, President Obama, Vice President Biden, Comey, then–acting attorney general Sally Yates and national-security adviser Susan Rice met to discuss withholding information about the Russia investigation from the incoming Trump administration. Andrew McCarthy writes:

> "It is easy to understand why Obama officials needed to discuss withholding information from Trump. They knew that the Trump campaign — not just some individuals tangentially connected to the campaign — was the subject of an ongoing FBI counterintelligence probe. Indeed, we now know that Obama's Justice Department had already commenced FISA surveillance on Trump campaign figures, and that it was preparing to return to the FISA court to seek renewal of the surveillance warrants. We also know that at least one informant was still deployed. And we know that the FBI withheld information about the investigation from the congressional "Gang of Eight" during quarterly briefings from July 2106 through early March 2017. ... Director Comey said Congress's most trusted leaders were not apprised of the investigation because "it was a matter of such sensitivity." Putting aside that the need to alert Congress to sensitive matters is exactly why there is a Gang of Eight, the palpable reason why the matter was deemed too "sensitive" for disclosure was that it involved the incumbent administration's investigation of the opposition campaign.
>
> Clearly, the Obama officials did not want Trump to know the full scope of their investigation of his campaign. But just as important, they wanted the investigation — an

"insurance policy" that promised to hamstring Trump's presidency — to continue.

So, how to accomplish these objectives? Plainly, the plan called for Comey to put the new president at ease by telling him he was not a suspect. This would not have been a credible assurance if Comey had informed Trump that his campaign had been under investigation for months, suspected of coordinating in Russia's cyber-espionage operation. So, information would be withheld. The intelligence chiefs would tell Trump only about Russia's espionage, not about the Trump campaign's suspected "coordination" with the Kremlin. Then, Comey would apprise Trump about only a sliver of the Steele dossier — just the lurid story about peeing prostitutes, not the dossier's principal allegations of a traitorous Trump-Russia conspiracy.

Shortly before he met with Trump, Comey consulted his top FBI advisers about the plan to tell Trump he was not a suspect. There was an objection from one of Comey's top advisers — we don't know which one. Comey recounted this disagreement for the Senate Intelligence Committee (my italics):

One of the members of the leadership team had a view that, although it was technically true [that] we did not have a counterintelligence file case open on then-President-elect Trump[,] . . . because we're looking at the potential . . . coordination between the campaign and Russia, because it was . . . President-elect Trump's campaign, this person's view was, inevitably, [Trump's] behavior, [Trump's] conduct will fall within the scope of that work.

the FBI did not regard Russia as the "target"; to the contrary, Comey said the focus of the investigation was whether Donald Trump's campaign had coordinated in Russia's election interference. And perspicaciously,

Comey's unidentified adviser connected the dots: Because (a) the FBI's investigation was about the campaign, and (b) the campaign was Trump's campaign, it was necessarily true that (c) Trump's own conduct was under FBI scrutiny.

So . . . what did the dossier say? The lion's share of it — the part Director Comey omitted from his briefing of Trump — alleged that the Trump campaign was conspiring with the Kremlin to corrupt the election, including by hacking and publicizing Democratic-party emails.[xc]

On January 6, 2017, Comey, Clapper, Brennan, and NSA chief Michael Rogers visited President-elect Trump in New York to brief him on the Intelligence Community Assessment (ICA) on Russian efforts to interfere in the presidential election. At Comey's request, Trump met alone with Comey afterwards to discuss "some personally sensitive" information gathered during the intelligence assessment.

James Clapper leaked information to CNN of Comey's briefing Trump on the dossier in order to add credibility to the dossier so the media would report on it.

For the first time in his career, Comey wrote a memo to himself documenting the meeting, as he would do in every subsequent meeting with President Trump. In the memo's remarks, Comey characterized the prostitute "golden showers" dossier allegation as "salacious and unverified." The memo remarks state that Comey also offered Trump unsolicited assurance during their one-on-one conversation that the FBI was not investigating him personally. Immediately after that meeting, Comey began typing out notes on what was discussed, according to his remarks. "I felt compelled to document my first conversation with the President-Elect in a memo. To ensure accuracy, I began to type it out on a laptop in an FBI vehicle outside Trump Tower the moment I walked out of the meeting," Comey testified. Comey wrote memos for nine one-on-one conversations over a period of four months — three of which were in-person, and six over the phone.

Comey assured Trump three different times that he was not the subject of an investigation. When President Trump asked him to publicly state that, Comey declined with a lame excuse. To Trump's great frustration, Comey then proceeded to publicly imply that Trump was the subject of an investigation. Andrew McCarthy writes the following about Comey's March 20, 2017 testimony:

> It is the testimony that launched the Mueller probe, and that sets (or, better, fails to set) the parameters of that probe — a flaw the nation has been discussing for a year.

> Comey's House testimony was breathtaking, not just because it confirmed the existence of a classified counterintelligence investigation, but because of what the bureau's then-director said about the Trump campaign (my italics):

> I have been authorized by the Department of Justice to confirm that the FBI, as part of our counterintelligence mission, is investigating the Russian government's efforts to interfere in the 2016 presidential election and that includes investigating the nature of any links between individuals associated with the Trump campaign and the Russian government and whether there was any coordination between the campaign and Russia's efforts. . ..

> That is an unambiguous declaration that the FBI was investigating the Trump campaign.

> But Comey went to extraordinary lengths to announce that the FBI was not merely zeroing in on individuals of varying ranks in the campaign; the main question was whether the Trump campaign itself — the entity — had "coordinated" in Russia's espionage operation.[xci]

Comey refused to answer questions on the dossier allegations in testimony before the House Intelligence Committee as Democrat Joaquin Castro read copiously from it and praised its accuracies. In this way, Comey left the impression that the dossier's allegations were true.

Comey purposely harmed Trump and his due process. As McCarthy explains "Under FBI protocols, the existence of investigations should not be acknowledged, much less their subject matters and potential targets —suspicions of wrongdoing should never be publicly announced until the government is prepared formally to charge and prove them in court."[xcii]

McCarthy said "Comey was not fired until May 9, but his days were clearly numbered after his March 20 House testimony. Fully aware of Trump's agitation, and against law-enforcement protocols, the director nevertheless asserted that the FBI's counterintelligence investigation of Russia's election interference was focusing on possible collusion between the Trump campaign and the Kremlin. He even added for good measure that the FBI would be assessing whether criminal violations had occurred. Concurrently, Comey confided in lawmakers that Trump was not a suspect in the investigation, but he declined to make that salient detail part of his public testimony. As anyone could have predicted, the media pounced. The FBI director, according to multiple reports, had made an extraordinary announcement that the president was a suspect in potential crimes involving collusion with the Putin regime. When he was not and Comey told him this privately."[xciii]

Comey testified that shortly after President Trump fired him, he authorized "a close friend" to leak the contents of his memos to the press in order to prompt a special counsel investigation. Comey wrote in one memo that President Trump told Comey, "I hope you can see your way clear to letting this go, to letting Flynn go. He is a good guy. I hope you can let this go." I replied by saying, 'I agree he is a good guy,' but said no more." On May 16, the New York Times ran a story headlined "Comey memo says

Trump Asked Him to End Investigation." In his testimony on June 8, 2017 at the Senate intelligence committee hearing, Comey spun the words "I hope..." into a strong implication of obstruction of justice:

> Sen. Jim Risch Do you know of any case where a person has been charged for obstruction of justice or, for that matter, any other criminal offense, where they said or thought they hoped for an outcome?
>
> COMEY: I don't know well enough to answer. The reason I keep saying his words is I took it as a direction.
>
> RISCH: Right.
>
> COMEY: I mean, this is a president of the United States with me alone saying I hope this. I took it as, this is what he wants me to do. I didn't obey that, but that's the way I took it.

Comey testified that:

> "I asked a friend of mine to share the content of a memo with the reporter," Comey said. "I didn't do it myself for a variety of reasons, but I asked him to because I thought that might prompt the appointment of a special counsel."
>
> "I don't think it's for me to say whether the conversation I had with the President was an effort to obstruct." "I'm sure the special counsel will work towards to find out the intention there and whether that's an offense."

A written account by White House Counsel, Don McGahn shows that President Trump did not try to obstruct justice: "It was unclear from the meeting with Yates whether an action could be taken without jeopardizing an ongoing investigation," McGahn further wrote in his memo. "President Trump asked

McGahn to further look into the issue as well as finding out more about the [Kislyak] calls."

McGahn's inclusion of the phrase "without jeopardizing an ongoing investigation" indicates the president was not trying to obstruct the Flynn probe.

Comey had testified before both the House Intelligence Committee and the Senate Judiciary Committee that the agents "saw nothing that indicated to them that [Flynn] knew he was lying to them."

A January 29, 2018 memo from President Trump's first legal team to special counsel Robert Mueller said "The White House counsel and chief of staff, as well as others surrounding the president, had every reason to believe at that time that the FBI was not investigating Lt. Gen. Flynn, especially in light of the fact that Lt. Gen. Flynn was allowed to keep his active security clearance. For all intents and purposes, and appearances, the FBI had accepted Flynn's account; concluded that he was confused but truthful; decided not to investigate him further; and let him retain his clearance." President Trump could not have intended to obstruct justice since he assumed there was no ongoing investigation of Flynn.

Rosenstein appointed Mueller as Special Counsel on May 17. Rosenstein is required to specify a crime in a Special Counsel appointment, but did not because he did not have one.

On May 18, the day after Mueller's appointment as Special Counsel, he recruited Peter Strzok. Shortly after midnight on May 19, 2017, Strzok solicited Lisa Page's opinion through a series of texts on whether he should accept the offer. Strzok first texted "No way" he would join the team because his career plan is to get a promotion to SAC (i.e., Special Agent in Charge), which he had already applied for, and then become an AD (i.e., Assistant Director) and "lead the Division." His subsequent texts list reasons why he should join the team, including:

- Strzok: "For me, and this case, I personally have a sense of unfinished business. \n\nI unleashed it with MYE [FBI acronym for the Clinton email investigation]. Now I need to fix it and finish it."
- Page: "You shouldn't take this on. I promise you, I would tell you if you should."
- Strzok: "Why not, re me?"
- Strzok: "Who gives a f*ck, one more AD [Assistant Director] like (Redacted) or whoever. \n\n An investigation leading to impeachment?"
- Strzok later texted "You and I both know the odds are nothing. If I thought it was likely, I'd be there no question. I hesitate in part because of my gut sense and concern there's no big there there."

Why did Strzok mention "impeachment?" Did Mueller or his recruiter mention "impeachment" to overcome Strzok's hesitancy to join the team?

The fast-moving sequence of events is very instructive. Comey was fired on May 9, his memos are published on May 16, Trump interviews Mueller for the FBI director on May 16 and Rosenstein rides with Mueller to the interview, Rosenstein appoints Comey's friend Mueller as Special Counsel on May 17, and Mueller recruits Strzok on May 18.

The extremely efficient process implies pre-planning and begets questions. Did Mueller talk to his friend Comey in 2017 before or after the firing? When did Mueller and Rosenstein discuss the Special Counsel? Did Comey discuss a Special Counsel with Rosenstein before he was fired?

Comey was in charge of the Trump/Russia investigation for 9 months and no crimes were found. Rosenstein knows that the DOJ regulations require specifying a crime for a Special Counsel appointment, but he did not do this because no crimes had been found. Why would Comey want a Special Counsel and why would Rosenstein appoint Mueller, a good friend of Comey's, immediately after Comey's memos were published?

As Ian Fleming said "Once is happenstance. Twice is coincidence. Three times is enemy action."

The conspirators' plot to set up President Trump consisted of the following:

- Provide the president with only selective information on the investigation and dossier to put him at ease
- Convince Jeff Sessions to unnecessarily recuse himself from any Trump/Russia investigations
- Comey writes memos on each meeting with the president
- Comey goads the president into firing him by publicly implicating him in the investigation
- Comey asks a friend to give the New York Times his memos with the objective of getting a Special Counsel appointed and to provide fodder to the media that the president was obstructing justice
- Rosenstein appoints Comey's friend Mueller as Special Prosecutor even though there is not a criminal factual predicate.
- Comey testifies that Trump directed him to stop the Flynn investigation.

22. Rosenstein and Mueller Join the Conspiracy

"The laws of the land are the inheritance and the right of every man before whatever tribunal he is brought." --Thomas Jefferson

The Special Counsel Appointment

Deputy Attorney General Rod Rosenstein wrote a memo on May 9, 2017 that strongly supported firing FBI director James Comey. Rosenstein concluded "The way the Director handled the conclusion of the email investigation was wrong. ... Having refused to admit his errors, the Director cannot be expected to implement the necessary corrective actions."

On May 9, 2017, President Trump sent Comey a termination letter stating that he accepted Rosenstein and AG Jeff Session's recommendations to fire him. Trump later stated that he had already decided to fire Comey before receiving Rosenstein's memo.

The Democrats seized on Trump's firing of Comey as an opportunity to accuse the president of obstructing the FBI's Russia investigation and they assailed Rosenstein for his memo justifying the firing. For example, Democratic Senator Christopher Murphy said: "You wrote a memo you knew would be used to perpetuate a lie. You own this debacle." The New York Times wrote that Rosenstein "grew concerned that his reputation had suffered harm," and he "became angry at Mr. Trump."

On September 21, 2018, a NY Times article, based on anonymous sources, said that FBI officials, including then-acting director Andrew McCabe, wrote internal memos documenting meetings with Rosenstein. Rosenstein suggested in several conversations with multiple FBI and Justice Department officials that he or a top FBI official, such as McCabe, would secretly record President Trump. The Times' sources said Rosenstein's intent in recording the president would be to expose him as being "unfit for office" in order to force his removal under the 25th Amendment.

Unbelievably, a few days after his memo justifying firing Comey, Rosenstein told FBI officials that he wished Comey were still FBI Director and that he hoped to get Comey's advice on the appointment of a special counsel.

Comey testified that he asked a friend to leak his memos on meetings with the president to get a special counsel appointed. The friend illegally leaked the memos to the NY Times. On May 16, 2017, the Times ran a story titled "Comey Memo Says Trump Asked Him to End the Flynn Investigation."

McCarthy writes "When Democratic pressure to appoint a special counsel reached fever pitch with the Times' publication of its report, based on a Comey leak, that Trump had pushed for the FBI to drop the Flynn investigation, Rosenstein decided to appoint a special counsel without specifying any crime against Trump."[xciv]

Robert Mueller was friends with James Comey, so he was probably angered by Comey's firing. On May 16, 2017, Mueller rode with Rosenstein to the White House for his job interview with the president for the FBI Director position. The next day, on May 17, Rosenstein appointed Mueller Special Counsel to investigate "any links and/or coordination between the Russian government and individuals associated with the campaign of President Donald Trump." This statement reflects Sergei Millian's allegations in the Steele dossier (the only "evidence" of such coordination) and was only 8 days after Comey's firing on May 9. Rosenstein had openly wished to get Comey's advice on the appointment of a special counsel, so one can deduce that he asked Mueller's advice in the car ride.

The day after Mueller's appointment as Special Counsel, he recruited Strzok. After the recruitment interview, Strzok texted Lisa Page that he could "fix and finish" the "unfinished business" he "unleashed" with the Clinton email exoneration, because the Special Counsel investigation could result in "impeachment?" Rosenstein wanted President Trump removed from office, and he openly contemplated using wiretaps to prove Trump was "unfit for office," so that he could be removed by the 25th Amendment. One can surmise from Strzok's reference to "impeachment" that Mueller and Rosenstein, perhaps in their car ride to the White House, discussed and decided that the best way to remove the president was an unbounded Special Counsel investigation to gather "evidence" for impeachment.

Jonathan Turley said that Rosenstein made a mistake in choosing Robert Mueller as the Special Counsel:

> *"Mueller interviewed for Comey's job, and Trump presumably spoke to Mueller about his reasons for firing Comey. Moreover, Mueller and Comey have a close prior professional history. Both men were involved in a historic moment during the George W. Bush administration where they stood side by side to oppose an unlawful surveillance program. It was a moment that would define the legacies of both men — and enjoin them in history."*

> *Rosenstein magnified that error with a mandate for Mueller that is strikingly broad. Yet this week, Rosenstein assured the public that "Bob Mueller understands and I understand the specific scope of the investigation, and so no, it's not a fishing expedition." If so, that understanding has remained strangely unstated.*

> *The special counsel provision found in 28 CFR 600 states that the attorney general (or in this case, the deputy attorney general) shall establish by jurisdiction of the special counsel "a specific factual statement of the matter to be investigated."*

The statement given to Robert Mueller was anything but specific."[xcv]

The FBI, under Comey, carried out the Trump campaign/Russia coordination counterterrorism investigation for 10 months without finding any substantial evidence of wrongdoing. Strzok was in charge of the FBI's Trump/Russia investigation for 10 months. He texted Lisa Page that "there's no big there there," and Page testified this meant there was a lack of evidence of Trump/Russia coordination.

Donald Trump received more than 62 million votes to become president. Rosenstein was angry at President Trump for harming his reputation. Driven by his bruised ego, Rosenstein, in an extremely narcissistic act, plotted to void the election by getting President Trump removed from office less than 4 months after the inauguration. Rosenstein found a willing partner in Mueller to reverse the will of the voters by aggressively investigating the president and his associates without any limits or probable cause to find evidence of some crimes so a democratic majority in Congress could impeach the president. Mueller and Rosenstein joined the conspiracy to harm President Trump using the justice system as a political weapon.

Rosenstein's Conflicts of Interest

Comey testified on June 8 that he is "sure" Mueller will investigate if Trump obstructed justice. Democratic Representative Rick Nolan said Rosenstein was asked repeatedly during testimony who told him to write the memo. Rosenstein would not say, adding that it was part of the Mueller probe.

Jonathan Turley writes:

> "If Mueller is pursuing obstruction allegations, that course will take him right over the desk of his superior: Rosenstein.

Rosenstein was consulted about firing Comey and supported the decision with a memorandum shredding the former FBI director. Moreover, when the White House initially made it sound like Rosenstein was the reason that Comey was fired (despite the fact that Trump had already decided to do so before receiving Rosenstein's memo in support of termination), Rosenstein reportedly demanded a correction.

Rosenstein will likely be a key witness on the obstruction issue. As someone who supported the firing, he may be as important to the defense as to the prosecution in showing the independent grounds for terminating Comey. He has much at stake professionally, as shown by his adamant response to the White House spin. The grand jury might want to know why Rosenstein did not act to protect Comey or why he did not confront Trump in any suggested desire to curtail the investigation.

It is a basic rule that prosecutor should immediately recuse himself from a matter where he may be a witness. In addition to the various grounds listed in the conflicts rule, recusal is appropriate in "circumstances other than those set forth in the regulation that would cause a reasonable person with knowledge of the facts to question an employee's impartiality." Rosenstein, who has recognized his problem as a potential witness, should have recused himself long ago.

Rosenstein clearly agreed with the recusal of Sessions (as did most of us) to avoid even an appearance of a conflict. The deputy attorney general has more than an appearance of a conflict. Not only did Rosenstein appoint someone with close ties to the main accuser of President Trump, but he himself reportedly clashed with the White House on its post-firing account on Comey. Yet, Rosenstein is reaffirming that he will continue to *make decisions on the scope and resources for the investigation.*"[xcvi]

McCarthy says "if reports are to be believed, Mueller is weighing whether the president is guilty of an obstruction crime. Putting aside my assessment that there would be no legal merit to such an allegation, there could be no doubting Comey's importance as a witness in such a case. Mueller would then have to consider an ethical dilemma that the National District Attorneys Association, in its National Prosecution Standards (third edition), has described in the section on conflicts of interest (Standard 1-3.3, at p. 7)."[xcvii]

Rosenstein violated DOJ regulations and lied to mislead the public

In an August 6 interview with Fox news, Chris Wallace asked Rosenstein about the New York Times report that Mueller is looking at Trump's finances and his family's finances, unrelated to Russia. Rosenstein replied that "the special counsel is subject to the rules and regulations of the Department of Justice, and we don't engage in fishing expeditions. Now, that order that you read, that doesn't detail specifically who may be the subject of the investigation because we don't reveal that publicly. But Bob Mueller understands and I understand the specific scope of the investigation and so, it's not a fishing expedition."

Wallace asks "In the course of his investigation of the issues that he is looking at, if he finds evidence of a crime, can he look at that?" Rosenstein replies "Well, Chris, if he finds evidence of a crime that's within the scope of what Director Mueller and I have agreed is the appropriate scope of the investigation, then he can. If it's something that's outside that scope, he needs to come to the acting attorney general, at this time, me, for a permission to expand his investigation. But we don't talk about that publicly."[xcviii]

McCarthy says:

"The scope of the special counsel's investigation remains unlimited, despite the deputy attorney general's claim that it's not a 'fishing expedition.'

To what should be the surprise of no one, Deputy Attorney General Rod Rosenstein has tried to defend his conferral of boundless jurisdiction to special counsel Robert Mueller's investigation of President Donald Trump. But the conferral is indefensible because Rosenstein failed to adhere to regulations that require a clear statement of the basis for a criminal investigation. This failure is not cured by the DAG's stubborn insistence that there really are limits to Mueller's jurisdiction . . . just not limits he can talk about.

Rosenstein maintains that DOJ officials (presumably including himself) are subject to "the rules and regulations of the Department of Justice." Yet, those rules and regulations expressly mandate that there be a basis for a criminal investigation or prosecution before a special counsel is appointed. The appropriate scope of the investigation is not supposed to be something to which the DAG and the special counsel agree in off-the-record conversations. It is governed by what is supposed to be the specified predicate for a criminal investigation without which there should be no special-counsel appointment in the first place.

Don't take my word for it. The regulation, 28 CFR Sec. 600.1, states that the Justice Department may appoint a special counsel when it is "determine[d] that criminal investigation of a person or matter is warranted," and that the Justice Department's handling of "that investigation or prosecution of that person or matter" in the normal course "would present a conflict of interest for the Department" (emphasis added).

The regulation does not permit the Justice Department to appoint a special counsel in order to determine whether there is a basis for a criminal investigation. To the contrary, the basis for a criminal investigation must pre-exist the appointment. It is the criminal investigation that triggers the special counsel, not the other way around. Rosenstein, instead, appointed a special counsel and unleashed him to sniff around and see if he could come up with a crime.

It is specious to claim, as Rosenstein does, that his citation of the Russia counterintelligence investigation is a sufficiently definite statement of the scope of the investigation. As we have frequently pointed out, a counterintelligence investigation is not a criminal investigation. There need be no suspicion of crime before a counterintelligence probe is commenced. The purpose of the latter is to collect information about a foreign power, not to investigate a suspected crime. "

Moreover, if citing the Russia counterintelligence investigation were a sufficiently definite statement of Mueller's "scope," Rosenstein and Mueller would not have had to agree on what the scope of the investigation is — as Rosenstein told Wallace they have done, privately.

Which brings us (yet again) to the regulation governing a special counsel's jurisdiction, 28 CFR 600.4. It states that the Justice Department will provide the special counsel "with a specific factual statement of the matter to be investigated." We know from the above-quoted reg (Sec. 600.1) that controls special-counsel appointments that this "matter to be investigated" must involve a suspected crime.

Patently, the order by which Rosenstein appointed Mueller to conduct the Russia counterintelligence investigation is not a specific factual statement of a transaction giving rise to a suspected crime. Nor is

Rosenstein relieved of the obligation to comply with the regulation because Justice Department officials prefer not to talk about investigations publicly.

It bears remembering that we have arrived at this point largely because, on March 20, 2017, former FBI director James Comey publicly disclosed the existence of the investigation into Russia's election-meddling. For good measure, Comey added that the investigation would include scrutiny of Trump-campaign ties to, and coordination with, the Putin regime, as well as an assessment of whether crimes were committed.

Comey testified that he had been authorized by the Justice Department to make this public announcement. How is it, then, that the Trump Justice Department, against law-enforcement protocols, authorized that public discussion of the investigation but now refuses to make disclosures regarding the investigation that are required by regulation?"[xcix]

Rosenstein took advantage of Jeff Sessions recusal to brazenly flout the DOJ regulations in order to give Mueller an investigative authority without limits to go after the president.

Rosenstein Used Sergei Millian's Allegation as Mueller's Authorization

Mueller ordered an FBI raid on the home of Paul Manafort to obtain documents regarding Manafort's consulting work for the Ukrainian president. Rosenstein prepared a letter one week after the FBI raid to give Mueller explicit authority to target Manafort over the financial aspects of his lobbying work for the Ukrainian government that ended in 2014 and was not related to Trump/Russia election collusion scope. This is a blatant example of Mueller doing a fishing expedition to look for crimes without probable cause and then Rosenstein preparing a post hoc justification of any crimes discovered.

A judge in Mueller's case against Paul Manafort required proof that Mueller had the authority to prosecute Manafort. As a result, Mueller unredacted a very small portion of Rosenstein's August 2, 2017 supplemental memorandum to Mueller citing the factual basis for the investigation. In the unredacted portion, Rosenstein wrote that:

"Mueller is authorized to investigate: Allegations that Paul Manafort . . . Committed a crime or crimes by colluding with Russian government officials with respect to the Russian government's efforts to interfere with the 2016 election."

The **only** evidence ever cited that Manafort colluded with Russia in the 2016 election is Millian's allegation in the Steele dossier. Shockingly, Rosenstein used Sergei Millian's easily disprovable allegations about Manafort in the Steele dossier as the "factual basis" for the investigation.

23. Mueller's Indictment Proves No Trump/Russia Collusion

The Intelligence Community Assessment (ICA) of January 6, 2017 had no confidence level assigned to the Key Judgement "We assess that the GRU operations resulted in the compromise of the personal e-mail accounts of Democratic Party officials and political figures. By May, the GRU had exfiltrated large volumes of data from the DNC." This was the only Key Judgement without a confidence level assigned.

The NSA and FBI continued to investigate the DNC computer hack and theft of emails after the ICA. They gathered incontrovertible evidence that Russian GRU intelligence officers hacked the computer systems of the DNC, DCCC, and Clinton campaign and stole emails and other documents, and that Guccifer 2.0 was a persona used by the GRU.

The Daily Beast reported that the investigators got a lucky break:

> *"Guccifer [2.0] was connecting through an anonymizing service called Elite VPN, a virtual private networking service that had an exit point in France but was headquartered in Russia. But on one occasion... Guccifer [2.0] failed to activate the VPN client before logging on. As a result, he left a real, Moscow-based Internet Protocol address in the server logs of an American social media company." "Working off the IP address, U.S. investigators identified Guccifer 2.0 as a particular GRU officer working out of the agency's headquarters on Grizodubovoy Street in Moscow."*[c]

As a result, the FBI and NSA were able to gather very detailed evidence about the GRU's hacking activities and identify 12 specific intelligence officers as the hackers. Rosenstein transferred the case and the FBI agents working on it to the

Mueller team in March 2018. Mueller's team then presented the evidence to a grand jury to obtain the indictment. In this way, the Special Counsel received the publicity and credit when Rosenstein announced the indictment on July 13. Rosenstein then sent the case back to the DOJ's National Security Division for prosecution.

Following are some examples of the very detailed and specific evidence in Mueller's indictment:

- In March 2016, GRU intelligence officers targeted over 300 people affiliated with the Clinton Campaign, DCCC, and DNC using the spear phishing technique to steal passwords.
- The GRU then searched for and identified computers within the DCCC and DNC networks that stored information related to the 2016 U.S. presidential election.
- The GRU used malware to move the stolen documents outside the DCCC and DNC networks through encrypted channels to leased computers in different states.
- Between May 25, 2016 and June 1, 2016, the GRU hacked the DNC Microsoft Exchange Server and stole thousands of emails from the work accounts of DNC employees.

The FBI and NSA were able to trace the activities of specific GRU officers by day. They found GRU officers capturing the keystrokes of DNC employees and taking pictures of their computer screens.

The GRU began the spear phishing campaign in March 2016, but they needed to plan the very complex hack and implement the infrastructure, such as the leased computers in different states, months before that. Paul Manafort and Carter Page just joined the Trump campaign team as unpaid volunteers in March, so Sergei Millian's allegation that they coordinated the hack with Russia is preposterous.

Mueller's evidence proves Clinton and the DNC falsely claimed that the Russians stole the emails to help Trump win the presidential election. The Russians tried and failed to hack the Republican National Committee's computer system. Guccifer 2.0 was a persona that the GRU used. The indictment details private messages Julian Assange/WikiLeaks sent to Guccifer 2.0 communicating the strategy to influence the election:

- On or about June 22, 2016, Organization 1 [WikiLeaks/Assange] sent a private message to Guccifer 2.0 to "[s]end any new material [stolen from the DNC] here for us to review and it will have a much higher impact than what you are doing."
- On or about July 6, 2016, Organization 1 [WikiLeaks/Assange] added, "if you have anything hillary related we want it in the next tweo [sic] days prefable [sic] because the DNC [Democratic National Convention] is approaching and she will solidify bernie supporters behind her after."
- The Conspirators [GRU/Guccifer 2.0] responded, "ok . . . i see."
- Organization 1 [WikiLeaks/Assange] explained, "we think trump has only a 25% chance of winning against hillary . . . so conflict between bernie and hillary is interesting."

The GRU was following WikiLeaks/Assange's advice, and that advice was to cause a conflict between Bernie Sanders and Hillary Clinton, which it did. Debbie Wasserman Schultz resigned after WikiLeaks published the emails because it showed the DNC favored Clinton. WikiLeaks/Assange believed that Trump had only a very slim chance to win. The Russians and WikiLeaks were trying to sow discord between Clinton and Sander's followers, they were not trying to help Trump win because Assange believed that he only had a 25% chance to win. House Intelligence Committee Chairman Devin Nunes said Mueller's indictment of 12 Russian officials on charges of hacking Democrats' computers during the 2016 campaign looks "ridiculous" because it left out the fact that Russians also targeted Republicans.

Rosenstein authorized the Special Counsel to investigate "any links and/or coordination between the Russian government and individuals associated with the campaign of President Donald Trump." On announcing the indictment of the 12 GRU officers, Rosenstein said he has no evidence that "any American was a knowing participant in the alleged unlawful activity." The NSA and FBI had emails between the GRU and WikiLeaks and details on individual GRU intelligence officers' computer activities. The indictment's incontrovertible evidence proves that no one in Donald Trump's campaign was involved in the GRU's hacking, and, therefore, Mueller's Special Counsel has no basis to continue its investigation of Trump campaign/Russia coordination.

24. The Steele Dossier – Real Russian Collusion

"Injustice anywhere is a threat to justice everywhere."

--Martin Luther King, Jr.

Hillary Clinton and Debbie Wasserman Schultz, then chair of the DNC, used intermediaries (aka "cutouts") to insulate themselves from the people carrying out their plot to falsely blame the Trump campaign for coordinating the DNC email hack with Russia. Clinton used the Clinton campaign and Wasserman Schultz used the DNC to instruct and pay the law firm, Perkins Coie, to hire Glenn Simpson's Fusion GPS company in April 2016. Simpson then hired Christopher Steele and Nellie Ohr, the wife of the third highest ranking DOJ official at the time.

In spite of the cutouts, Clinton left fingerprints indicating her direct participation in the development, dissemination, and use of the Steele dossier:

- Clinton's close confidantes, Sidney Blumenthal and Cody Shearer, worked on creating false Trump/Russia collusion information and gave it to Steele. They most likely did this at Clinton's request since the Steele dossier was not public knowledge at the time.
- James Baker, who served as FBI's general counsel at the time, testified to Congress that Michael Sussmann, a lawyer for the firm Perkins Coie, provided documents and electronic media related to Russian meddling in the election. Clinton likely instructed Sussman to do this, since Sussman would not do this unilaterally without his client's request and approval.[ci]
- After Wikileaks posted thousands of DNC documents on July 22, 2016, Clinton's campaign manager, Robby Mook, publicly announced that the Russian government

was behind the release of DNC documents on WikiLeaks as a way to help Trump.

- Hillary Clinton harped on Russia hacking the DNC emails and Trump supporting Putin beginning in July 2016 in her speeches and ads, and in the debates with Trump.
- Clinton's friends at the State Department worked with Steele to pass the dossier onto the FBI.

Christopher Steele, who had not been to Russia in over 15 years, makes the patently absurd claim in his dossier that he had inside sources providing him with the private conversations of top Russian officials, including President Putin, Prime Minister Dmitry Medvedev, and close Putin confidante, Igor Sechin. The UK could replace all of its MI6 Russia experts with Steele if this fantasy were true.

Steele's dossier alleges that Sechin offered Carter Page money to reduce US sanctions against Russia. This was not the first time that Steele accused Igor Sechin of wrongdoing. England lost hosting the 2018 World Cup to Russia and the FBI investigated to find out if corruption was involved. Ken Bensinger's book "Red Card" says "one of Steele's best sources" informed him that the then Deputy Prime Minister, Igor Sechin, is suspected of having travelled to Qatar "to swap World Cup votes." In 2015 the US DOJ indicted fourteen people in connection with a hundred and fifty million dollars in bribes and kickbacks. Russia and Sechin were not implicated.

The evidence in Mueller's indictment of 12 Russian intelligence officers incontrovertibly proves that Trump's campaign did not coordinate the Russian DNC hack, and clearly proves that the information and allegations in Steele's dossier are absurd. Examples of Steele's false allegations:

- Carter Page and Paul Manafort coordinated the DNC hack with Russia.

- The leak of emails "had been conducted with the full knowledge and support of TRUMP and senior members of his campaign team."
- Russian diplomatic staff in key U.S. cities used the émigré 'pension' distribution system to reward the U.S. Russian émigré hackers.
- Michael Cohen met with Russian officials in Prague to discuss "how deniable cash payments were to be made to hackers who had worked in Europe under Kremlin direction against the CLINTON campaign."
- Hacking experts Aleksei Gubarov and Seva Kapsubovich were recruited under duress by the Russian Federal Security Service and were significant players in the DNC hack.

The Mueller indictment evidence proved without a doubt that 12 Russian GRU officers located in a specific building in Moscow hacked the DNC servers, stole the emails, and had them published on WikiLeaks. No other parties were involved in hacking the DNC in 2016 to steal the emails. Julian Assange urged the GRU officers to publish the DNC emails on WikiLeaks to promote conflict between supporters of Bernie Sanders and Hillary Clinton. Assange and the Russians did not publish the emails to help Trump because Assange assessed Trump only had a 25% probability of winning. The Russians did not publish Republican documents because they could not successfully hack their computer systems. Trump campaign team members, including Carter Page, Paul Manafort and Michael Cohen, were not involved. There were no U.S. Russian émigré hackers. Aleksei Gubarov, a millionaire business owner, and Seva Kapsubovich, a convicted pedophile in a remote Russian gulag, were also not involved. Steele created his preposterous allegations at the behest of Clinton and the DNC to blame the Trump campaign for coordinating the DNC hack with Russia in order to help Clinton win the election.

As documented in his dossier, Steele worked with senior Russian officials to gather false information that the conspirators used to influence the 2016 presidential election. Steele paid former and current Russian government officials to provide negative information on Trump that Steele used to create a 35-page dossier of false allegations against Trump and his associates. "The dossier quotes from a large number of anonymous sources. It cites 'a former top level Russian intelligence officer still active inside the Kremlin', 'a senior Russian foreign ministry figure' and "a senior Russian financial official'."[cii]

Hillary Clinton, her campaign, Debbie Wasserman Schultz, the DNC, Perkins Coie, Fusion GPS, Glenn Simpson, Nellie Ohr, Sydney Blumenthal, Cody Shearer, and the others involved in the Steele dossier conspired with a hostile nation, Russia, and a foreign national, Steele, to subvert a federal election. They received something of value from Russian government officials and the UK citizen in the form of the Steele dossier's false evidence. The conspirators used the Steele dossier's false evidence to influence the election to help Hillary Clinton win.

A partner at Perkins Coie, Robert Bauer, stated that a campaign finance law prohibits foreign nationals from providing "anything of value ... in connection with" an election and it is criminally enforceable. Perkins Coie is one of the conspirators. They hired Fusion GPS for Clinton and the DNC. The Perkins Coie attorney, Michael Sussman, a former DOJ lawyer, provided the FBI's General Counsel, James Baker, with documents and a thumb drive related to Russian interference in the election, hacking and possible Trump connections.[ciii] Obviously Sussman would do this only at the instruction of his clients, Hillary Clinton and the DNC.

The conspirators in the DOJ, the FBI, the State Department, and intelligence services used the false Steele Dossier allegations and foreign nationals to help Clinton win the election so they could remain in power.

Hillary Clinton used Steele's false evidence of Trump/Russia collusion throughout her 2016 presidential campaign in ads, speeches, and the debates. Clinton and the DNC had their vendors, Fusion GPS and Steele, disseminate the false allegations to the media, the DOJ, and the FBI. Clinton and the DNC's scam lives on in the Mueller investigation and is part of the biggest scandal in US history.

Clinton, Debbie Wasserman Schultz, and the DNC betrayed the United States by paying for and disseminating fraudulent information about the presidential candidate, Donald Trump, provided by Russian government officials and a foreign national, Steele, whose stated objective was to stop Donald Trump from being president. Clinton, Wasserman Schultz, the DNC and their co-conspirators are traitors because they colluded with foreign nationals to subvert the democratic election process in order to gain power. They actually did change the election results because an unknown millions of votes were cast for Clinton instead of Trump because of Clinton and the DNC's Trump/Russia collusion scam.

25. Mueller's Major Conflict-of-Interest

Mueller and Comey have worked together for 25 years, have praised each other publicly, and are friends. During the George W. Bush administration, Comey was the deputy attorney general and Mueller was FBI director. Comey succeeded Mueller as FBI director.

The vast majority of Americans trust the Department of Justice and the FBI. Americans trusted James Comey as the FBI Director, and many wanted the Mueller Special Counsel investigation after President Trump fired Comey.

James Comey was one of the primary conspirators to use the DOJ and FBI as a political weapon to elect Hillary Clinton president and harm Donald Trump. As detailed previously, Comey wanted to be fired and he set President Trump up to accomplish this. Comey's objective was to leak to the press his memos on meetings with the president to demonstrate that the president fired him to obstruct justice in the Russia investigation. Comey testified that he leaked the memos to get a Special Counsel appointed.

Comey is President Trump's accuser. While Rosenstein and Mueller viciously investigated the president and his associates without any probable cause looking for unknown crimes, they protected Comey, the accuser. Comey committed multiple felonies and deserved to be fired and prosecuted. Comey's felonies include:

- Comey approved the original Carter Page FISA warrant application and two renewals. The applications contained material misrepresentations and failed to properly follow the Woods Procedures requiring accuracy of facts by the sworn declarants. The applications violated Page's Fourth Amendment protections against omissions of material facts that would undermine or negate probable cause to search because they withheld material and exculpatory evidence.

- Comey deceived the Foreign Intelligence Surveillance Court (FISC) in the warrant application. The FISA application cited both the Steele dossier and the Yahoo News article based on an interview with Steele as key evidence that Carter Page was a Russian agent. Steele's major allegations were easily disprovable and Steele himself was extremely biased. Based on Steele's phony evidence, the FISA application essentially called Page a traitor by stating "The FBI believes that Page has been collaborating and conspiring with the Russian government. The FBI submits that there is probable cause to believe that Page . . . knowingly engage in clandestine intelligence activities (other than intelligence gathering activities) for or on behalf of such foreign power, or knowingly conspires with other persons to engage in such activities, and there, is an agent of a foreign power."

- Comey illegally violated Page's Fourth Amendment protections because the FISA application that his department prepared and that he approved hid the fact that Clinton and the DNC funded the dossier, it did not identify Steele's extreme bias, and it did not state that, as Comey testified, the allegations were unverified. McCabe testified in December 2017 that no surveillance warrant would have been sought from the FISC without the Steele dossier information.

- Comey leaked his memos on meetings with President Trump to the press, some of which were classified.

- Comey used a covert agent, Stefan Halper, to spy on Stephen Miller and Carter Page without probable cause. Halper's contact with Miller was in May 2016, and Halper's graduate assistant contacted Page in late May or early June. Both contacts predate the Trump/Russia collusion investigation that was initiated on July 31, 2016. Comey may have used other covert agents at an earlier date. On December 28, 2015, Peter Strzok texted the FBI attorney Lisa Page: "you get all your ocunus lures approved?" OCUNUS stands for Outside of the Continental United States. Was this regarding Mifsud and Papadopoulos?

- Comey used contractors to perform illegal searches in the FISA 702 database, permitting the contractors to illegally spy on U.S. citizens. The contractors were reported to be associated with Fusion GPS and the Clinton campaign. Following is an excerpt from the applicable Foreign Intelligence Surveillance Court's MEMORANDUM OPINION AND ORDER:[civ]

On March 9, 2016, DOJ oversight personnel conducting a minimization review at the FBI's [Redacted] learned that the FBI had disclosed raw FISA information, including but not limited to Section 702-acquired information, to a [Redacted] Compliance Report at 92. [Redacted] is part of the [Redacted] and "is largely staffed by private contractors" [Redacted] certain [Redacted] contractors had access to raw FISA information on FBI storage systems [Redacted].

Private contractors, employed by the FBI, were given full access to raw FISA data. FISA data that, once in their possession, could not be traced.

The apparent purpose for the FBI's granting such access was to receive analytical assistance from [Redacted]. Nonetheless, the [Redacted] contractors had access to raw FISA information that went well beyond what was necessary to respond to the FBI's requests; [Redacted]. The FBI discontinued the above-described access to raw FISA information as of April 18, 2016.

Comey committed various felonies in the Clinton email investigation:

- Illegally permitted Clinton's aides to represent her as attorneys
- Conspired with defense attorneys to hide obstruction of justice evidence
- Permitted a false attorney-client privilege between Clinton and her aides
- Conspired with defense attorneys to destroy evidence
- Permitted subjects of the investigation to attend Clinton's interview

Comey committed perjury multiple times:

- Comey falsely certified to Congress that the FBI had "reviewed all of the communications" discovered on a personal laptop used by Clinton aide, Huma Abedin, and her husband, Anthony Weiner. Comey testified to Congress that "thanks to the wizardry of our technology," the FBI was able to eliminate the vast majority of messages as "duplicates" of emails they'd previously seen. Tireless agents, he claimed, then worked "night after night after night" to scrutinize the remaining material. In fact, only 3,077 of the 694,000 emails were directly reviewed for classified or incriminating information. Three FBI officials completed that work in a single 12-hour spurt the day before Comey again cleared Clinton of criminal charges.
- Comey testified that the FBI included the dossier allegations in the FISA applications because Steele was considered reliable due to his past work with the FBI. Comey was guilty of perjury because he and others in the DOJ and FBI knew that Steele told Bruce Ohr that he was "desperate that Donald Trump not get elected and was passionate about him not being president." Comey also knew that Hillary Clinton and the DNC financed Steele's

dossier. Comey testified that the dossier allegations were salacious and unverified, but Strzok could have easily disproved the most important allegations if he had attempted to do so. The FBI judged Christopher Steele's anti-Trump information as only "minimally corroborated," according to a document declassified as of September 6, 2018.

- Comey lied when he testified that he had no knowledge of the parameters of Attorney General Sessions' recusal in the Russia investigation. A DOJ statement on June 8, 2017, says "In his testimony, Mr. Comey stated that he was "not *** aware of" "any kind of memorandum issued from the Attorney General or the Department of Justice to the FBI outlining the parameters of [the Attorney General's] recusal." However, on March 2, 2017, the Attorney General's Chief of Staff sent the attached email specifically informing Mr. Comey and other relevant Department officials of the recusal and its parameters, and advising that each of them instruct their staff "not to brief the Attorney General *** about, or otherwise involve the Attorney General *** in, any such matters described.""

- Comey lied in May 2017 about the scope of the email investigation into Clinton, Abedin, and Weiner. He testified that Huma Abedin "forwarded hundreds and thousands of emails" from Clinton's private email server to her husband, former congressman Anthony Weiner, as part of a "regular practice" of forwarding emails for Weiner to print out for Clinton, and ..." Devlin Barrett reported in the Washington Post that this is false because "The investigation found that Abedin did occasionally forward emails to her husband for printing, but it was a far smaller number than described by Comey, and it wasn't a "regular practice."

26. Rosenstein and Mueller's True Objective

"Law is often but the tyrant's will, and always so when it violates the right of an individual." --Thomas Jefferson

Mueller and Rosenstein are violating the Fourth Amendment of the Constitution

Rosenstein cannot specify the basis for a criminal investigation because there is none. Clinton and the DNC funded the Steele dossier to blame the DNC hack on the Trump campaign colluding with Russia. Steele used one source, Sergei Millian, to allege that the Trump campaign colluded with Russia to steal and publish the DNC emails. Comey could have easily disproved this allegation, but he instead used it to justify the FBI's counterterrorism investigation and obtain a FISA warrant to surveille Carter Page. Rosenstein hides the fact there is no evidence of a crime by saying he cannot speak publicly about the scope.

Despite having no evidentiary basis of a crime, Mueller, with Rosenstein's complicity, has very aggressively hired an extraordinary number of attorneys, most of which are democratic donors, to pursue investigations unrelated to Trump campaign/Russia coordination. For example, they have investigated previous Trump transactions and business deals such as the 2013 Miss Universe pageant in Moscow and Trump's sale of a Florida mansion to a Russian oligarch in 2008.

Mueller is investigating Paul Manafort for 2005 tax crimes, 2010 bank fraud crimes and 2013 foreign agent crimes completely unrelated to the 2016 campaign. Mueller conducted a predawn raid of Manafort's Virginia home, even though he had been cooperating. Trump attorney, John Dowd, accused investigators of committing a "gross abuse of the judicial process" for the sake of "shock value" – and employing tactics normally seen "in Russia not America."

John Eastman writes:

> "The special counsel will not to track down the details of a crime known to have been committed and determine "who dunnit," but will scour the personal and business affairs of a select group of people—the President of the United States, members of his family, his business associates, and members of his presidential campaign and transition teams—to see if any crime can be found (or worse, manufactured by luring someone into making a conflicting statement at some point). This is not a proper use of prosecutorial power, but a "witch hunt," as President Trump himself correctly observed. Or, to put it more in terms of legalese, this special prosecutor has effectively been given a "writ of assistance" and the power to exercise a "general warrant" against this select group of people, including the President of the United States, recently elected by a fairly wide margin of the electoral vote."

> "That is the very kind of thing our Fourth Amendment was adopted to prevent. Indeed, the issuance of general warrants and writs of assistance is quite arguably the spark that ignited America's war for independence."

> The Fourth Amendment "...protects people against unreasonable searches of their "persons, houses, papers, and effects" (contra the writs of assistance), and requires that warrants be issued only "upon probable cause, . . . particularly describing the place to be searched, and the persons or things to be seized" (contra the general warrant)."

> "No such limitation seems to be in place with the special prosecutor. He is reportedly looking into the financial records and meeting schedules of several top aides to President Trump, for example, including Trump's son-in-

law Jared Kushner. It is hard to imagine that a court would issue 'probable cause' warrants for such things, when there is no evidence of an underlying crime, but 'probable cause' has given way to political pressure."

"...the power to deploy the full resources of the United States government against a select group of individuals, to churn up the soil and turn over every rock on their personal path of life, to see if ever a crime had been committed along the way, is a dangerous threat to the liberty of all of us. It is intolerable under the Fourth Amendment. And it should be intolerable in any nation committed to principles of liberty."[cv]

Rosenstein and Mueller's Act II

Fusion GPS developed the Steele dossier and used its many DOJ and reporter contacts to spread their false Russia conspiracy story. Their Russia collusion campaign was so successful that a Special Counsel is now investigating it to the great detriment to President Trump. William Jacobson, a Cornell law professor, wrote that the Mueller investigation is Act I and that Act II is foreshadowed by the NY Times Op-Ed written by the Fusion GPS co-founders:[cvi]

Mueller, has subpoenaed Trump Organization business records as part of his inquiry into Russian interference in the presidential election.

Those documents — and records recently seized by the F.B.I. from the president's personal lawyer Michael Cohen — might answer a question raised by the president's critics: Have certain real estate investors used Trump-branded properties to launder the proceeds of criminal activity around the world?

Jacobson notes "That Act II, even more so than Act I, is a more direct attack on Trump's business dealings and history than Mueller could justify keeping under his jurisdiction." Michael Cohen is a former attorney for Donald Trump. The Michael Cohen case perfectly illustrates Act II.

Rosenstein and Mueller referred Michael Cohen's case to the Southern District of New York (SDNY). Rosenstein has not recused himself from Mueller's investigation even though he has a very strong conflict of interest. The malevolent Rosenstein though ordered Geoffrey Berman, President Trump's appointed SDNY U.S. attorney, to recuse himself from Cohen's case, so that Robert Khuzami was in charge of it. As soon as Mueller referred Cohen to the SDNY, the long-time Clinton defender, Lanny Davis, became Cohen's attorney. Cohen immediately turned against President Trump. Davis got Cohen to accept a plea deal. In addition to tax evasion, Cohen pled guilty to a felony campaign finance law violation for paying $280,000 of hush-money payments on behalf of Trump prior to the election. The $280,000 payment is probably not a felony campaign finance violation, and, if it were, even large violations such as the 2008 $2 million Obama campaign violation are usually settled with a fine rather than a felony conviction. Why then did Lanny Davis and Robert Khuzami create this guilty plea deal for Michael Cohen. The answer is that they wanted to make President Trump an unindicted co-conspirator to a felony offense, which would give Mueller evidence for a report that substantiates a recommendation for impeachment. Unbelievably, Hillary somehow got her long-time confidante, defender and friend, Lanny Davis, involved in helping Mueller to prosecute the president and obtain "evidence" for impeachment.

Harvard law professor Alan Dershowitz downplayed the significance of election law violations saying "every" administration and presidential candidate commits them. Here, they're trying to elevate this into an impeachable offense or a felony against the president. Naming someone as an un-indicted co-conspirator is very unfair because he has no opportunity to defend himself or herself. And yet that may happen."

Mueller likely referred the case to the SDNY so that Cohen could continue composing crimes, under the guiding hand of Clinton confidante Lanny Davis, against the Trump Organization, Donald Trump Jr., Jared Kushner, and Ivanka Trump, all located in the DOJ's New York jurisdiction.

Rosenstein and Mueller are conducting a vicious personal vendetta against the president, his family, associates, and business so legal defenses used in a good faith investigation are not applicable. Mueller and Rosenstein's objective has always been impeachment, and they may well achieve this if the Democrats win congressional majorities this November as some polls indicate.

27. The Conspirators' Many Crimes

Government officials conspired ("conspirators") to elect Hillary Clinton president by violating multiple laws to wrongfully exonerate her in the email investigation and harming candidate Donald Trump's electability through fraud:

Former Attorney General, Loretta Lynch, former FBI Director, James Comey, FBI Deputy Director Andrew McCabe, and others violated federal laws in wrongfully exonerating Hillary Clinton in the email investigation so that she could be the Democratic presidential candidate.

Lynch, Comey, Peter Strzok, and the other conspirators violated federal laws to harm candidate Donald Trump's electability, and, after the election, continued to violate federal laws to harm President Trump.

Some of the conspirators many felonies are listed below.

Violated the RICO Act

The Racketeer Influenced and Corrupt Organizations Act ("RICO") - 18 USC §1962 1 is designed to combat organized crime in the United States, and can be used to prosecute government officials. McCarthy explains "Under RICO, an "enterprise" can be any association of people, informal or formal, illegitimate or legitimate — it could be a Mafia family, an ostensibly charitable foundation, or a department of government. It is a racketeering enterprise if its affairs are conducted through "a pattern of racketeering activity." A "pattern" means merely two or more violations of federal or state law; these violations constitute "racketeering activity" if they are included among the extensive list of felonies laid out in the statute."cvii

The RICO Act is applicable to this conspiracy. The statute provides that a public official can be charged with a RICO violation "through the commission of two or more chargeable or indictable or punishable predicate offenses."

Comey, Lynch, and others (the "conspirators") violated multiple laws, including RICO Act predicate offenses, to wrongfully exonerate Clinton in the email investigation. Some examples of laws that the conspirators violated are listed below, with the RICO Act predicate offenses noted in italics:

Bribed witnesses in violation of 18 U.S. Code § 201 - Bribery of public officials and witnesses, and in violation of 18 U.S. Code § 1510 - Obstruction of criminal investigations, *both of which are RICO Act predicate offenses.* Bribery under the law includes offering something of value to witnesses with the intent of influencing their testimony. Subjects of the investigation, such as Clinton's aides, were at risk of being indicted. The conspirators did not use a grand jury, and instead gave unnecessary immunity deals, did not investigate suspects with confidential emails on their laptop computers, allowed subjects of the investigation to attend Clinton's interview, and accepted a false attorney-client privilege (all of which are something of value) to protect subjects of the investigations so that they would not testify against Clinton.

Conspired with defense attorneys to hide evidence of obstruction of justice by agreeing to limit the search of Mills and Samuelson's laptops to no later than January 31, 2015. This prevented the FBI from discovering the March 31, 2015 destruction of Clinton's emails. Also gave unnecessary immunity so the person destroying the emails would not testify about it. These violated 18 U.S. Code § 1512 - Tampering with a witness, victim, or an informant (*a RICO Act predicate offense*), because they corruptly concealed an object (evidence of email destruction) with intent to impair the object's availability for use in an official proceeding (the email investigation).

Conspired with defense attorneys to destroy evidence, the laptop computers of Clinton aides, Mills and Samuelson. This violated 18 U.S. Code § 1512 - Tampering with a witness, victim, or an informant (*a RICO Act predicate offense*), because they corruptly concealed an object (evidence on the laptops) with intent to impair the object's availability for use in an official proceeding (the email investigation). It also violated 18 U.S. Code § 1519 - Destruction, alteration, or falsification of records in Federal investigations and bankruptcy.

Violated the Hatch Act, which prohibits government employees from using their positions to influence an election, by violating multiple laws to wrongfully exonerate Clinton so that she could be the Democratic candidate for president. Comey also violated the Hatch Act by making false statements and material omissions in his press conference to recommend exoneration.

Violated 18 U.S. Code § 371 - Conspiracy to commit offense or to defraud United States by violating multiple laws to wrongfully exonerate Clinton so that she could be the Democratic candidate for president.

Violated 18 U.S. Code § 1001 (Statements or entries generally) by violating multiple laws to conceal and cover up material facts in the Clinton email investigation.

Violated 18 U.S. Code § 207 - Restrictions on former officers, employees, and elected officials of the executive and legislative branches, by permitting Mills and Samuelson to act as Clinton's attorneys to justify a fraudulent attorney-client privilege.

The conspirators violated laws to harm candidate Trump and benefit candidate Clinton in the presidential election, and afterwards to harm president Trump. They did this by creating and publishing the false narrative that the Trump campaign coordinated with Putin to direct the GRU to hack the DNC computer system and publish the stolen emails in order to harm Clinton's electability and help Trump. They also harmed Trump by 1) initiating an investigation, based on false evidence, of the

Trump campaign coordinating with Russia to influence the election and, 2) political spying and promoting misinformation.

Some examples of laws that the conspirators violated are listed below, with the RICO predicate offenses noted in italics:

Devised the false Russia narrative as a scheme to defraud the American voters into electing Clinton, using television, radio and wire (i.e., internet), in order to keep their high-level government positions and associated power and money. This is in violation of 18 U.S.C. § 1343, *a RICO Act predicate offense.*

Made materially false, fictitious, and fraudulent statements, representations, and documents about the Russia narrative in violation of 18 U.S. Code § 1001.

Conspired to commit offense and to defraud the U.S. about the false Russia narrative in violation of 18 U.S. Code § 371

Committed perjury at congressional hearings about the false Russia narrative in violation of 18 U.S.C. § 1621

Initiated an investigation, based on false evidence, of the Trump campaign coordinating with Russia to influence the election and engaged in political spying and promoting misinformation in violation of probable cause and due process protected by the Fourth and Fifth Amendments of the constitution. This violated Section 242 of Title 18 because the conspirators acted under color of any law and also violated Section 241 of Title 18, the civil rights conspiracy statute.

Had subordinates prepare the fraudulent applications for a FISA surveillance warrant on Carter Page, and leak information to the media. The boss/subordinate relationship indirectly and corruptly is an offer or promise of something of value (e.g., salary increase, promotion) to influence such public official to commit or aid in committing, or collude in, or allow, any fraud, or make opportunity for the commission of any fraud, on the United

States. This violates 18 U.S. Code § 201 - Bribery of public officials and witnesses, *a RICO Act predicate offense.*

Corruptly concealed evidence (i.e., an object) by agreeing to limit the search of emails to specified dates that would hide obstruction of justice in deleting emails under a preservation order. This was done with the intent to impair the evidence's availability for use in an official proceeding (the Clinton email investigation). This violates 18 U.S. Code § 1512 - Tampering with a witness, victim, or an informant, *a RICO Act predicate offense.*

Committed a Brady violation by failing to turn over exculpatory Trump campaign evidence (e.g., the FBI's Peter Strzok purposely did not try to verify the easily disprovable Millian allegations in the Steele dossier that Carter Page and Paul Manafort coordinated the DNC hack with Russia to steal the emails).

Used their official authority or influence for the purpose of interfering with or affecting the result of an election violating 5 U.S. Code § 7323 - Political activity authorized; prohibitions.

James Comey's many felonies are described in Chapter 25.

Violated Due Process by Political Spying

James Clapper, Obama's director of national intelligence, admitted that there was foreign and domestic surveillance of Trump in 2015 and 2016. Congressman Devin Nunes revealed that Trump and his transition team were "monitored" by U.S. intelligence agencies before and after the elections.

McCarthy explains that the FBI, CIA, and NSA are responsible to collect intelligence, perform investigations, do analysis, and prepare intelligence reports. These agencies would unmask names of U.S. citizens in the reports only in extremely rare cases of an intelligence need and in compliance with "minimization" standards. Comey testified that they are "obsessive" in their determination to protect the identities and privacy of Americans.[cviii]

Susan Rice, President Obama's National Security Adviser, called for the "unmasking" of Trump campaign and transition officials whose identities and communications were captured in the collection of U.S. intelligence on foreign targets. Rice, as a White House staff person, receives intelligence reports, but should not determine the content.[cix] Rice admittedly knew President-elect Trump was under surveillance. McCarthy writes that Rice had no intelligence need to unmask names; "it was to fulfill a political desire based on Democratic-party interests."

During a press conference, a reporter asked Representative Devin Nunes "Was the president [i.e., Trump] included in that incidental collection — his communication?" Nunes responded, "Yes." Based on the little that has been reported, the interception and handling of these communications seems more disturbing because, according to Nunes, they have nothing to do with any known government intelligence investigations of Russia. Unless there is some legitimate connection to foreign activities, the specter of political spying hovers.[cx] McCarthy poses "two central questions: (1) Did the Obama administration take active steps to capture communications of Trump officials, whether by particularized FISA warrant or by intentionally exploiting their "incidental" intelligence-collection authority? And (2) if such active steps were taken, was it in connection with a good-faith suspicion of collusion in Russian sabotage, or was it Watergate-style political spying?"[cxi]

The Fourth Amendment protects U.S. citizens against unreasonable searches, but the Obama administration spied on Trump and his associates before and after the election, violating the privacy protection of masking the identities of Americans whose communications were incidentally recorded in foreign surveillance.

Violated Due Process by Promoting Misinformation

Fusion GPS is a U.S. company that does political opposition research. For example, Democrats hired them in 2012 to find negative information on presidential candidate Mitt Romney. Hillary Clinton, through her campaign, and the DNC, chaired by Debbie Wasserman Schultz, hired Fusion GPS through the Perkins Coie law firm in April 2016. Glenn Simpson of Fusion GPS hired Christopher Steele, a former British intelligence officer, and Nellie Ohr, the wife of the third-highest DOJ official, to work on the project. They fabricated evidence blaming the Trump campaign for coordinating the DNC hack with Russia and documented it in the Steele dossier. During the same period, Fusion GPS also worked "on behalf of the Russian government" to fight U.S. sanctions.[cxii] Steele paid former and current Russian government officials to provide negative information on Trump that Steele used to create his 35-page dossier of unfounded allegations against Trump and his associates. "The dossier quotes from a large number of anonymous sources. It cites 'a former top level Russian intelligence officer still active inside the Kremlin', 'a senior Russian foreign ministry figure' and "a senior Russian financial official'."[cxiii] The dossier contained allegations by Sergei Millian that the Trump campaign worked with Russian agents to hack the DNC server in order to steal emails and publish them on Wikileaks. The FBI purposely did not attempt to verify this easily disprovable allegation because they used it as the sole "evidence" to initiate the Trump/Russia collusion counterintelligence investigation and to obtain a FISA surveillance warrant on Carter Page. None of the significant allegations have been substantiated.

One person targeted in the dossier's allegations sued Steele for defamation. Steele admitted during the trial that the allegation was not verified. Steele's lawyers at the trial said Fusion GPS asked Steele to disseminate the dossier's allegations to certain news media: 'The journalists initially briefed at the end of September 2016 by the Second Defendant (Steele) and Fusion at Fusion's instruction were from the New York Times, the Washington Post, Yahoo News, the New Yorker and CNN,' and he "verbally and in person" briefed the first three organizations in mid-October and a reporter from Mother Jones via Skype."cxiv

The information was widely published before the election. Eight days before the election, Mother Jones published an article titled "Veteran Spy Has Given the FBI Information Alleging a Russian Operation to Cultivate Donald Trump. Has the bureau investigated this material?"   Other news sources such The Atlantic picked this up and followed with their own articles.

The Steele dossier is a clear-cut case of Americans working with foreign governments to influence the presidential election. The Steele dossier is actual Russian government misinformation solicited and propagated by Americans that did in fact hurt Trump and help Clinton in the election. This is in stark contrast to the Trump/Russia coordination narrative investigated by many over a long period of time and ultimately disproven by evidence in a Mueller indictment against 12 Russian intelligence officers. Although Comey had evidence in hand of coordination between the Russian government and Fusion GPS/Steele, that was funded by Hillary Clinton and the DNC, to influence the election, he did not investigate it. Comey used the dossier's misinformation in the Trump/Russia investigation and lent credibility to it. For example, Comey:

- offered to pay Steele $50,000 to continue his "investigation"
- used a dossier allegation to obtain a FISA warrant on Carter Page
- used dossier allegations to brief Congress and national security community as indicated in a letter that senate minority leader, Harry Reid, wrote to Comey in October 2016 stating "In my communications with you and other top officials in the national security community, it has become clear that you possess explosive information

about close ties and coordination between Donald Trump, his top advisors, and the Russian government

- included a dossier summary in his briefing of Obama and Trump in January 2017 on the final intelligence community report regarding Russian meddling in the election.
- refused to answer questions on the dossier allegations in testimony before the House Intelligence Committee as Democrat Joaquin Castro read copiously from it and praised its accuracies.[cxv] In this way, Comey subtly left the impression that the dossier's allegations were true.

The Clinton campaign and DNC funded the Steele dossier, and their vendors, Fusion GPS and Christopher Steele, obtained false information from Russian officials to blame the Trump campaign for coordinating with Russia the hack the DNC, steal the DNC emails, and publish the emails on WikiLeaks.

Comey violated Donald Trump's probable cause and due process rights protected by the Fourth and Fifth Amendments of the constitution.

Violated Due Process by Deceptive Testimony

Comey purposely harmed Trump and his due process and probable cause rights protected by the Fourth and Fifth Amendments of the constitution. As McCarthy explains "Under FBI protocols, the existence of investigations should not be acknowledged, much less their subject matters and potential targets —suspicions of wrongdoing should never be publicly announced until the government is prepared formally to charge and prove them in court."[cxvi]

McCarthy said "Comey was not fired until May 9, but his days were clearly numbered after his March 20 House testimony. Fully aware of Trump's agitation, and against law-enforcement protocols, the director nevertheless asserted that the FBI's counterintelligence investigation of Russia's election interference was focusing on possible collusion between the Trump campaign and the Kremlin. He even added for good measure that the FBI would be assessing whether criminal violations had occurred. Concurrently, Comey confided in lawmakers that Trump was not a suspect in the investigation, but he declined to make that salient detail part of his public testimony.[cxvii]

As anyone could have predicted, the media pounced. The FBI director, according to multiple reports, had made an extraordinary announcement that the president was a suspect in potential crimes involving collusion with the Putin regime. When he was not and Comey told him this privately."[cxviii]

This is in stark contrast to Comey's acquiescence to Lynch's order to mislead the public by referring to the Clinton email investigation as a "matter," which coincided with the Clinton campaign's characterization.

Violated Due Process by Leaks

Comey testified that the FBI used espionage information about Americans without a warrant only when it was "lawfully collected, carefully overseen and checked." A FISA Court judge refuted this stating he was "extremely concerned" over the FBI and NSA failing to comply with minimization requirements.

McCarthy explains that FISA minimization "procedures *categorically prohibited NSA analysts from using U.S.-person identifiers* to query the results of upstream Internet collection" (emphasis added). This meant the NSA was not supposed to use an American's phone number, e-mail address, or other "identifier" in running searches through its upstream database. It is this prohibition that the NSA routinely and extensively violated. The violation was so broad that, at the time the Obama administration ended, its scope had still not been determined.[cxix]

McCarthy added that "more officials were given unmasking authority. At the same time, President Obama loosened restrictions to allow wider access to raw intelligence collection and wider dissemination of intelligence reports. This geometrically increased the likelihood that classified information would be leaked — as did the Obama administration's encouragement to Congress to demand disclosure of intelligence related to the Trump campaign (the purported Trump–Russia connection). And of course, there has been a stunning amount of leaking of classified information to the media."cxx

The Obama administration violated due process by illegally searching for specific Americans in the NSA database and unmasking the names to facilitate unlawful leaks of classified and unauthorized government information.

Comey wrote memos documenting each of Trump's meetings with him even though the president had not said or done anything illegal. Comey did not write a memo, resign, or tell anyone of the numerous, egregious felony offenses in the email investigation's criminal justice process because he was part of a conspiracy with Lynch and others to exonerate Clinton and falsely prosecute Trump. Comey's purpose for the memos was obviously to hurt Trump.

After Trump fired him, Comey illegally gave a memo to a friend to leak to the press. Jonathan Turley explains

"These [memos] were documents prepared on an FBI computer addressing a highly sensitive investigation on facts that he considered material to that investigation. Indeed, he conveyed that information confidentially to his top aides and later said that he wanted the information to be given to the special counsel because it was important to the investigation. ... he used these memos not as a shield but a sword."

Besides being subject to nondisclosure agreements, Comey falls under federal laws governing the disclosure of classified and unclassified information. Assuming that the memos were not classified (though it seems odd that it would not be classified even on the confidential level), there is 18 U.S.C. § 641, which makes it a crime to steal, sell, or convey "any record, voucher, money, or thing of value of the United States or of any department or agency thereof."[cxxi]

Acted under color of law to violate probable cause

Rosenstein and Mueller are investigating the Trump campaign coordination with Russia without defining the crime. They violated Section 242 of Title 18 because they acted under color of any law to willfully deprive Trump of his probable cause right protected by the Fourth Amendment. They violated Section 241 of Title 18 by agreeing together to injure, threaten, and intimidate Trump in the free exercise or enjoyment of his probable cause right secured to him by the Fourth Amendment of the Constitution.

The Trump/Russia investigation is in stark contrast to the Clinton email and Clinton foundation investigations. The evidence in Mueller's of 12 GRU officers clearly proves that Trump and his campaign did not coordinate with Russia to influence the election. On the other hand, both Clinton investigations have massive amounts of evidence, but Comey, Lynch, and others violated multiple laws to exonerate Clinton in the email investigation.

Overwhelming evidence indicates that Comey, Lynch, Hillary Clinton, Glenn Simpson and many other conspirators committed felonies regarding the baseless Trump/Russia collusion investigation. Rosenstein and Mueller conducted a selective prosecution based on political party. The U.S. Supreme Court has held that selective prosecution exists where the enforcement or prosecution of a Criminal Law is "directed so exclusively against a particular class of persons ... with a mind so unequal and oppressive" that the administration of the criminal law amounts to a practical denial of Equal Protection of the law. The conspirators deprived Trump of Equal Protection because he is a Republican (particular class of persons).

The conspirator, Glenn Simpson, committed perjury

Simpson committed perjury in his November 14, 2017 testimony to the House Permanent Select Committee on Intelligence:

Simpson falsely testified that he did not have contact with any FBI or DOJ officials regarding the Steele dossier until after the 2016 election. Bruce Ohr's emails prove that Ohr and Simpson were in contact as early as August 2016.

In answer to the question "Do you have any information there have been reports about potential communications between a server at [Alfa] Bank and potentially servers that belong to the Trump organization or Trump?" – Simpson falsely answered that people gave him information, but "I did not draw any conclusions from the data." Bruce Ohr's notes of a December 2016 meeting with Simpson contradict Simpson's testimony. Ohr noted that Simpson said: "The New York Times story on Oct. 31 downplaying the connection between Alfa servers and the Trump campaign was incorrect. There was communication and it wasn't spam."

Simpson testified that, postelection, he had no anti-Trump clients. Daniel Jones, a former senior Feinstein staffer, told the FBI in March 2017 that he had raised $50 million from seven to 10 wealthy donors to investigate Mr. Trump, and that he hired Fusion GPS (Simpson) and Steele. In a letter to the DOJ, Senator Chuck Grassley wrote "Where we do have actual evidence of misleading testimony in Committee interviews, we should treat it seriously. For example, when the Committee staff interviewed

Glenn Simpson in August of 2017, Majority staff asked him: 'So you didn't do any work on the Trump matter after the election date, that was the end of your work?' Mr. Simpson answered: 'I had no client after the election.' As we now know, that was extremely misleading, if not an outright lie."

28. Potential Rosenstein and Special Counsel Crimes

"The most sacred of the duties of a government [is] to do equal and impartial justice to all its citizens." --Thomas Jefferson

Sergei Millian's allegations in the Steele Dossier are the very foundation of the Trump/Russia collusion investigations by the FBI and subsequently by the Special Counsel. Hillary Clinton and the DNC funded and used this misinformation to blame the Trump campaign for colluding with Russia to steal the DNC emails. Mueller's own indictment of 12 Russian GRU intelligence officers contains incontrovertible evidence that the Trump campaign did not coordinate the DNC computer system hack with Russia.

The following evidence suggests that Rosenstein, Mueller, and the Mueller team may be guilty of: a) Bias and General Prosecutorial Misconduct, b) Abuse of Investigative or Prosecutorial Authority, Overzealous Prosecution and Selective prosecution by political affiliation, c) Constitutional and Civil Rights Violations, and d) Failure to Provide Exculpatory Information to Defendants.

No one is above the law, including a Special Counsel. President Trump should order an investigation of Mueller's 16 month-long investigation to determine if Mueller, Rosenstein, and the Special Counsel team committed criminal misconduct.

Bias and General Prosecutorial Misconduct

Was Mueller and Rosenstein's objective to impeach President Trump?

Peter Strzok and Lisa Page's texts demonstrate that they have an extraordinary bias against President Trump and they performed work on Mueller's team. Strzok headed the Clinton email investigation and the Russia probe. Their text exchange In August 2016 encapsulates Strzok's intent:

> Page texted to Strzok "[Trump's] not ever going to become president, right? Right?!"

> "No. No he won't. We'll stop it," Strzok replied.

The day after Mueller's appointment as Special Counsel, he recruited Strzok. After the recruitment interview, Strzok texted that he could "fix and finish" the "unfinished business" he "unleashed" with the Clinton email exoneration, because the Special Counsel investigation could result in "impeachment?"

Strzok was the FBI agent in charge of the Trump/Russia investigation for 10 months, and he was hesitant to join Mueller's team because 1) "there's no big there there," and 2) Strzok wanted to get a promotion within the FBI. Immediately after he was recruited, Strzok told Page the reasons why he should join. Did Strzok's words reflect what Mueller or his recruiter told him? Did Mueller or his recruiter try to convince Strzok to join the team, by telling him it is "the most important case of our lives," and that Strzok could "fix and finish" the "unfinished business" he "unleashed" with the Clinton email exoneration, because the Special Counsel investigation could result in "impeachment?"

The investigation of prosecutorial misconduct (Recommendation III in Chapter 31) should include:

Work that Page and Strzok did in the Special Counsel investigation

Any communications on impeachment within the team (e.g., to recruit Strzok, as an objective in

gathering evidence, in the impeachment trap questions for President Trump).

Any communications by a team member or Rosenstein indicating an objective to harm the president instead of a non-biased investigation into Trump/Russia collusion.

Mueller and Rosenstein should be referred to the Special Counsel of Recommendation II (Chapter 31.) for criminal investigation if prosecutorial misconduct is discovered.

<u>Did Mueller and Rosenstein attempt to illegally entrap Papadopoulos?</u>

As detailed in Chapter 8 "The George Papadopoulos Setup," Charles Tawil and David Ha'ivri, an Israeli, gave Papadopoulos $10,000 in an apparent illegal entrapment attempt. A 2006 WikiLeaks document show Tawil worked as an FBI and CIA intelligence asset. An investigation of prosecutorial misconduct should find out if Mueller's team created the entrapment. The investigation should answer the following questions:

- Was Peter Strzok working on Mueller's Papadopoulos indictment and was he or another person on Mueller's team involved with enlisting Tawil and David Ha'ivri as covert agents?
- Was Strzok involved with the 2016 Papadopoulos entrapment attempts by covert agents: Joseph Mifsud, Alexander Downer, Stefan Halper, and Sergei Millian?
- Was Tawil and/or David Ha'ivri working as an FBI or CIA covert agent in meeting with Papadopoulos and, if so, who provided the $10,000 to Tawil?

(Note: Mueller's written submission to the court states that Papadopoulos agreed, in advance, to pay a fine of $9,500, and that he has the money in cash, ready and waiting, locked in a safe to await the day of sentencing. Under sentencing guidelines, $9,500 is the maximum fine for the offense. Mueller's indictment states *The defendant provided information about $10,000 in cash he received from a foreign national whom he believed was likely an intelligence officer of a foreign country (other than Russia).* If the government gave Tawil $10,000 to entrap Papadopoulos, then Mueller's $9,500 fine is aimed at reimbursing the government.

Papadopoulos's wife said he "pled guilty because [Mueller's prosecutors] threatened to charge him with being an Israeli agent."

If Mueller did use Tawil to entrap Papadopoulos, his threat to charge him as an Israeli agent to get him to plead guilty is an outrageous abuse of power. The investigation of prosecutorial misconduct (Recommendation III in Chapter 31) should find out if Mueller used covert agents to entrap Papadopoulos. If he did, Mueller and Rosenstein should be referred to the Special Counsel of Recommendation II (Chapter 31.) for criminal investigation.

<u>Did Rosenstein and Mueller use Cohen as a Pawn to make the president an unindicted co-conspirator?</u>

As soon as Mueller referred Cohen to the SDNY, the long-time Clinton defender and confidante, Lanny Davis, became Cohen's attorney. Cohen immediately turned against President Trump.

Rosenstein did not recuse himself from the Special Counsel investigation even though he has many major conflicts of interest. The malevolent Rosenstein ordered Geoffrey Berman, President Trump's appointed SDNY U.S. attorney, to recuse from Cohen's case. Rosenstein's objective in ordering Berman's recusal is apparently to put Robert Khuzami in charge of Michael Cohen's case.

Davis got Cohen a plea deal with Khuzami. In addition to tax evasion, Cohen pled guilty to a felony campaign finance law violation for paying $280,000 of hush-money payments on behalf of Trump prior to the election. It is very disputable that the $280,000 hush-money payment, a relatively very small amount of money, is even a campaign contribution violation. Usually the DOJ treats serious campaign-finance transgressions as administrative violations, not felonies. For example, the 2008 Obama campaign accepted nearly $2 million in illegal campaign contributions, but only paid a fine. Why would his attorney, Clinton confidante Lanny Davis, get Cohen to plead guilty to this phony campaign finance felony charge and why would Khuzami agree to it? Davis and Khuzami apparently wanted the felony guilty plea for this instead of a fine in order to make the president an unindicted co-conspirator to a felony, which would give Mueller evidence for a report that substantiates a recommendation for impeachment. Hillary has her confidante, Lanny Davis, successfully helping Mueller and Rosenstein gather impeachment "evidence" on the president by conspiring with the SDNY's Khuzami to use an extremely unethical plea bargain.

Harvard law professor Alan Dershowitz downplayed the significance of election law violations saying "every" administration and presidential candidate commits them. Here, they're trying to elevate this into an impeachable offense or a felony against the president. Naming someone as an un-indicted co-conspirator is very unfair because he has no opportunity to defend himself or herself. And yet that may happen."

Mueller likely referred the case to the SDNY so that Cohen could continue composing crimes against the Trump Organization, Donald Trump Jr., Jared Kushner, and Ivanka Trump, all located in New York's jurisdiction.

The investigation of prosecutorial misconduct (Recommendation III in Chapter 31) should find out if Mueller, Rosenstein, Lanny Davis, and Khuzami plotted to create a plea deal that would implicate President Trump as an unindicted co-conspirator. **Mueller, Rosenstein, Davis, and Khuzami should be referred to the Special Counsel of Recommendation II (Chapter 31.) for criminal investigation if facts uncovered in the investigation indicate that they conspired to create a plea deal with a false felony in order to make the president an unindicted co-conspirator. Also, if evidence indicates that they had a defendant plead guilty to a felony he did not commit in order to make another person an unindicted co-conspirator, then Sessions should 1) refer them to the Bar Association for disbarment, 2) fire Khuzami and 3) order Berman to unrecuse himself from Cohen's case.**

Abuse of Investigative or Prosecutorial Authority, Overzealous Prosecution and Selective prosecution by political affiliation

Rosenstein said in his letter appointing Mueller that "The Special Counsel is authorized to conduct the investigation confirmed by then-FBI Director James B. Comey in testimony before the House Permanent Select Committee on Intelligence on March 20, 2017, "any links and/or coordination between individuals associated with the Trump campaign and the Russian government."

In his March 20, 2017 testimony, Comey defined the counterintelligence investigation scope as the Russian government's efforts to interfere in the 2016 presidential election, including links between Trump's campaign and Russia's efforts to interfere. Comey did not define the investigation of Trump/Russia links in isolation with no association with Russia's election interference because such links are not a crime. However, Rosenstein pointedly did not specifically state "the Russian government's efforts to interfere in the 2016 presidential election" in Mueller's scope to make it an unbounded investigation.

Subsequent to the appointment of Mueller, the DOJ's Inspector General and Congressional committees have discovered much exculpatory evidence. They have also discovered much damning evidence of the Clinton campaign, the DNC, and some Obama administration officials conspiring to influence the election by coordinating with foreign nationals to falsely frame Donald Trump and his campaign for coordinating with Russia to influence the election.

The misconduct investigation should find out if Rosenstein and Mueller's team were prejudicial in the investigation by 1) not examining exculpatory evidence of collusion by Donald Trump and his campaign, 2) not examining any evidence of guilt by people not associated with Trump, but who committed crimes related to the Russia investigation, and 3) overzealous prosecution of persons because they are associated with Donald Trump. Following are some examples.

In his August 2, 2017 supplemental memorandum to Mueller citing the factual basis for the investigation, Rosenstein wrote that "Mueller is authorized to investigate: Allegations that Paul Manafort . . . Committed a crime or crimes by colluding with Russian government officials with respect to the Russian government's efforts to interfere with the 2016 election." Shockingly, Rosenstein used Sergei Millian's easily disprovable allegations in the Steele dossier as the "factual basis" for Mueller's investigation. Did Mueller investigate this easily disprovable allegation? As detailed in Chapter 6, it was not only impossible for Manafort and Carter Page to coordinate the complex hack of the DNC computers with Russia in April 2017, but Sergei Millian is an extremely unreliable source with no means to obtain any such information.

If they are investigating Donald Trump Jr.'s meeting at Trump Tower as Russia collusion, are they also investigating Glenn Simpson of Fusion GPS for his role in the meeting? Simpson met with the Russian lawyer, Veselnitskaya, before and after her meeting with Trump Jr. Simpson was hired by Clinton and the DNC to provide evidence of Trump/Russia collusion, so he likely devised the meeting as a trap for Trump Jr. Veselnitskaya said Mueller has not contacted her and accused him of 'not working to discover the truth.'

Has Mueller's team investigated the exculpatory evidence such as the false Steele dossier allegations funded by Clinton and the DNC, the FISA warrant applications based on the dossier, political spying and unmasking by Obama officials, the FBI contractors performing illegal searches of the raw 702 FISA data, etc.?

Has Mueller's team investigated James Comey, the president's accuser, who committed multiple felonies related to the Trump/Russia collusion scam. Examples of Comey's criminal misconduct related to the Trump/Russia Collusion investigation include:

- Used FBI spies in Trump's campaign prior to the initiation of the counterintelligence investigation violated probable cause
- Committed perjury multiple times
- Used the Clinton/DNC funded Steele dossier false allegations in the investigation and in the ICA. The FBI could have easily disproved the major allegations.
- Approved and submitted a deceptive application to the FISA court in order to obtain a surveillance warrant for Carter Page

A close friend of the Clintons, Cody Shearer, wrote a memo on Trump/Russia collusion that was given to Steele, who forwarded it to the FBI. Shearer is dubbed "the fixer" because he has helped the Clintons for decades. Another close Clinton friend, Sidney Blumenthal was involved by passing Shearer's memo to Jonathan Winer, a State Department special envoy. Winer then passed it to Steele. The only way Shearer and Blumenthal would know about Steele's secret dossier work on Trump/Russia collusion would be through their friend, Hillary Clinton. This and other evidence support the conclusion that Hillary Clinton was directly involved in the creation, dissemination, and use of the Steele dossier. Are Rosenstein and the Special Counsel investigating the DNC and Hillary Clinton's involvement in the fraudulent allegations used to actually change voter decisions in the 2016 presidential election?

The DOJ's IG, Michael Horowitz, informed Mueller of Peter Strzok and Lisa Page's extremely biased texts expressing animosity against Donald Trump. Strzok testified that Mueller dismissed him without pressing him on the texts or asking him whether that showed any bias in the probe. Did Mueller investigate Strzok and Lisa Page actions as exculpatory evidence in the Trump Campaign/Russia Collusion investigation. A September 10, 2018 letter from Congressional representative Mark Meadows to Rod Rosenstein gives examples of Strzok and Lisa Page texting that they leaked information to the media in order to use press reports of their leaked information as "evidence" to pursue the Trump/Russia collusion investigation.

- April 10, 2017: (former FBI Special Agent) Peter Strzok contacts (former FBI Attorney) Lisa Page to discuss a "media leak strategy." Specifically, the text says: "I had literally just gone to find this phone to tell you I want to talk to you about media leak strategy with DOJ before you go."
- April 12, 2017: Peter Strzok congratulates Lisa Page on a job well done while referring to two derogatory articles about Carter Page. In the text, Strzok warns Page two articles are coming out, one which is "worse" than the other about Lisa's "namesake"." Strzok added: "Well done, Page."

Comey and Strzok used Sergei Millian's false allegations in the Steele dossier to initiate the Trump/Russia investigation and a summary of the dossier was used in the ICA preparation. A different source than Millian in Steele's dossier alleges that Michael Cohen met with Russian officials in Prague to coordinate payments to hackers. Cohen was never in Prague so the allegation is easily disprovable. When Mueller investigated Michael Cohen, did he investigate the Prague allegation?

Overwhelming evidence indicates the conspirators in the Obama administration, such as Comey, McCabe, Lynch, and Strzok committed felonies in the Trump/Russia investigation to falsely persecute Donald Trump and his associates and help elect Clinton. Mueller has not indicted any of them. On the other hand, Mueller indicted General Flynn, Paul Manafort, Rick Gates, George Papadopoulos and others associated with Donald Trump on charges not related to any collusion between the Trump campaign and Russia to interfere with the election. Some of his indictments are abusive, overzealous, and targeting political affiliation:

- Mueller's indictment of Michael Flynn successfully concluded the Comey, McCabe, and Yates' Flynn setup as described in Chapter 10 "The Michael Flynn Setup." Strzok and FBI agent, Joe Pientka, thought Flynn was truthful during their "ambush" interview. Comey testified Flynn may have had some honest failures of recollection. Mueller coerced Flynn into pleading guilty to lying by threatening to indict his son, and putting Flynn at risk of five years in prison and a $250,000 fine if found guilty. Mueller's indictment had nothing to do with Trump/Russia collusion.
- Mueller indicted Papadopoulos for lying about the timing and scope of his contact with Joseph Mifsud. McCarthy writes "When one looks carefully at Mueller's statement of the offense, and at the one-count criminal-information to which Papadopoulos pled guilty, one realizes Mueller

is not claiming that Mifsud and his associates truly were Kremlin operatives — only that Papadopoulos was under the impression that they were. That is, Papadopoulos is accused of misrepresenting his subjective state of mind, not objective reality." Mueller's indictment had nothing to do with Trump/Russia collusion.

- Mueller indicted Paul Manafort for various charges that he committed years before joining the Trump campaign. For example, Mueller charged Manafort for failing to register with the government under the Foreign Agent Registration Act because he lobbied for foreign interests. This is an example of overzealous prosecution because as Manafort's defense team argued "The United States government has only used that offense six times since 1966 and only resulted in one conviction." Tony Podesta, the brother of Clinton's campaign manager, worked with Manafort to lobby on behalf of Ukrainian interests in the United States, without properly registering at the time under the Foreign Agent Registration Act (FARA). Mueller gave Tony Podesta immunity to testify against Manafort, and prosecuted Manafort for the same rarely used felony. This is another example of Mueller targeting political affiliation. Mueller's indictments of Manafort had nothing to do with Trump/Russia collusion.
- Mueller indicted Michael Cohen for tax evasion, lying on a loan application, and campaign finance violations, which are not related to Trump/Russia collusion.
- Mueller continues to request an interview with President Trump. Mueller's questions clearly show he is investigating the president for obstruction of justice in firing Comey and Mueller set a perjury trap for the president similar to the perjury trap set by Comey, Yates and McCabe for General Flynn.

Mueller seemingly ignores the fast-growing evidence of serious criminal wrongdoing by top Obama administration officials in the FBI and DOJ, including Mueller's friend and the president's accuser, James Comey. Mueller's indictment of 12 Russian GRU intelligence officers contains incontrovertible evidence that the Trump campaign did not coordinate the GRU's hack of the DNC computer system. Mueller and Rosenstein had this evidence sometime prior to March 2018, and yet Mueller's investigation continues.

The investigation of prosecutorial misconduct (Recommendation III in Chapter 31) should find out if there is evidence that Mueller and Rosenstein are conducting an abusive, overzealous, and selective prosecution by political affiliation (i.e., only people associated with Donald Trump). **If such evidence is found, Mueller and Rosenstein should be referred to the Special Counsel of Recommendation II in Chapter 31 for criminal investigation for Abuse of Investigative or Prosecutorial Authority, Overzealous Prosecution, and Selective prosecution by political affiliation. The investigation of prosecutorial misconduct should determine if Rosenstein and Mueller's Special Counsel team violated 18 U.S. Code § 242 - Deprivation of rights under color of law and 18 U.S. Code § 241 - Conspiracy against rights for harshly prosecuting people because they are associated with Donald Trump or his campaign.**

Constitutional and Civil Rights Violations

Mueller ordered an FBI raid on the home of Paul Manafort to obtain documents regarding Manafort's consulting work for the Ukrainian president. Rosenstein wrote a supplemental memorandum on August 2, 2017, one week after the FBI raid, to give Mueller explicit authority to target Manafort over the financial aspects of his lobbying work for the Ukrainian government that ended in 2014 and was not related to Trump/Russia election collusion scope. This is a blatant example of Mueller doing a fishing expedition to look for crimes committed by Trump associates without probable cause and then Rosenstein preparing a post hoc justification of any crimes discovered.

The judge in the Manafort trial required Rosenstein to reveal the factual basis for Mueller's investigation of Manafort. To satisfy the judge's request, Rosenstein unredacted a very small portion of his August 2, 2017 supplemental memo in which he wrote that "Mueller is authorized to investigate: "Allegations that Paul Manafort . . . Committed a crime or crimes by colluding with Russian government officials with respect to the Russian government's efforts to interfere with the 2016 election." Rosenstein obviously used Sergei Millian's false allegation because no other public source for this allegation has ever surfaced. Rosenstein demonstrates once again that Millian is the most influential person in the United States. It is reprehensible that Rosenstein used the purposely unverified, but easily disprovable, Clinton and DNC-funded Steele dossier allegations for the "factual" basis for the crimes Mueller is authorized to investigate.

Rosenstein also approved one renewal of the application for the Carter Page FISA warrant at the end of June 2017. The application relied almost wholly on the Steele dossier's false allegations that Sergei Millian made. Comey had previously testified that the dossier allegations were salacious and unverified. Steele, who was being sued for defamation by a company named in his dossier, admitted in a British court in April 2017 that his dossier was "unsolicited," "raw" intelligence that "needed to be further investigated." Rosenstein gave the lame excuse that he did not read the application. Rosenstein authorized a Special Counsel to investigate the president of the United States and his associates, so Rosenstein has the highest obligation to assure that a FISA surveillance warrant related to the case is proper. The FISA warrant violated Carter Page's constitutional right of probable cause, and it targeted him because he was associated with the Trump campaign. The FBI may have surveilled other people in the Trump campaign and the

Trump administration due to the FISA surveillance warrant "two-hop" rule.[cxxii] Rosenstein should be prosecuted if the Page FISA warrant did result in the surveillance of anyone in the Trump administration.

The investigation of prosecutorial misconduct (Recommendation III in Chapter 31) should find out if Mueller and Rosenstein are investigating people for crimes not related to Russia collusion and without probable cause, and if such evidence is found, Mueller and Rosenstein should be referred to the Special Counsel of Recommendation II in Chapter 31 for criminal investigation (e.g., violations of 18 U.S. Code § 241 - Conspiracy against rights).

Failure to Provide Exculpatory Information to Defendants

Peter Strzok and another FBI agent interviewed Michael Flynn on January 24, 2017. Mueller charged Flynn of "willfully and knowingly make materially false, fictitious, and fraudulent statements" in the Strzok interview about his conversations with Russian Ambassador Sergey Kislyak. Flynn pleaded guilty to one count of lying to FBI agents.

Mueller should have provided all exculpatory information to Flynn such as:

- The agents performing the interview did not think Flynn was lying.
- Charles Grassley pointed out to Rosenstein that General Mike Flynn was a witness against Andrew McCabe in a sex abuse case when McCabe sent agents to interview him.
- John Dowd noted that "There are reports that Gen. Flynn referred to the FISA wiretap of Ambassador Sergey Kislyak conversation at the outset of the FBI interview. If

those reports are true, his reference to the complete and accurate wiretap precludes any charge of false statement."

The law professor, Jonathan Turley said "The broader collusion case appears to be thin," adding that there are new questions as to whether prosecutors even initially believed Flynn did anything wrong involving Russia. He cited a 1963 Supreme Court case, Brady v. Maryland, in which the court decided that exculpatory evidence - evidence that may help prove innocence - must be presented to the defendant by the prosecution. "It's very hard to make this catwalk backward" out of a guilty plea," Turley said. "Mueller would also get out of it [then, and] load up on charges and go after [Flynn's] son."

FBI employees Peter Strzok, Lisa Page, and Kevin Clinesmith were extremely biased against President Trump as evidenced by their texts, and the DOJ IG's report. All were on Mueller's Special Counsel team and their bias may have unjustly prejudiced the evidence in some of Mueller's indictments.

The investigation of prosecutorial misconduct (Recommendation III in Chapter 31) should find out if biased members of Mueller's team tainted any cases, and if Mueller provided all exculpatory evidence to the indicted defendants prior to making a plea bargain or trying the case in court. The investigators should inform the DOJ of any tainted cases or undisclosed exculpatory evidence so it can take proper action.

29. Miscellaneous Potential Crimes

The DOJ might have suppressed a national security case of high interest to Clinton and Wasserman Schultz

Debbie Wasserman Schultz is a primary conspirator in the Trump/Russia collusion hoax. As head of the DNC, she and Clinton hired Fusion GPS to create false evidence of Trump campaign collusion with Russia to hack the DNC and steal the DNC emails.

Imran Awan is a confidante of Wasserman Schultz, who had access to her computers and those of 40 other Congressional members. Awan also had access to the DNC computer and Wasserman Schultz's iPad. Awan and his associates illegally collected data, including emails, from Congressional computers. An attorney who is a very close friend of the Clintons represented Awan in a federal fraud case, even though Hillary Clinton has no association with this low-level IT technician. As part of the case, Wasserman Schultz publicly fought to prevent the government from gaining access to Awan's laptop computer. In his illegal hacking endeavors, Awan may have found information on Wasserman Schultz and Clinton's plan to frame Donald Trump.

The investigative reporter Luke Rosiak of The Daily Caller News Foundation uncovered many of the details described below.[cxxiii]

Details

Imran Awan was born in Pakistan and became a U.S. citizen in 2004. Awan was first hired by Rep. Xavier Becerra (D-Calif.), and four other Democratic House members in 2004. Debbie Wasserman Schultz hired Awan as her congressional IT aide in 2005. Awan and six other family members and friends ('Awan group') worked as shared IT employees for 44 House Democrats and had access to the House members' emails, calendars, constituents' data, and personal files.

None of 44 members requested a background check on the Awan group even though they had access to sensitive information on servers used by House members and their staff dealing in areas such as intelligence, homeland security, terrorism, and foreign affairs. A background check would have found lawsuits against them, fraud, criminal convictions, and two million-dollar bankruptcies. McCarthy said Awan could not possibly have qualified for a security clearance.

The House Office of Inspector General (IG) initiated an investigation of the Awan group for fraudulent purchase and theft of equipment, and, upon identifying IT irregularities, began a cybersecurity investigation. The IG found that the Awan group hacked Congressional members' computers and transferred information. Following is a summary:

On September 20, 2016, the House Office of Inspector General warned House leadership and the Committee on House Administration that five members of the Awan group (two left the Congressional payroll before the investigation began) had made unauthorized logins on systems of House members they were not employed by, and in some cases continued to log in to the computers of members who had previously fired them. They also logged in using the personal credentials of congressmen.

On September 30, 2016, IG provided another briefing stating that "during September 2016, shared employee continued to use Democratic Caucus computers in anomalous ways:

- Logged onto laptop as system administrator
- Changed identity and logged onto Democratic Caucus server using 17 other user account credentials
- Some credentials belonged to Members
- The shared employee did not work for 9 of the 17 offices to which these user accounts belonged."

Xavier Becerra led the House Democratic Caucus, a sister group of the DNC, from 2013 to January 2017, when he became California's attorney general. The IG found that the Awan group made excessive logons to the House Democratic Caucus server, an average of 27 times a day, and, in a briefing, said "Excessive logons are an indication that the server is being used for nefarious purposes and elevated the risk that individuals could be reading and/or removing information. Their "pattern of login activity suggests steps [were] being taken to conceal their activity." This included the use of active role servers, which could have been used to grant access on a temporary basis and could have been used to evade network monitoring. The Democratic Caucus server "could be used to store documents taken from other offices or evidence of other illicit activity," according to the IG presentation. The unusual login activity could also indicate computers were "used as a launching point to access other systems for which access may be unauthorized."

The Awan group installed Dropbox, in violation of House policy, on two Democratic Caucus computers. Dropbox could be used to transfer data out of Congressional network to other parties. The IG noted "While file sharing sites, such as Dropbox, have legitimate business purposes, use of such sites is also a classic method for insiders to exfiltrate data from an organization."

The House Democratic Caucus server was physically stolen immediately after an IG report in September 2016 named it as evidence in their investigation.

Imran Awan allegedly routed data from numerous House Democrats to a secret server connected to the House Democratic Caucus server. On Jan. 24, 2017, Becerra vacated his congressional seat to become California's attorney general. "He wanted to wipe his server, and we brought to his attention it was under investigation. The light-off was we asked for an image of the server, and they deliberately turned over a fake server," the senior official said. Capitol Police considered the fake image a sign that the Awans knew exactly what they were doing and were going to great lengths to try to cover it up, the senior official said. Authorities considered the false image they received to be interference in a criminal investigation. As a result, the House banned the Awan group from the House network on February 2, 2017.

Imran Awan took frequent trips to Pakistan and told associates he worked remotely from that country. Imran reportedly bragged he had the power to "change the U.S. president."

Luke Rosiak, an investigative reporter with The Daily Caller News Foundation discovered that in addition to hacking congressional servers, the Awan group is alleged to have committed fraud, theft, tax evasion, purchase order falsification, lying on House financial disclosure forms, and money laundering. Imran's own wife, Hina Alvi, said in a suit filed in Pakistan on September 13, 2017, that Imran "threatened [her] of dire consequences, he also threatened to harm the lives of family of [Hina] if she intervenes."cxxiv

Andrew McCarthy listed grounds to suspect the Awan group was blackmailing members of Congress:cxxv cxxvi

- the staggering sums of money paid to the Awan group over the years. For example, Imran's 20-year-old brother was paid $160,000 a year and the average Congressional staff salary is $40,000. Imran's friend was hired as an IT aide after being fired from McDonald's.
- the sensitive congressional communications to which they had access,
- the alleged involvement of Imran Awan and one of his brothers in a blackmail-extortion scheme against their stepmother, and
- Wasserman Schultz's months of protecting Awan and potentially impeding the investigation. She paid him for

six months as her congressional IT aide even though he could not do his job because the police revoked his IT access. After learning the Awan group was under investigation, Debbie Wasserman Schultz created a second IT aide position to employ his wife, Hina Alvi.

In another sign of blackmail, Democratic members of Congress impeded the IG's investigation in multiple ways.

- Democrats refused to press charges and asserted the "Speech and Debate Clause" of the Constitution, which protects lawmakers' legislative comments, to block prosecutors from evidence.
- Rep. Yvette Clarke approved a $120,000 write-off rather than press charges against Awan's brother, Abid, for stolen computer equipment.
- Rep. Xavier Becerra was head of the Democratic caucus when the IG briefed House members. Right after the IG briefing identified the Democratic caucus server as evidence, the server was physically removed and disappeared.
- Capitol Police determined that an image they asked Imran Awan to provide of Xavier Becerra's server was falsified, believing it to be a "deliberate attempt to conceal the activities that they knew were against House policy and the law."
- The House did not ban the Awan group from the congressional network until February 2, five months after the IG briefed congress on their hacking.

After the IG briefed congress, Imran Awan and his wife, Hina Alvi, fraudulently acquired $283,000 and wired it to Pakistan on January 18, 2017. Hina Alvi flew to Pakistan in March 2017. The FBI allowed her, a co-conspirator, to go to Pakistan after briefly detaining her at the airport, even though they had grounds to arrest her. Imran was arrested at the airport on July 25, 2017 waiting for a flight to Pakistan. A grand jury indicted Imran and his wife in August in the U.S. District Court for the District of Columbia. Prosecutors said in court papers that they believe rounding up that money and wiring it overseas was part of a plan to flee from the underlying investigation. "Based on the suspicious timing of that transaction, Awan and Alvi likely knew they were under investigation at that time."

Awan hid a laptop in a tiny former phone booth room in the Rayburn House Office Building, along with copies of his IDs, letters addressed to acting U.S. Attorney for the District of Columbia, and notes in a composition notebook marked "attorney-client privilege." The Capitol police found it on April 6, 2017. At a May 18 congressional hearing on the Capitol Police budget, Wasserman Schultz threatened "consequences" if the police chief, Matthew Verderosa, did not return the laptop to her. Verderosa told her the laptop could not be returned because it was tied to a criminal suspect. Wasserman Schultz said in an Aug. 3 interview "This was not my laptop, I have never seen that laptop. I don't know what's on the laptop," and she sought only to protect Awan's rights.[cxxvii]

Debbie Wasserman Schultz was the head of the DNC when the DNC worked with a Ukrainian-American consultant to develop the Trump/Russia collusion narrative and the DNC along with the Clinton campaign paid for the Steele dossier. Imran Awan had Wasserman Shultz's password and could access the DNC server, and he had access to her congressional server. Awan's history of hacking and fraud, and his access to the DNC server make him a prime witness.

Wasserman Schultz hired an outside attorney to argue in the Awan case that police and prosecutors should not be allowed to keep or look at Awan's laptop because it was full of sensitive legislative information. This argument does not make sense because Awan is an IT aide who should not have any "sensitive legislative information," and Wasserman Schultz previously said she did not know what was on the computer.

The FBI arrested Awan on July 24, 2017 and a federal grand jury indicted him on August 17th. Assistant U.S. Attorney Michael Mirando said that when Imran was arrested at Dulles International Airport a cellphone found on him "had been wiped clean just a few hours before." The prosecutor said "When we arrested him there was a Whatsapp message from his lawyer asking to speak with his client indicating he may have had reason to believe he was about to be arrested." The high-priced attorney, Chris Gowen, is an old and dear friend of Hillary and Bill Clinton. Hillary obviously provided Imran Awan, through an intermediary, with Gowen's phone number to put on his speed dial in case he was arrested. Hillary did not do this out of the goodness of her heart. Awan likely has damaging information on Clinton and the DNC.

The DOJ's District of Columbia office's indictment alleges that Awan and his wife engaged in a conspiracy to obtain home equity lines of credit from the Congressional Federal Credit Union by giving false information about two properties, and then sending the proceeds to individuals in Pakistan.

Andrew McCarthy described the indictment as "an exercise in omission," and said "The office is low-keying the Awan prosecution. The indictment itself is drawn very narrowly. All four charges flow from a financial-fraud conspiracy of short duration. Only Imran Awan and his wife are named as defendants. There is no reference to Awan family perfidy in connection with the House communications system." The indictment is "incredibly beneficial" to Awan and his wife, co-conspirators in financial fraud, by 1) omitting the strongest evidence (i.e., fleeing the country after sending fraudulently obtained money to Pakistan), 2) citing dates beneficial to Awan (a similar ploy to the DOJ limiting the FBI's investigation to certain dates in order to hide destruction of evidence in the Clinton email investigation), 3) omitting theft of information and equipment from Congress.[cxxviii]

Steven Wasserman, Debbie Wasserman Schultz's brother, has been an assistant U.S. attorney in the Washington D.C. office for many years. He has no role in prosecuting the case, but, as a senior attorney, he may try to used his influence behind the scenes to protect his sister. In August, he publicly used his influence when he tweeted an editorial titled "The non-case against Debbie Wasserman Schultz."

The Congressional IG performed a cyber security investigation and found forensic evidence that Imran Awan, Hina Alvi and others in the Awan group frequently made unauthorized access to data and emails of House members that they were not employed by, copied data from the computers of House members to other computers, changed identity and logged onto Democratic Caucus server using 17 other user account credentials, and stole equipment.

At the sentencing hearing on August 22, 2018, the DOJ said it did not find any evidence that supported criminal charges and could substantiate only the bank fraud charge. The judge gave Imran three months of supervised release.

The prosecutors said in the plea deal with Awan that the government interviewed 40 witnesses, took custody of the House Democratic Caucus server and other devices, reviewed electronic communications between House employees and questioned Awan during multiple voluntary interviews. The DOJ's claim is simply outrageous because their interviews and email reviews simply cannot disprove the Congressional IG's forensic evidence from a cybersecurity investigation. The original House Democratic Caucus server was physically stolen immediately after the September 2016 IG report named it as evidence in their investigation, so the DOJ statement that they took custody of the House Democratic Caucus server in their investigation is obviously intended to deceive. There is a major conflict of interest if the 40 witnesses interviewed by the DOJ included the 40 Democratic House members who employed the Awan group.

Rep. Louis Gohmert said there were at least 5,400 unauthorized accesses to then Congressman Xavier Becerra's computer. Gohmert said "it turns out the Awans had loaded different congress members' iClouds and servers onto one so that anybody could access it without authorization. It's terribly incredible. There are hundreds of potential federal charges here."

The Inspector General found that the Awan group illegally transferred massive amounts of data off of the Congressional network. After the IG's report, evidence disappeared and evidence was falsified. The Awan group possibly could have transferred sensitive security information out of the country. In an article titled "Debbie Wasserman Schultz and the Pakistani IT Scammers" McCarthy wrote "This is not about bank fraud. The Awan family swindles are plentiful, but they are just window-dressing. This appears to be a real conspiracy, aimed at undermining American national security."[cxxix]

Was the Washington D.C. DOJ office guilty of criminal misconduct in covering up the Awan national security crimes to protect congressional representative Debbie Wasserman Schultz, whose brother is a prosecutor in the office?

How did Christopher Gowen, a high-priced attorney and close Clinton friend, come to represent a low-level unknown IT aide accused of fraud the day after his arrest? Where did Awan get the money shortly after his arrest to pay off the fraudulent loan? Why would Gowen and Wasserman Schultz's attorney argue so strenuously against using Awan's laptop for evidence in the case? Why would Hillary Clinton have an interest in the fraud or in Awan's laptop? A very plausible answer is that Imran Awan has incriminating evidence on Clinton and Wasserman Schultz that he collected accessing Wasserman Schultz's computers and the DNC network.

The Special Counsel of Recommendation II in Chapter 31 should investigate the Awan group to determine if they are witnesses or have evidence regarding Hillary Clinton, the Clinton campaign, the DNC, and/or Debbie Wasserman Schultz perpetrating their criminal Trump/Russia collusion fraud to help Clinton win the presidential election. The Special Counsel should coordinate their investigation with the DOJ to determine if there is a factual predicate to initiate: 1) a national security investigation into the Awan group's congressional hacking and downloading of data, and 2) a criminal misconduct case against the DOJ's Washington D.C. office for covering up any Awan national security crimes.

CrowdStrike Created False Evidence

The DNC hired CrowdStrike to work on their hacked computer system May 4, 2016. Debbie Wasserman Schultz was chair of the DNC at the time. In June, 2016, CrowdStrike had medium confidence that the Russian military intelligence service (GRU) was hacked the DNC and placed the APT28 malware (Fancy Bear) on the DNC servers. On December 22, 2016, Dmitri Alperovitch, a co-founder of CrowdStrike, raised his confidence level to high based on strong new evidence. "CrowdStrike found that a variant of the Fancy Bear [X-Agent] malware that was used to penetrate the DNC's network in April 2016 was also used to hack an Android app developed by the Ukrainian army to help artillery troops more efficiently train their antiquated howitzers on targets. The Fancy Bear crew evidently hacked the app, allowing the GRU to use the phone's GPS coordinates to track the Ukrainian troops' position. In that way, the Russian military could then target the Ukrainian army with artillery and other weaponry. The Android app was useful in helping the Russian troops locate Ukrainian artillery positions. According to the International Institute for Strategic

Studies, Ukrainian artillery forces lost more than 50 percent of their weapons in the two years of conflict."cxxx CrowdStrike said this resulted in Ukraine losing 80% of its D-30 howitzers from late 2014 through 2016.cxxxi

Alperovitch said "we wanted to produce more evidence that raises the level of confidence that we have, even internally, that this is Russian intelligence agency called the GRU. And when you think about, well, who would be interested in targeting Ukraine artillerymen in eastern Ukraine who has interest in hacking the Democratic Party, Russia government comes to mind, but specifically, Russian military that would have operational [control] over forces in the Ukraine and would target these artillerymen."cxxxii

The International Institute for Strategic Studies (IISS) told the Voice of America that CrowdStrike misinterpreted their data and hadn't reached out beforehand for comment or clarification. IISS flatly rejected the assertion of artillery combat losses. The Ukrainian Ministry of Defense issued a statement saying artillery losses from the ongoing fighting with separatists are "several times smaller than the number reported by [CrowdStrike] and are not associated with the specified cause" of Russian hacking. The apps developer, Jaroslav Sherstuk, said CrowdStrike's report was "delusional."cxxxiii

The cybersecurity expert, Jeffrey Carr investigated Alperovitch's claim through hours of interviews and background research with Ukrainian hackers, soldiers, and an independent analysis of the malware by CrySys Lab. Carr found out in an interview with Sherstuk that "The first iteration of the POPR-D30 Android app designed by Ukrainian military officer Jaroslav Sherstuk (and the only iteration allegedly impacted by this malware) was a simple ballistics program that calculated corrections for humidity, atmospheric pressure, and other environmental factors that determine accuracy of the D-30 Howitzer. It did not have the capability to connect to Wi-Fi, nor to receive or transmit any data. The Android APK malware doesn't use GPS nor does it ask for GPS location information from the infected phone or tablet.

CrowdStrike hasn't provided any evidence that the malware-infected Android app was used by even a single Ukrainian soldier. Crowdstrike invented a 'devastating' cyber attack out of thin air and called it DNA evidence of Russian government involvement."cxxxiv Carr said "Crowdstrike hasn't said how many of Sherstuck's devices were infected (the answer is zero), nor have they attempted to contact Sherstuck himself. If they had, they would have saved themselves the embarrassment of claiming an effect that would be impossible for the malware to execute on that app. The company found one piece of malware and one video, and from that flimsy evidence built an entire house of cards whose only purpose was to grab headlines and reinforce their DNC [Russian hacking conclusion]. This kind of irresponsible behavior should not be tolerated by the U.S. government or CrowdStrike's customers."cxxxv

Carr's research is the "smoking gun" that proves CrowdStrike fabricated false evidence in order to demonstrate the GRU hacked the DNC. Based on this false evidence, CrowdStrike raised their confidence level of GRU hacking to high. CrowdStrike created and promoted this false evidence in the press in December.

Christopher Steele prepared the last dossier misinformation report in December 2016 and CrowdStrike created this false evidence in December. Clinton and the DNC, or their intermediaries, may have instructed them to do this in order to provide additional evidence for the preparers of the Intelligence Community Assessment, who were writing it in December and published on January 6, 2017.

CrowdStrike prepared an intelligence report titled "Danger Close: Fancy Bear Tracking of Ukrainian Field Artillery Units" describing the fabricated evidence. **The Special Counsel of Recommendation II in Chapter 31 should find out if**

CrowdStrike conspired to defraud the government by providing this intelligence report with false evidence to the government, and also investigate who requested CrowdStrike to do this.

CrowdStrike's incompetence

On a side note, CrowdStrike is not only dishonest, but was extremely incompetent in dealing with the DNC hacking intrusion as revealed in Mueller's indictment of 12 GRU intelligence officers.

After it discovered its computers were hacked on April 28, 2016, the DNC hired the cybersecurity company, CrowdStrike, on May 4, 2016 to help. On May 5 CrowdStrike had installed its Falcon software that supposedly "profiled every action that occurred at a programme level on the hundreds of machines owned by the DNC."cxxxvi

In addition to Falcon, the DNC used Overwatch, a service where an elite team of CrowdStrike cybersecurity experts monitors the servers 24/7. The team of experts "proactively hunt, investigate and advise on threat activity in your environment."

In June 2016, CrowdStrike wrote on their website that when the DNC asked them to respond to a suspected breach "We deployed our IR [Incident Response] team and technology and immediately identified two sophisticated adversaries on the network – COZY BEAR and FANCY BEAR. We've had lots of experience with both of these actors attempting to target our customers in the past and know them well." CrowdStrike said Fancy Bear (APT28) is the Russian GRU military intelligence service, and Cozy Bear (APT29) is the Russian SVR/FSB intelligence service.

On the weekend starting Friday June 10, 2016, CrowdStrike secretly replaced the DNC's software on all computers to cleanse the system. CrowdStrike said that all hackers were expelled from the DNC's network in a "major computer cleanup campaign."

Shawn Henry is the president of CrowdStrike Services and CSO. Before joining CrowdStrike in 2012, Henry was a retired executive assistant director of the FBI, who oversaw global computer crime investigations.

In an October 24, 2016 Esquire article Henry said that Cozy Bear (the Russian SVR/FSB intelligence service) had been stealing emails from the DNC for more than a year. "Henry led a CrowdStrike forensics team that over a two-week period retraced the hackers' steps and pieced together the pathology of the breach."[cxxxvii]

One can conclude from the CrowdStrike and DNC publicity described above that CrowdStrike quickly identified and monitored the hackers, cleansed the DNC system from malware, and prevented the hackers from doing any additional damage after CrowdStrike deployed their Falcon software and Overwatch monitoring on May 4. Nothing could be further from the truth!

The evidence in the Mueller indictment is eye opening, and demonstrates CrowdStrike's incompetence:

- Per Henry, CrowdStrike's "forensics team" determined Cozy Bear stole the emails, but Mueller's incontrovertible evidence identified Fancy Bear (the GRU) as the hacker stealing the emails. So CrowdStrike's forensics experts lost the 50/50-coin toss on that one.
- Henry said the hackers were stealing the emails from the DNC for more than a year, but Mueller's indictment states "Between May 25, 2016 and June 1, 2016, the GRU hacked the DNC Microsoft Exchange Server and stole

thousands of emails from the work accounts of DNC employees."

- The CrowdStrike Overwatch's elite team of cybersecurity experts were monitoring the DNC servers 24/7. Mueller's evidence proves that the GRU stole the emails under this elite team's nose "Between May 25, 2016 and June 1, 2016."

- CrowdStrike claimed to have cleansed the DNC computer system on the weekend of June 10 and expelled all intruders. Mueller's evidence found that a malicious program "remained on the DNC network until in or around October 2016." In addition, the GRU also gained access to DNC computers hosted on a third-party cloud-computing service around September 2016, which enabled them to steal data from the DNC by creating backups, or snapshots, of the DNC's cloud-based systems.

30. The Media and Democrats – The Conspiracy Enablers

The Mainstream Media

The mainstream media is a very effective propaganda machine for the Democrats. In October 2017, the Pew Research Center found the media was three times more negative and eight times less positive toward Trump than it was to Obama, and the media was also significantly more biased against Trump compared to presidents Clinton and Bush II. A Harvard study in May 2017 said Trump set "a new standard for unfavorable press coverage of a president."

The DOJ's Inspector General, Michael Horowitz, issued a report titled "A Review of Various Actions by the Federal Bureau of Investigation and Department of Justice in Advance of the 2016 Election."[cxxxviii] Horowitz found that officials in the FBI at "all levels of the organization" leaked information to reporters without authorization. The FBI's strict media relations policy on disclosures was "widely ignored" during the Clinton email probe and afterwards. The report said "We have profound concerns about the volume and extent of unauthorized media contacts by FBI personnel." A chart showed dozens of FBI officials who spoke to reporters without permission, including several special agents, special agents in charge, secretaries, management and program analysts, attorneys, an "FBI executive," a deputy assistant director and an assistant director.

The Obama administration's conspirators Andrew McCabe, Peter Strzok, James Baker, and Lisa Page all leaked classified information to the press to get stories published in a beneficial way for them. James Comey, who committed multiple felonies, successfully leaked his memos to the press with the objective of getting a special counsel appointed.

The mainstream media allied with the conspirators and the Democrats to successfully cover up the biggest scandal by far in U.S. history. The New York Times and Washington Post publish stories handed to them by the conspirators, referred to as "anonymous sources," to deftly cover up the conspirators' wrongdoing and promote the Clinton and DNC's hoax that the Trump campaign colluded with Russia to hack the DNC. Sergei Millian's allegations are the raison d'être of Mueller's special counsel investigation. The mainstream media's many "investigative journalists" could have easily uncovered the facts about Sergei Millian and his false allegations, but did not. The mainstream media's objectives are to harm President Trump and help the Democrats achieve their impeachment goal, so disproving Millian's allegations would undermine these goals.

In September 2016, editors at the New York Times, Dean Baquet, and Washington Post, Bob Woodward, publicly displayed faux courage by saying that they would risk jail time if it meant they could publish then Republican nominee Donald Trump's tax returns. The traitorous conspirators in the Obama administration tried to turn the U.S. into a police state by using the DOJ, FBI, and intelligence community to help Hillary Clinton become president. This is by far the biggest scandal in U.S. history. If Baquet or Woodward had their journalists uncover this scandal, it would have shown real courage.

The New York Times and Washington Post have been extremely successful propaganda outlets for the Democrats and conspirators because much of the public trusts them for unbiased reporting. Hitler and Stalin would be envious.

Democrats

The United States is unique in the world in its peaceful presidential elections and smooth transfer of power to the winner. The transfer from President Bush to President Obama went smoothly, but the transfer from President Obama to

President Trump was marred from the beginning by angry protests, violence, and lawsuits.

Donald Trump won the election, but Democrats planned for his impeachment before the inauguration, when Democratic senators, including Elizabeth Warren, introduced a bill in December 2106 to require a president to divest any assets that could raise a conflict of interest and failure to do so would constitute high crimes and misdemeanors "under the impeachment clause of the U.S. Constitution." Democrats formed PAC's as early as February 2017 aimed at Trump's impeachment because 1) his businesses had conflicts of interest that violated the Foreign Emoluments Clause, or 2) his coordination with Russia in the DNC hack to influence the 2016 election.

When President Trump fired James Comey in May 2017, the Democrats discussed impeachment on the grounds of obstruction of justice. On July 12, a representative introduced an Article of Impeachment in the House that accused the President Trump of obstructing justice in the Trump campaign/Russia collusion investigation. It did not pass, but the Democrats could conceivably impeach the president if they take control of the House in the midterm elections.

In furtherance of their impeachment strategy, Democratic senators and representatives try to impede congressional committees' investigations into potential Obama administration wrongdoing in the Clinton investigations and the Trump/Russia investigation. Rosenstein helps them by stonewalling congressional requests for documents, and making unnecessary extensive redactions. The Democrats' goal is to cover up this scandal in the hope that they win congressional majorities in the midterm elections. When they are in the majority, the Democrats can terminate the congressional committee investigations into DOJ and FBI wrongdoing in the Clinton investigations and the Trump/Russia investigation.

After the midterm election, Mueller will issue a report of the Special Counsel findings that the Democrats, if in the majority, can use to impeach President Trump.

It would be a grievous miscarriage of justice if the Democrats impeach President Trump under the pretense that he obstructed justice in an investigation that only exists because of the false Sergei Millian allegations in the Hillary Clinton and DNC funded Steele dossier. Mueller and Rosenstein know that Trump's campaign did not collude with Russia because of the evidence in their indictment of 12 Russian intelligence officers.

Donald Trump is the democratically elected president. The Democrats with the help of the mainstream media, Rosenstein, and Mueller are aiming to overturn the will of the voters by impeachment based on the false allegations of Sergei Millian – the most influential person in America.

Clinton, the DNC, and their co-conspirators betrayed the United States by subverting the democratic election process through fraud in order to gain power. Congressional Democrats and the mainstream media betrayed the United States by covering up the biggest scandal in US history. The conspirators actually did change the election results because an unknown millions of votes were cast for Clinton instead of Trump because of Clinton and the DNC's Trump/Russia collusion scam.

31. Recommendations

"[To save] the Republic... is the first and supreme law." --
Thomas Jefferson

President Trump's attorneys probably advised him against taking any action related to the Trump/Russia probe because Watergate's "Saturday Night Massacre" resulted in the downfall of President Nixon. This is a completely different situation though because President Trump is innocent and President Nixon was not. President Trump's attorneys should heed Thomas Jefferson's advice "In an encampment expecting daily attack from a powerful enemy, self-preservation is paramount to all law."

President Trump holds all of the aces – the truth! The truth is that the Obama administration, Hillary Clinton, and the DNC colluded with foreign nationals in the UK, Australia, Ukraine, Russia, Malta, and other nations to create and disseminate the false Trump/Russia collusion story to influence the 2016 presidential elections.

Most Americans do not know that Clinton and the DNC successfully perpetrated a huge fraud with their Trump/Russia collusion story that did in fact sway millions of votes from Trump to Clinton. President Trump's advisers have him sitting on the sidelines like a deer in the headlights while Rosenstein and Mueller continue their vendetta. They will continue to threaten and scare Michael Cohen to compose crimes, under the guidance of Clinton confidante Lanny Davis, to prosecute the president's associates, family, and business organization with the ultimate goal of impeachment. Hillary Clinton may yet defeat Donald Trump if the Democrats win congressional majorities in the midterm elections and use her false Trump/Russia collusion hoax to impeach the president. The president needs to take urgent and drastic action by implementing the following recommendations.

Recommendation I

Recommend that the president order Jeff Sessions to fire Rod Rosenstein for failure to comply with DOJ regulations.

Rosenstein did not comply with several DOJ regulations: 1) he did not define the crime for the Special Counsel investigation, 2) he approved a FISA warrant application submitted to the FISC without informing the court that the basis was a Clinton campaign opposition document, 3) as a witness, he did not recuse himself from the Special Counsel investigation into obstruction of justice for firing James Comey, and 4) Rosenstein dishonestly did not terminate the Special Counsel when Mueller's own evidence in the 12 Russian GRU intelligence officer indictment proved that no one in Trump's campaign coordinated with Russia.

The DOJ's regulation 28 CFR Sec. 600.1, states that the Justice Department may appoint a special counsel when it is "determine[d] that criminal investigation of a person or matter is warranted." Regulation 28 CFR 600.4 states that the Justice Department will provide the special counsel "with a specific factual statement of the matter to be investigated." Rosenstein did not comply with these regulations because he did not define the crime to be investigated.

Rosenstein should have recused himself in the Special Counsel investigation because he is a potential witness. Rosenstein wrote a letter recommending James Comey's dismissal, so he would be a witness in any Special Counsel probe into Comey's dismissal as an obstruction of justice.

Rosenstein approved an application for a FISA warrant based on the unverified Steele dossier allegations, and the application was very deceptive because it did not state that Clinton and the DNC funded the information justifying the warrant to spy on a Trump campaign person. Rosenstein violated the FBI's Domestic Investigations and Operations Guide requiring that "only documented and verified information may be used to support FBI applications to the [FISA] court."

Rosenstein's letter justified the dismissal of FBI Director James Comey because he did not follow "a well-established process," he "ignored another longstanding principle," and he "refused to admit his errors." President Trump's firing of Rosenstein would be consistent with the justification Rosenstein gave in his letter for firing Comey because Rosenstein violated DOJ regulations and refused to admit his errors.

Mueller's indictment of 12 Russian intelligence officers for stealing the DNC emails and publishing them on WikiLeaks proves that no one in Donald Trump's campaign was involved. The indictment's incontrovertible evidence proves that there is no justification at all for Mueller's Special Counsel to investigate Trump campaign/Russia coordination. Rosenstein should have admitted his error and terminated the Mueller Special Counsel investigation. Instead, he dishonestly did nothing, and President Trump should fire him for this among the many other reasons.

Recommendation II

Recommend that the president order Jeff Sessions to appoint a Special Counsel to investigate the criminal misconduct committed by the conspirators in the Clinton email investigation, the Clinton Foundation investigation, and the Trump Campaign/Russia investigation.

President Trump should order Jeff Sessions to appoint the person specified by the president as Special Counsel.

President Trump should request the British government to initiate an investigation of people in Britain participating in the plot to subvert the 2016 U.S. presidential election, and for British investigators to work with his Special Counsel.

Since Special Counsels/Independent Counsels have always abused their authority, they should arguably never be used. However, this conspiracy is a perfect storm, and a Special Counsel is absolutely needed for the following reasons:

A Special Counsel is needed because the DOJ and FBI have proven that they cannot be trusted to investigate themselves. The DOJ and FBI have a) stonewalled in providing documents requested by Congress, b) heavily and unnecessarily redacted documents finally provided, c) leaked information to the press, including an anonymous attack on a Congressional staffer. Andrew McCarthy writes that the "outrageous redactions" to conceal the truth about their actions indicates that "the Justice Department and the FBI cannot be trusted to decide what the public gets to learn about their decision-making." The FBI and DOJ are trying to run out the clock until the midterm elections in hopes that Democrats will control committees.

A Special Counsel is also needed due to the tremendous breadth of the conspiracy extending to the highest levels of government in multiple countries.

- The conspiracy includes people in high positions at the DOJ, FBI, CIA, Office of the Director of National Intelligence, State Department, and others. House Intelligence Committee Chairman Devin Nunes said that Hillary Clinton's campaign "colluded" with nearly every top official in the Justice Department and FBI.
- The conspiracy is international and includes people in the UK, Ukraine, Russia, Australia, Italy and other countries. Much of the evidence for the Trump/Russia collusion investigation came from the UK.

- The conspiracy may well implicate former President Obama, Robert Hannigan, former head of the British GCHQ intelligence agency, and Alexander Downer, an Australian ambassador.
- Although the highest-level people leading the conspiracy are no longer in their positions, the volume of leaks suggests that career employee conspirators are still in place.

A Special Counsel is required for this investigation because many more prosecutors and FBI agents are required than any one DOJ district or FBI office could reasonably provide. The diversity of a Special Counsel team drawn from the best prosecutors and FBI agents throughout the country would give the country assurance of a fair investigation free from bias and assure a high-performing team. Prosecutors and agents from the Washington D.C. DOJ or FBI headquarters in their positions prior to the Trump administration should be excluded from the team unless thoroughly vetted to assure they were not complicit with the criminal conspiracy.

Fusion GPS and Steele used Sergei Millian to provide the dossier's major allegation that Carter Page and Paul Manafort colluded with Russia to hack and steal the DNC emails and publish them on WikiLeaks. Based solely on Millian's false information, the DOJ and FBI obtained a FISA warrant to surveille the innocent and patriotic Carter Page for one year, and Rosenstein used it for Mueller's Special Counsel appointment and for authorization to investigate Manafort. Millian's name was shown as the source in the FBI's copy of Steele's dossier, but the FBI used his allegation to surveille Page rather than investigate Millian to verify it. **The DOJ or special counsel should immediately locate and put Sergei Millian in the Witness Security Program, as he had previously requested, and investigate his allegations to find out who was involved in creating this phony information.**

Other preparatory actions that the DOJ or Special Counsel can take immediately include:

- Obtain a grand jury indictment of James Comey for multiple felonies.
- Obtain a grand jury indictment of Glenn Simpson for perjury
- Investigate who was surveilled, including anyone in the Trump administration, using the Carter Page FISA surveillance warrant and the 2-hop rule for FISA warrants.[cxxxix]
- Investigate to identify all covert agents used for the Trump campaign, including any foreign covert agents such as Joseph Mifsud involved in the setups of Trump campaign members.
- Interview Gina Haspel to find out what she knew about the covert agents and setups in London while she was the CIA's London Chief of Station (COS) in 2016. (Section A4 of the Appendix has examples of pertinent interview topics.)

The conspirators' objective was to elect Hillary Clinton president by 1) criminally corrupting the justice process to wrongfully exonerate her in the email investigation, 2) terminating the validly predicated Clinton Foundation investigation, and 3) harming candidate Trump by using the Clinton/DNC fraudulent story that the Trump campaign colluded with Russia to steal the DNC emails and publish them on WikiLeaks to help Clinton win the election. The Special Counsel's scope of this recommendation should include all three investigations because they are interconnected.

Recommendation III

Recommend that the president order Jeff Sessions to terminate the Special Counsel since the evidence in

the Mueller indictment of 12 Russian intelligence officers proves there is no basis for the investigation.

Refer any unfinished investigations with a valid factual predicate to the DOJ.

Order Sessions to investigate Rosenstein, Mueller, and the Mueller team for: a) Bias and General Prosecutorial Misconduct, b) Abuse of Investigative or Prosecutorial Authority, Overzealous Prosecution and Selective prosecution by political affiliation, c) Constitutional and Civil Rights Violations, and d) Failure to Provide Exculpatory Information to Defendants.

If a factual predicate for a criminal case is identified, refer it to the Special Counsel of Recommendation II.

No one is above the law, including a Special Counsel. The DNC and Hillary Clinton created the false Russia collusion story to blame the DNC email theft on Donald Trump and his campaign colluding with Russia. The evidence in Mueller's indictment of 12 Russian GRU intelligence officers proves this allegation is false, so there was never any basis for Rosenstein to appoint a Special Counsel to investigate this.

Recommendation IV

Recommend that the president order Jeff Sessions to reopen the Clinton email and Clinton Foundation investigations as one investigation since they are related.

The president should order Sessions to assign the investigation to a DOJ office outside of Washington D.C. and exclude the DOJ's Eastern

District of New York. Exclude anyone from the investigation team who worked on the Clinton email investigation or the Trump Campaign/Russia Investigation. The investigation should exclude the DOJ's National Security Division, and the FBI's Counterintelligence Division.

The DOJ and the FBI corrupted the federal criminal justice process to exonerate Hillary Clinton in the email investigation, so this case should be reopened.

In 2016, FBI agents on the Clinton Foundation case in the SDNY office requested to review the emails on Mills' and Samuelson's nongovernment laptop computers acquired in the Clinton email investigation. Prosecutors at the EDNY refused the request. After the EDNY rejected their request, the FBI agents requested permission to ask federal prosecutors in SDNY. FBI Deputy Director Andrew McCabe refused, saying they could not "go prosecutor-shopping." The DOJ and FBI shut down the Clinton Foundation investigation even though McCabe admitted that it is validly predicated.

McCarthy said that "Comey found that Hillary Clinton quite plainly mishandled classified information and exposed the United States to a heightened risk of national-security harm. But he forgot to explain the reason she did so — to keep her business, both public and private, beyond the reach of public scrutiny. She did all of this to avoid congressional oversight, FOIA requests, and accountability to the public. Comey's decision simply ensures that she was successful in avoiding that accountability." "While Clinton may not have been motivated to harm our national security, she was precisely motivated to conceal the corrupt interplay of the State Department and the Clinton Foundation. That was the real objective of the home-brew server system... and, critically, it perfectly explains why she deleted and attempted to destroy 33,000 e-mails." "Were it not for the Clinton Foundation, there probably would not be a Clinton email scandal. Mrs. Clinton's home-brew communications system was designed to conceal the degree to which the State Department was put in the service of Foundation donors who transformed the 'dead broke' Clintons into hundred-millionaires."[cxl]

Jedd Babbin, a former deputy undersecretary of defense, wrote that "Hillary Clinton established a private, non-government email system for her and her aides to use with the obvious intent of preventing anyone from knowing what she did that would violate laws against public corruption (such as her dealings with foreign governments to benefit the Clinton Foundation)." [cxli]

The Clinton email investigation and the Clinton Foundation investigation should be consolidated into one investigation because, as McCarthy and Babbin described, they are interconnected.

Recommendation V

Recommend that the president order the DOJ and FBI to provide the documents that Congress requests without delay and without unnecessary redactions.

The president should order that no redactions are permitted unless approved by the President's assigned representative on this matter.

The DOJ and FBI have continually delayed for months in providing documents requested by Congress, and the documents that they finally give are very heavily redacted. Upon pressure, the DOJ and FBI will remove some of the redactions and it is obvious there was no valid reason to redact in the first place except to cover up their own questionable judgments.

As summarized below, Andrew McCarthy has repeatedly written about this and expressed frustration that President Trump does not order his subordinates at the DOJ and FBI to comply with congressional requests. I suspect the president has not done so because his attorneys have advised against it. The congressional committees have uncovered much wrongdoing by the Obama administration in the Trump/Russia investigation. It is in the president's best interest to order the DOJ and FBI to respond in a timely manner to congressional requests and declassify as much as possible.

In a May 2018 article titled "Outrageous Redactions to the Russia Report," McCarthy writes:

> "Cute how this works: Kick off the week with some "the Department of Justice is not going to be extorted" bombast from Deputy Attorney General Rod Rosenstein, by which he rationalizes that his defiance of subpoenas and slow-walking document production to Congress — which is probing investigative irregularities related to the 2016 campaign — is required by DOJ policy and "the rule of law." Then end the week with the Friday-night bad-news dump: the grudging removal of DOJ and FBI redactions from a House Intelligence Committee report on Russia's election meddling.

> Now that we can see what they wanted to conceal, it is clear, yet again, that the Justice Department and the FBI cannot be trusted to decide what the public gets to learn about their decision-making"

> They tell us that their lack of transparency is necessary for the protection of national security, vital intelligence, and investigative operations. But what we find out is that they were concealing their own questionable judgments and conflicting explanations for their actions; their use of foreign-intelligence and criminal-investigative authorities to investigate Michael Flynn, Trump's top campaign

supporter and former national-security adviser; and their explicitly stated belief that Flynn did not lie in the FBI interview for which Special Counsel Robert Mueller has since prosecuted him on false-statements charges.

What happened with these redactions is inexcusable.

There is no defending the redactions that have now been disclosed. Especially in light of recent history, this powerfully suggests that there is no justification for withholding much else that the Justice Department refuses to reveal.

*The president has not only the authority but the duty to ensure that his subordinates honor lawful disclosure requests from Congress. Republican committees can carp all they like about Deputy Attorney General Rosenstein. The buck stops with the president."*cxlii

McCarthy writes in an August 2017 article titled "Why Doesn't Trump Just Unmask the Unmasking?":

"I can't get past a nagging question: Why must we speculate about whether the Obama administration abusively exploited its foreign-intelligence-collection powers in order to spy on Donald Trump's political campaign? After all, Trump is president now. If he was victimized, he's in a position to tell us all about it.

*The president is in charge of the executive branch, including its intelligence agencies. He has the authority to decide what intelligence information, and intelligence abuses, can be declassified and made public."*cxliii

The president tweeted on May 19 "If the FBI or DOJ was infiltrating a campaign for the benefit of another campaign, that is a really big deal. Only the release or review of documents that the House Intelligence Committee (also, Senate Judiciary) is asking for can give the conclusive answers. Drain the Swamp!"

All of the recommendations are for President Trump to give direct orders – not Tweets. Tweets are useless. As Andrew McCarthy said regarding documents requested by Devin Nunes "It is simply ridiculous for President Trump to continue bloviating about this situation on Twitter and in friendly media interviews, and for congressional Republicans to continue pretending that the problem is Justice Department and FBI leadership — as if Trump were not responsible for his own administration's actions. The president has not only the authority but the duty to ensure that his subordinates honor lawful disclosure requests from Congress."[cxliv]

32. Jeff Sessions Can Immediately Restore Justice

Jeff Sessions only recused himself from "any existing or future investigations of any matters related in any way to the campaigns for President of the United States." Robert Barnes writes:

> "This recusal letter limits the scope of Sessions' recusal to the 2016 campaigns; it does not authorize Sessions' recusal for anything beyond that. Constitutionally, Sessions has a "duty to direct and supervise litigation" conducted by the Department of Justice. Ethically, professionally, and legally, Sessions cannot ignore his supervisory obligations for cases that are not related to the 'campaigns for President.'" "Sessions himself has exclusive authority to appoint a special counsel for non-collusion charges"[cxlv]

Rosenstein and Mueller have gone way beyond that scope of Sessions' recusal. Mueller is prosecuting Paul Manafort for 2005 tax crimes, 2010 bank fraud crimes and 2013 foreign agent crimes. Barnes notes that

> "if Rosenstein's authorization could be interpreted so broadly, it would make Mueller a de facto Attorney General of the United States, which the Appointments Clause does not permit, rendering such an authorization in violation; second, if it could be interpreted as broadly as Mueller has done so, then it failed to conform to the statutes and regulations governing special counsel authorizations."

> "Sessions limiting Mueller would enforce the limits intended on Rosenstein's letter authorization. Contrary to anti-Trump critics, Mueller's mandate was not 'get Trump,' 'indict anybody who ever worked for Trump.' Mueller's authority is limited to 'links between the Russian government and individuals associated with the campaign

of President Donald Trump.' Any subject matter that does not concern 'the campaign,' is a subject matter that Sessions Constitutionally must directly supervise Mueller. This includes Sessions power to notify Mueller and formally revoke Mueller's authority at any time in cases that do not concern the campaign itself. Sessions can remove Mueller's authority to request search warrants, subpoena grand jury testimony, subpoena grand jury records, target individuals, or issue indictments unless the subject matter is constricted to the campaign itself. Sessions can return power over the existing indictments to regular DOJ prosecutors, as both the Constitution and the statutes compel. Sessions can dismiss existing indictments as an excess of authority of Mueller's team (a team already infamous for acting outside their authority in the past, whether it be ethical abuses or over-broad, unconstitutional interpretations of federal criminal law)."

A federal district court held: "the special counsel cannot act outside the bounds of either his limited jurisdiction or without regard for Department of Justice policies and regulations. As such, the Special Counsel does not wield unlimited authority." Indeed, a special counsel's "authority is therefore confined to the narrow objective of accomplishing the specific mandate he was given."[cxlvi]

Mueller's indictment of 12 Russian GRU intelligence officers proves that no one on Trump's campaign team coordinated the hacks with Russia, but Mueller's Special Counsel investigation still continues unabated. Hillary Clinton and the DNC perpetrated a hugely successful hoax. The whole basis of the Trump campaign/Russia collusion investigation consists of Sergei Millian's accusations in the Steele dossier. Sergei Millian is the most influential person in America.

No matter what Jeff Sessions accomplishes as Attorney General, history will undoubtedly judge him as the worst Attorney General in U.S. history because he not only allowed the

Rosenstein/Mueller special counsel travesty to proceed unbounded, but he also abetted it by stonewalling information requests by Congressional committees investigating criminal misconduct by the FBI and Department of Justice. Jeff Sessions has been the prime enabler in perpetuating the Clinton/DNC hoax.

Jeff Sessions has betrayed his country by permitting the conspirators in the DOJ and Mueller investigation to use the Clinton/DNC hoax to gravely harm the democratically elected president with the ultimate goal of impeachment.

Jeff Sessions can redeem himself and immediately restore justice

Overwhelming evidence in this book demonstrates without a doubt that the conspirators in the DOJ, FBI, and intelligence community corrupted the justice system to get Hillary Clinton elected president and harm Donald Trump.

In a cowardly avoidance of any political controversy, Sessions has passively observed the Rosenstein and Mueller's baseless investigation carry out a vendetta against the president. Mueller's own evidence proves President Trump and his campaign are innocent of collusion with the Russians, which is the very foundation of the Special Counsel investigation. Sessions has a moral and ethical obligation to protect the innocent and he should heed Thomas Jefferson's advice that "It [is] more a duty [of the Attorney General] to save an innocent than to convict a guilty man."

The biggest scandal in US history will not remain hidden forever as more evidence continually emerges. The DOJ's Inspector General is still investigating criminal wrongdoing in the Clinton email investigation. Investigators in media outlets searching for the unbiased truth discover new evidence, as do thousands of patriotic internet researchers. My hope is that people seeking the truth will leverage off of the evidence and conclusions presented in this book to expedite exposing the scandal.

The truth will undoubtedly be manifested sooner or later. Thomas Jefferson made this very clear: "No nation however powerful, any more than an individual, can be unjust with impunity. Sooner or later, public opinion, an instrument merely moral in the beginning, will find occasion physically to inflict its sentences on the unjust... The lesson is useful to the weak as well as the strong."

But there is no need to wait because Jeff Sessions has it in his power to immediately restore justice and heal the nation. Sessions should unrecuse himself because Mueller's own evidence absolves the Trump campaign of any collusion with Russia.

- Jeff Sessions can fire Rod Rosenstein for cause and appoint a Special Counsel to investigate the criminal misconduct committed by the conspirators in the Clinton email investigation, the Clinton Foundation investigation, and the Trump Campaign/Russia investigation.
- Jeff Sessions can terminate the Special Counsel since the evidence in the Mueller indictment of 12 Russian intelligence officers proves there is no basis for the investigation. Sessions can refer any unfinished investigations with a valid factual predicate to the DOJ and can order an investigation of Rosenstein, Mueller, and the Mueller team for the potential crimes described in Chapter 28.
- Jeff Sessions can reopen the Clinton email and Clinton Foundation investigations as one investigation.
- Jeff Sessions can order the DOJ and FBI to provide the documents that Congress requests without delay and without unnecessary redactions.

By doing this, Jeff Sessions will give a tremendous gift to his employees at the Department of Justice. He will let the wonderful people in the DOJ and FBI restore the reputation of these precious institutions that was tainted by a few bad eggs at the top who attempted to use the DOJ and FBI as a political weapon.

Thomas Jefferson said ""Equal and exact justice to all men, of whatever state or persuasion, religious or political, I deem [one of] the essential principles of our Government." My fervent hope is that many people in the FBI and DOJ and Americans of all political beliefs deluge Attorney General Jeff Sessions with petitions to take these actions for the good of the nation.

33. How to Expose the Biggest Scandal in U.S. History

Hillary Clinton and the DNC perpetrated the biggest hoax in history by framing Donald Trump's campaign for coordinating with Russia to steal the DNC emails. Obama administration officials criminally subverted the justice system to wrongly: 1) exonerate Clinton in the email investigation, 2) terminate the Clinton Foundation investigation, and 3) conduct a criminal investigation of President Trump and his associates based on Hillary Clinton and the DNC's Trump/Russia collusion scam.

Mueller and Rosenstein's objective has always been impeachment, and they may well achieve this if the Democrats win majorities in Congress this November as some polls indicate. Rosenstein and Wray are stonewalling Devin Nunes and Chuck Grassley's requests for documents in hopes the Democrats take control of Congress and shut down the investigations.

President Trump holds all of the aces – the truth! The truth is that the Obama administration, Hillary Clinton, and the DNC colluded with foreign nationals in the UK, Australia, Ukraine, Russia, and Italy to create the false Trump/Russia collusion story to influence the 2016 presidential elections.

This is by far the biggest scandal in American history and the vast majority of Americans do not know the truth because the mainstream media and the Democrats in Congress disseminate lies and hide the truth.

The Democrats and mainstream media own this scandal. Only a few weeks remain before the midterm elections. The Republicans are at risk of losing control of the Senate and House, which would seriously undermine the Trump presidency's agenda and possibly result in President Trump's impeachment due to the Clinton/DNC hoax.

To avert this disastrous scenario, I recommend that the RNC convene a conference of major Republican donors and heads of the RNC to develop a strategy to highlight the Democrat's huge scandal. Following are some suggestions for the strategy:

Civil Lawsuits

Very large civil lawsuits would bring immediate public attention to the Clinton/DNC hoax and the criminal conspiracy to elect Clinton president and prosecute Donald Trump and his associates.

1. File a $100 million countersuit against the DNC and Hillary Clinton.

The DNC filed a lawsuit alleging that "the Trump campaign solicited Russia's illegal assistance, and maintained secret communications with individuals tied to the Russian government, including one of the intelligence agencies responsible for attacking the DNC. Through these communications, the Trump campaign, Trump's closest advisers, and Russian agents formed an agreement to promote Donald Trump's candidacy through illegal means" most notably, the hacking and leak of the DNC's own email accounts and documents.

The DNC lawsuit asserts that various combinations of Russia-tied and Trump-tied people violated computer crime, racketeering, wiretapping, and even copyright statutes because of this conspiracy — and are seeking millions of dollars in damages.

The countersuit would be filed on behalf of the Trump campaign, Donald Trump Jr., Paul Manafort, Jared Kushner, George Papadopoulos, and Richard Gates, who are defendants in the DNC lawsuit.

In addition to the DNC, the countersuit's defendants would include Hillary Clinton, Debbie Wasserman Schultz, Glenn Simpson, Fusion GPS, Nellie Ohr, and Christopher Steele.

The countersuit would assert that Mueller's indictment of 12 GRU intelligence officers proves that no members of the Trump campaign communicated with Russia to coordinate the theft of the DNC emails through a hack. The DNC and other defendants conspired to falsely blame Donald Trump's campaign for Russian collusion by creating, disseminating and using the provably false Steele dossier allegations.

2. File a $100 million lawsuit on behalf of Carter Page and any other people surveilled against the conspirators that obtained a FISA surveillance warrant on false pretenses.

The defendants would be any official involved in preparing the FISA warrant application or in approving the renewals including: Loretta Lynch, James Comey, Andrew McCabe, Peter Strzok, Lisa Page, Sally Yates, Rod Rosenstein, Dana Boente, John Carlin, and any others. The Plaintiffs would be Carter Page and any other people surveilled under the Carter Page FISA surveillance warrant. The FISA warrant 2-hop rule greatly expands the people surveilled, and likely included the entire Trump campaign team, and perhaps even people in the Trump administration. (Note: Carter Page just filed a lawsuit against the DNC and Perkins Coie for an insignificant $75,000. The conspirators severely damage our nation so there needs to be substantial punitive consequences. Page needs a good pro bono attorney.)

3. File a $100 billion lawsuit on behalf of the American people against the conspirators for criminal actions to elect Hillary Clinton president and harm

President Trump and his associates by subverting the justice process.

The lawsuit's allegations are that the defendants criminally conspired to subvert the justice system to wrongly: 1) exonerate Clinton in the email investigation, 2) terminate the Clinton Foundation investigation, and 3) conduct a criminal investigation of President Trump and his associates based on Hillary Clinton and the DNC's Trump/Russia collusion scam. Based on overwhelming evidence, the conspirators' criminal misconduct wrongfully exonerated Clinton in the email investigation and terminated the factually predicated Clinton Foundation investigation so that Hillary Clinton would be the Democratic presidential nominee. Their criminal actions, without a doubt, changed the 2016 presidential election results because Bernie Sanders would have been the Democratic nominee if Clinton had been indicted, and because the false Trump/Russia collusion story caused unknown millions of votes to be cast for Clinton instead of Trump.

After Donald Trump won the 2016 presidential election, the conspirators used Sergei Millian's allegations in the Steele dossier as the basis to appoint Robert Mueller as Special Counsel to investigate Trump/Russia collusion. The Mueller investigation continues to greatly harm the country by significantly weakening the elected president and his agenda.

The $100 billion damages requested on behalf of the American people for the great harm the conspirators caused to the United States amounts to only about $300 per person.

Multi-Media Blitz

The strategy should include a multi-media blitz to disseminate the overwhelming factual evidence of the criminal conspiracy to elect Clinton president and harm Donald Trump. In addition to the evidence in this book, much public evidence is available from Michael Horowitz's Inspector General report on the Clinton email investigation, Congressional committee reports, and reports by investigative journalists. The media blitz would include short documentaries on different elements of the conspiracy. Examples of bite sized stories to parcel out are 1) the Carter Page setup, 2) Hillary Clinton and the DNC's Trump/Russia collusion scam, 3) the General Flynn setup, 4) James Comey's felonies, 5) the criminal misconduct to obtain the Page FISA warrant, 6) Glenn Simpson and Fusion GPS.

Appendix

A1. Intelligence Services' Links to London Setups

Christopher Steele, Stefan Halper, Alexander Downer, Sir Andrew Wood, Robert Hannigan, and Sir Richard Dearlove are based in London. They all have relationships with UK intelligence, are pro-Clinton and/or anti-Trump, and played a role in the false Trump/Russia collusion story. A brief background of each is described below.

Christopher Steele

Christopher Steele is a former officer in Britain's Secret Intelligence Service known as MI6. He joined MI6 when he graduated from the University of Cambridge in 1986. MI6 stationed the 26-year-old Steele in Moscow in 1990 as the second secretary in the UK chancery division at the embassy. After two years in Russia, he returned to London where he stayed until 1998, when he took a post in Paris. In 1999 Steele was on a leaked list of MI6 officers, and Russia prohibited him from entering the country. MI6 moved Steele to London's Russia desk in 2006.

Steele left MI6 in 2009 and formed Orbis Business Intelligence Ltd. with Christopher Burrows to provide intelligence and investigative services. Soon after its founding, Orbis began working with Fusion GPS on various projects. As part of this ongoing relationship, Fusion GPS hired Steele in the Spring of 2016 to work on the DNC and Clinton campaign's project. In June 2016, Steele began writing a series of 16 reports totaling 35 pages, known as the "Steele dossier," on Trump's supposed collusion with the Russian government to influence the election. He completed his last report in early November.

Steele began giving his dossier reports to the FBI beginning in late July or early August. Steele told Bruce Ohr, the third highest ranking DOJ official, that he "was desperate that Donald Trump not get elected."

Stefan Halper

Glenn Simpson testified that Steele told him the FBI had a human source in the Trump campaign. The Washington Post described the informant as "a top-secret intelligence source" and "a U.S. citizen who has provided intelligence to the CIA and FBI." The source was Stefan Halper, a Cambridge University professor, and a CIA operative going back to the Nixon administration. While on the Reagan campaign, he allegedly led CIA operatives to steal briefing materials from Jimmy Carter's campaign.

Halper is a professor at Cambridge University and he works with Sir Richard Dearlove, a former chief of MI6, in directing the Cambridge Security Initiative (CSi), a non-profit intelligence consulting group. The private UK intelligence firm, Hakluyt & Company (now called Holdingham) was founded by former officials of MI6. Halper co-wrote a book with Jonathan Clarke, Hakluyt's Director of United States operations.

Halper attended Cambridge with Bill Clinton. Halper told the press that he feared a Trump presidency, as it could harm the "special relationship" between the United States and Great Britain.

Alexander Downer

Alexander Downer was the Australian High Commissioner to the United Kingdom from 2014 to 2018. Downer has close ties to UK intelligence. He was on the advisory board of a private UK intelligence firm, Hakluyt & Company (now called Holdingham), from 2008 to 2014, and attended corporate meetings through 2015. Hakluyt was founded by former officials of MI6. Dearlove is a close friend of a founder, Mike Reynolds. Halper co-wrote a book with Jonathan Clarke, Hakluyt Director of United States operations, and he was a speaker at a seminar with Downer. Downer arranged a $25 million Australian donation to the Clinton Foundation in 2006, jointly signing the Memorandum of Understanding with Bill Clinton.

Sir Andrew Wood

After the election asked Sir Andrew Wood, a former British Ambassador to Moscow, to tell Senator John McCain about the dossier. Wood is an unpaid informal adviser to Orbis. In late November, Wood discussed the dossier with McCain at the Halifax International Security Forum. McCain asked a former aide, David Kramer, to go to England to meet Steele. Steele gave Kramer a copy of the dossier. Kramer provided it to McCain, who gave it to Comey.

Robert Hannigan

The Government Communications Headquarters (GCHQ) is an intelligence and security organization responsible for providing signals intelligence (SIGINT) and information assurance to the government and armed forces of the United Kingdom

European intelligence began in 2015 to look for collusion as described in The Guardian:[cxlvii]

> GCHQ [a UK intelligence agency] first became aware in late 2015 of suspicious "interactions" between figures connected to Trump and known or suspected Russian agents, a source close to UK intelligence said. This

intelligence was passed to the US as part of a routine exchange of information, they added.

Over the next six months, until summer 2016, a number of western agencies shared further information on contacts between Trump's inner circle and Russians, sources said.

The head of GCHQ at the time, Robert Hannigan, came to the U.S. in the summer of 2016 to personally give Brennan highly sensitive information about Trump/Russia collusion. Hannigan should have provided the information to his U.S. counterpart, the NSA director, Mike Rogers, but did not. This begs the question: Was Brennan directing and coordinating the overseas covert operations against the Trump campaign with the British? Hannigan abruptly quit after Donald Trump won the election.

In September 2018, President Trump ordered the DOJ and Office of the Director of National Intelligence to initiate the "immediate declassification" of selective portions of the Foreign Intelligence Surveillance Act application on former Trump foreign policy aide Carter Page. Shortly after the announcement the president delayed the declassification because two foreign allies pleaded with him not to declassify documents related to the Russia investigation. Did the UK request the president not declassify the documents because it would reveal their role in using covert agents based in London to entrap Trump campaign team members?

Did Hannigan or any other British government officials participate in the covert agent operations on Trump campaign members or work with the CIA and/or FBI to spy on American citizens? An affirmative answer would mean that the British government interfered in the 2016 US presidential election to help Hillary Clinton win.

Sir Richard Dearlove

Sir Richard Dearlove was head of the British Secret Intelligence Service (MI6) from 1999 until May 2004. He currently serves as Chair of Board of Trustees of University of London. He previously served as Master of Pembroke College at University of Cambridge from 2004 to 2015.

The FBI informant, Halper, is very good friends with Dearlove. Dearlove and Halper co-direct the Cambridge Security Initiative (CSi), a non-profit intelligence consulting group. Steele and his business partner, Chris Burrows, worked for Dearlove at MI6 as intelligence officers, and they met with Dearlove during the dossier preparation process to discuss it and obtain advice. Halper and Dearlove are also friends of the covert agent, Alexander Downer.

A2. Joseph Mifsud

Joseph Mifsud framed the Trump campaign adviser, George Papadopoulos, to appear as a Russian collaborator. Mifsud is the most important covert agent because his successful trap for George Papadopoulos resulted in the "evidence" that the FBI supposedly used to create the Trump/Russia Collusion investigation.

The media portrays Mifsud as the "shadowy professor" or a Russian spy. The Democrats on the House Permanent Select Committee on Intelligence asserted that "In their approach to Papadopoulos, the Russians used common tradecraft and employed a cutout—a Maltese professor named Joseph Mifsud."

In actuality, Mifsud is well-known in his academic circles, and he is a UK covert agent, not a Russian spy. His link to UK intelligence is not obvious, so the following background is fairly detailed to explain the connection.

Mifsud's Academic and Diplomatic background

Mifsud is a Maltese university academic. He taught at the University of Malta and was a senior lecturer when he left in 2007. Mifsud excels in networking with influential people, collaborating on international projects, and forming educational partnerships. The multi-lingual Mifsud is in high demand to speak and teach throughout the world. Mifsud's history is easily found online and his list of positions and accomplishments is impressive:

He was a member of the world football FIFA Executive Committee

Prior to Malta joining the EU, Mifsud was head of the University of Malta's European Unit, which he established, and was on the EU Socrates Committee for educational programs and on the EU Committee for Higher Education. He significantly increased educational opportunities for Maltese students and upgrades in Maltese schools.

He was a member of the team that negotiated Malta's 2004 accession into the European Union.

He was Malta's representative at UNESCO

Mifsud and associates worked with Vincenzo Scotti, a former Italian Minister, to obtain approval to open a University of Malta branch in Rome. It was the first foreign university authorized to operate in Italy. The name was changed to LINK Campus University. Scotti is the President.

Mifsud was elected the first president of the new Euro-Mediterranean University in Slovenia in 11/26/2008. EMUNI was co-founded by four universities with the objective of becoming an international, post-graduate, higher-education and research institution. Mifsud joined when EMUNI had no students and developed the university until he resigned in July 2012.

He joined the London Academy of Diplomacy of the highly rated University of East Anglia (UEA) in 2012 and became a director in 2013. Mifsud received an honorary professorship from UEA.

Mifsud was a "professorial teaching fellow" at the University of Stirling, one of Scotland's best universities. The University of Stirling announced in July 2017 that their "Professor Joseph Mifsud" worked with other experts in Europe on recommendations for EU and UK Brexit negotiators.

He is a Member of the European Council on Foreign Relations (ECFR)

Mifsud also committed some relatively minor transgressions. He allegedly had $48,550 of ineligible expenses to EMUNI, and $79,000 in a fraud scheme at another university. Mifsud brags about connections and accomplishments that are not true. For example, he boasts of knowing Boris Johnson, Vladimir Putin, and Sergei Lavrov after he attended events that they also attended. His biography falsely states that he was president of the non-existent Comité du Risque, established by the office of the French president, and he falsely claimed he had been an ambassador.

Mifsud purposely led a high-profile career because the better known he was, the more money he made. In a highly competitive market, people hired Mifsud to teach at seminars and universities, hold conferences, speak at events, and consult because of his reputation and his influential contacts. Mifsud also used his acclaim to recruit students for the LAD and LINK. Success begot success for him.

Since 2013 Mifsud was the director of the London Academy of Diplomacy (LAD), originally founded and run by the notable University of East Anglia (UEA). In 2014, UEA decided to close its London campus, so in September 2014 the University of Stirling took over in accrediting its courses. Due to large financial losses, which could be the reason UEA moved its campus out of London, LAD advised its staff in 2015 that it would close in 2016, which it did. The University of Stirling's deputy principal, John Gardner, said the professor had "truly global contacts in the world of diplomacy and is on first name terms with a wide variety of ambassadors from across the globe."

Mifsud and Russia

Despite Mifsud's high profile, the media calls him the "mysterious professor" and they characterize Mifsud as a Russian spy because 1) he has associated with Russians and 2) he told Papadopoulos that the Russians have dirt on Hillary and thousands of her emails. The following explains Mifsud's Russian associations.

The LAD often had foreign visitors from many countries, but the media focused on Mifsud's meetings with Russians visitors. Mifsud entered into collaboration agreements with universities, including Russian universities. For example, he signed a "wide ranging cooperation agreement" with Moscow State University, which included "shared research, student and teacher exchanges" and "a commitment to hold conferences together and to publish joint research." His meetings with a Russian university delegation would sometimes include someone from the Russian embassy.

The distinguished Professor Nabil Ayad of the UEA is the original founder of the LAD and worked with Mifsud there. Regarding Mifsud's connections with Russia, he said "Russia was a place where we had an exchange programme at the Moscow Diplomatic Academy. But I don't think he has reached that level [of influence] unless by chance Putin happened to be at a place he was teaching. There's nothing sinister about him."

Mifsud has been associated with the LINK Campus University in Rome since he helped found it in 1999. He is LINK's Dean of the Bachelor of Arts degree program in political sciences and international relations and is a visiting professor. LINK has 25 partner universities, of which seven are Russian. The three British institutions listed are London Academy of Diplomacy, the University of East Anglia and LSE Enterprise (the "business and consultancy arm" of the London School of Economics).

Mifsud's worldwide travels to speak at academic seminars and conferences included trips to Moscow. Mifsud was invited to attend the annual Russian Valdai Discussion Club that Vladimir Putin hosts. Leading politicians, public figures, and scholars from around the world participate in Valdai. More than 1,000 representatives of the international scholarly community from 63 countries have taken part in the Club's work. They include professors from major world universities and think tanks, including Harvard, Columbia, Georgetown, Stanford, Carleton Universities, the University of London, etc.

Dr. Stephen Roh is a multi-millionaire friend of Mifsud. Roh was a visiting lecturer at LAD and, at Mifsud's suggestion, he bought 5% of Link Campus in 2014. Roh hired Mifsud in 2015 as a business development consultant. Roh and Thierry Pastor co-authored a book titled "The Faking of Russia-gate: The Papadopoulos Case, an Investigative Analysis." Pastor said Mifsud "was supposed to introduce him [Roh] to business figures and officials. Stephan has had an office in Moscow since 2000. He hired Joseph because he wanted to have higher-level contacts. But it turned out Joseph didn't have those contacts in Russia." Pastor and Roh write that far from being a Russian spy, Mifsud "had only one master: the Western Political, Diplomatic and Intelligence World, his only home, of which he is still deeply dependent."

Mifsud and Western Intelligence

Although Mifsud's Russian connections are only academic and diplomatic, he has a strong association with Western intelligence at LAD and LINK. Claire Smith was a member of the UK's Joint Intelligence Committee (JIC), a supervisory body overseeing all UK intelligence agencies. The JIC is part of the Cabinet Office and reports directly to the Prime Minister. She was also an eight-year member of the UK Cabinet Office Security Vetting Appeals Panel, which oversees the vetting process for UK intelligence placement. Smith and Mifsud were involved with an international security training program for high level Italian military officers that was organized by LINK and LAD in 2012. Claire Smith was a visiting professor at LAD from 2013-2014. Charles Crawford, a former MI6 officer, and Robert Whalley, former UK Director for Counter Terrorism and Intelligence at the Home Office and the Cabinet Office, also taught there.

Link Campus is a private university, accredited by Italy's education ministry, with six Italian politicians on its governing body, including two former foreign ministers. One of the university's courses is a MA degree in Intelligence and Security. LINK runs the Consortium for Research on Intelligence and Security Services (CRISS). CRISS is an Italian consortium of Defense and Technology sector companies specializing in the high tech, security and intelligence sectors. CRISS operates in five main areas: Territorial Security, Intelligence, Security Devices, Systems and Infrastructures, Training and Support Systems. LINK also offers anti-drug trafficking studies.

LINK Campus has trained intelligence and police personnel from the West for years. In 2004 the CIA arranged a conference on terrorism there. David Ignatius of the Washington Post wrote about the conference saying "'New Frontiers of Intelligence Analysis' brought together officials from intelligence and police agencies of nearly 30 countries."

The FBI has trained students at Link since 2010. In September 2016, or two months after the FBI opened its Russia investigation, the FBI's legal attaché working out of the U.S. Embassy in Rome sent Special Agent Preston Ackerman to conduct a seminar at Link.

The London Centre of International Law and Practice

The London Centre of International Law and Practice (LCILP) was incorporated in April 2014. It provides legal services, forums, and training in eleven areas of international law expertise. Nagi Idris, LCILP's founding director, was connected to Mifsud in several ways. LCILP's first event after its founding was held at the LAD and Idris is a visiting professor at LINK Campus University in Rome. Mifsud appears to have joined LCILP in November or December 2015 as "board adviser" and the Director of International Strategic Development.

Majed Garoub is a prominent Saudi lawyer whose law firm handles sport for the Saudi Kingdom. Nagi is a consultant at Garoub's law firm. In late 2015, LCILP signed a cooperation agreement with Garoub's Saudi Law Training Centre (STLC) "to collaborate on training programmes, legal events and consultancy."

George Papadopoulos graduated from college in 2009. He spent four years as an unpaid intern and a contact researcher at the Hudson Institute from 2011 to 2015 and worked on Ben Carson's campaign starting in December 2015 for six weeks.

Papadopoulos joined LCILP in February 2016 as the Director of the Centre for International Energy and Natural Resources Law & Security and he left in April 2016. His appointment to that position was ludicrous because he had no qualifications for it. For example, Papadopoulos attended LCILP and STLP's "1st Annual Conference on Energy Arbitration and Dispute Resolution in the Middle East and Africa" held in London from March 7 to 9 in 2016. The International Court of Arbitration announced that it was pleased to be one of 21 prominent global organizations lending their support to LCILP, STLP and their conference. The conference's "Session Chairs" included the former Senior Vice President of the American Arbitration Association, the Editor in Chief of the Arab Bankers Association, and the Former Legal Director & Member of Executive Committee of Royal Dutch Shell Plc.

Papadopoulos was way out of his league at that conference, so obviously LCILP did not hire him as a director for his knowledge or experience.

A photo at an LCILP conference shows with Papadopoulos seated with Garoub. The Saudis and Italians would play an important role in Mifsud's future career so Garoub's early association with Papadopoulos is an important fact.

A3. George Papadopoulos – Timeline

On March 6, 2016, Papadopoulos joined the Trump campaign team as a foreign policy adviser. Carson's campaign manager, Barry Bennett, said that he would not have recommended Papadopoulos to the Trump campaign if he had been asked because he found him unimpressive. Papadopoulos knew that one of the campaign's foreign policy priorities was to improve US relations with Russia.

On March 14, 2016, Papadopoulos travelled to Rome as part of a visiting LCILP delegation of eight people. Mifsud joined them in dining, and Papadopoulos mentioned that he joined the Trump campaign team. Mifsud told Papadopoulos that he had substantial connections with Russian government officials. Papadopoulos thought these Russian connections could increase his importance as a policy advisor to the campaign, so he pursued meeting with Mifsud.

As subsequent events would show, the real reason LCILP hired Papadopoulos in a prestigious position he was not qualified for was to arrange this "chance" meeting with Mifsud without raising suspicion.

On March 24, 2016, Papadopoulos, Mifsud, a lady named Olga Polonskaya (maiden name Olga Vinogradova) and an unknown fourth party met in a London cafe. Mifsud introduced Polonskaya as Putin's niece. Polonskaya is a 30-year-old Russian from St. Petersburg and the former manager of a wine distribution company. Putin has no niece. Mifsud later said in an interview after Papadopoulos was indicted that Polonskaya was "a simple student, very beautiful." Prasenjit Kumar owns the London School of Executive Training (LSET) which had "a partnership" with LAD. Kumar told "The Observer" that he did know Polonskaya and that "She was just a normal student. Very nice. An ordinary girl." Kumar met her at Link Campus University in Rome.

Polonskaya's brother, Sergei Vinogradova, said she was in London discussing a possible internship with Mr. Mifsud, a friend of hers, the morning before the meeting with Mr. Papadopoulos. He insisted that she had no connections to the Russian government and never portrayed herself as Mr. Putin's niece. He said that she only exchanged pleasantries with Papadopoulos. Polonskaya told her brother that she understood only about half of the discussion "Because my English was bad."

Mifsud introduced Polonskaya/Vinogradova to Papadopoulos as someone with high-profile ties to the Russian government, which was then seeking better relations with the U.S. and an end to western economic sanctions imposed over Russian aggression in Ukraine. One Papadopoulos email to Trump campaign officials said that the woman had offered "to arrange a meeting between us and the Russian leadership to discuss U.S.-Russia ties under President Trump."

After Papadopoulos asked for help arranging a trip to Moscow, Polonskaya/Vinogradova said in an April email "I have already alerted my personal links to our conversation and your request." "As mentioned we are all very excited by the possibility of a good relationship with Mr. Trump. The Russian Federation would love to welcome him once his candidature would be officially announced," she added.

Polonskaya's email was clearly written by someone with excellent English. For example, the proper use of the word "candidature" is too sophisticated for a non-native speaker without an excellent command of English.

Papadopoulos continued corresponding with Vinogradova throughout the spring of 2016, including multiple efforts to arrange a meeting in Russia between the Trump campaign and government connections Vinogradova purported to have.

On April 18, 2016, Mifsud introduced Papadopoulos by email to Dr. Ivan Timofeev, a Russian scholar, who Mifsud said had connections to the Russian Ministry of Foreign Affairs.

Timofeev is the Director of Programs at the Russian International Affairs Council (RIAC), a Russian non-profit academic and diplomatic think tank. Timofeev is responsible for its intellectual performance. The RIAC's defined mission is "organizing greater cooperation between Russian scientific institutions and foreign analytical centers/scholars on the major issues of international relations." Dr. Timofeev is an author and co-author of more than 80 publications, issued in Russian and foreign academic press.

Mifsud made the email introduction one day before he appeared on a panel with Timofeev and Dr. Roh at the Valdai Discussion Club in Russia. Over the next several weeks, Papadopoulos and Timofeev had multiple conversations over Skype and email about setting "the groundwork" for a "potential" meeting between the Campaign and Russian government official.

Between March and September 2016, Papadopoulos made at least six requests to campaign officials for Trump or representatives of his campaign to meet in Russia with Russian politicians. In May, campaign chairman Paul Manafort forwarded one such request to his deputy Rick Gates, saying "We need someone to communicate that [Trump] is not doing these trips."

On April 26, 2016, Mifsud told Papadopoulos at a breakfast meeting that high-level Russian government officials said "They [the Russians] have dirt on her;" "the Russians had emails of Clinton;" "they have thousands of emails."

Papadopoulos later said he believes that the emails in question were the 30,000-plus emails that Clinton deleted before turning her State Department emails over to the agency.

On May 10, 2016, Papadopoulos met Alexander Downer at a London bar. Downer requested the meeting. Some accounts say that Papadopoulos told Downer the Russians have dirt on Clinton in the form of emails, but Downer disputes that. Downer stated in an Australian interview "He [Papadopoulos] didn't say dirt, he said material that could be damaging to her. He didn't say what it was." Downer noted "Nothing he said in that conversation indicated Trump himself had been conspiring with the Russians to collect information on Hillary Clinton."

Footnote 5 of Rep. Adam Schiff's memorandum responding to Devin Nunes on Foreign Intelligence Surveillance Act abuse verifies that the FBI only knew that the Russians had damaging information on Clinton, as Downer had said, but nothing about emails. Margot Cleveland says "Papadopoulos merely stated that 'Russians might use material that they have on Hillary Clinton in the lead-up to the election, which may be damaging.' That statement cannot possibly justify opening a counterintelligence investigation on a presidential campaign. Half the world expected that at the time."[cxlviii]

In the same interview, Downer said he officially reported the Papadopoulos meeting back to Australia "the following day or a day or two after," as it "seemed quite interesting." The story nonchalantly notes that "after a period of time, Australia's ambassador to the US, Joe Hockey, passed the information on to Washington."

Kimberly Strassel of the Wall Street Journal, said "A diplomatic source tells me Mr. Hockey neither transmitted any information to the FBI nor was approached by the U.S. about the tip. Rather, it was Mr. Downer who at some point decided to convey his information—to the U.S. Embassy in London."[cxlix] As required by the Five Eyes Agreement with the US, Downer should have reported it to Australian intelligence and they would have communicated the information to US intelligence. Instead, the information was provided to the embassy's then-chargé d'affaires, Elizabeth Dibble, who previously served as a principal deputy assistant secretary in Mrs. Clinton's State Department.

Strassel asks "When did all this happen, and what came next? Did the info go straight to U.S. intelligence? Or did it instead filter to the wider State Department team, who we already know were helping foment Russia-Trump conspiracy theories? Jonathan Winer, a former deputy assistant secretary of state, has publicly admitted to communicating in the summer of 2016 with his friend Christopher Steele, author of the infamous dossier."[cl]

On July 22, 2016, WikiLeaks began publishing the DNC emails.

On July 22, 2016, Sergei Millian, who was not associated with the Trump campaign in any way, made an unsolicited contact with Papadopoulos and requested a meeting. They met several times during the 2016 election campaign. In a setup attempt, Millian proposed that he and Papadopoulos "form an energy-related business that would be financed by influential Russian billionaires." Although Papadopoulos declined, Millian and he became friends.[cli]

On July 31, 2016, Peter Strzok, the FBI's deputy chief of counterintelligence at the time, opened and oversaw the Russia probe. Devin Nunes said no foreign intelligence was used to open the investigation. Downer certainly did not have any useable foreign intelligence. The Downer information was simply that the supposed Russian spy, Mifsud, told Papadopoulos that he could assist with a meeting between the Trump campaign and Russian officials, and that Russia might use damaging material on Hillary Clinton prior to the election. No meeting between Russia and the Trump campaign ever occurred, and there was nothing illegal about Papadopoulos learning the Russians had damaging information on Clinton. Strzok initiated the Russia probe without a valid predicate, which is a violation of DOJ/FBI regulations.

On August 2, 2016, Strzok travelled to London to interview Downer at the Australian embassy.

On August 29, 2016, Stefan Halper sent Sam Clovis, the Trump campaign's national co-chairman, an email stating that he was a professor at Cambridge University, had met Carter Page at a Cambridge conference, and suggested that he and Clovis meet. When they met several days later, Halper offered to help the campaign by sharing research on foreign policy. Clovis later told a reporter "This is just my speculation — I have no knowledge. I think [Halper] was using his meeting with me to give him bona fides to talk to George Papadopoulos. He used Carter Page to get to me and he used me to get to George. George was the target. I think George was the target all along."

In a September 2, 2016 email, Stefan Halper offered Papadopoulos $3,000 to write a policy paper on issues related to Turkey, Cyprus, Israel and the Leviathan natural gas field. Halper also offered to pay for Papadopoulos's flight and a three-night stay in London. Papadopoulos accepted the proposal, flew to England, and met with Halper. He delivered the paper electronically Oct. 2 and received payment.

While in London, Papadopoulos had dinner multiple times with Halper and a Turkish woman described as his assistant. Sources familiar with Papadopoulos's version of their meetings said Halper randomly asked Papadopoulos whether he knew about Democratic National Committee emails that had been hacked and leaked by Russians. Papadopoulos strongly denied the allegation. Halper grew agitated and pressed Papadopoulos on the topic.

Halper's assistant, who is named Azra Turk, brought up Russians and emails over drinks with Papadopoulos. Turk also flirted heavily with Papadopoulos and attempted to meet him in Chicago, where he lived.

In September 2016, At Millian's request, Papadopoulos tried unsuccessfully to schedule a meeting with Millian and Boris Epshteyn, a Trump campaign advisor. A Steele intermediary probably paid Millian to schedule this meeting. Millian was not a member of the Trump campaign team, so he had no reason to meet with Epshteyn, who is a successful political strategist, investment banker, and attorney. Epshteyn is a Russian-American, who was born in Moscow. Steele's dossier refers to one source as an ethnic Russian associate of Trump. Simpson and Steele likely wanted Millian to meet with Epshteyn to set him up in a manner similar to the Donald Trump Jr. setup meeting with Russians offering dirt on Clinton.

After November 8, 2016, After Donald Trump won the election, Millian offered Papadopoulos $30,000 per month "while he worked inside the Trump administration." Millian did not have the financial resources or connections to do this, so Steele obviously had his intermediaries pay Millian to make these entrapment offers. Papadopoulos told associates he felt such a relationship would have been illegal, and turned it down.

A4. Mifsud's Reward?

Mifsud told his staff in 2015 that the LAD would close in 2016 because of financial losses. This was very bad news for Mifsud's career because LAD was not only his main income stream, but also his reputation as the director of the prestigious LAD spawned influential contacts and income-producing requests to teach at seminars and universities, hold conferences, speak at events, and consult.

After his covert Papadopoulos entrapment operation, however, Mifsud's career blossomed. Influential people in Saudi Arabia and Italy were behind his rapidly rising career trajectory.

Mifsud's two significant Saudi connections are Nawaf Obaid and Majed Garoub:

- Nawaf Obaid was a "visiting fellow" at the LAD. He is a counselor to both Prince Mohammad bin Nawaf, Saudi ambassador to the United Kingdom, and Prince Turki Al Faisal, and he is an adjunct fellow at the King Faisal CSIS headed by Turki al-Faisal. Obaid is the CEO of the Essam and Dalal Obaid Foundation (EDOF). Turki al-Faisal ran the Saudi foreign intelligence service for almost a quarter of a century, from 1977 until 2001. Turki al-Faisal has been a friend of Bill Clinton since their college days at Georgetown University and a very large donor to the Clinton Foundation.
- Majed Garoub signed the cooperation agreement with LCILP, at around the same time that Mifsud joined LCILP.

Mifsud's two significant Italian connections are Vincenzo Scotti and Gianni Pittelli:

- Vincenzo Scotti, a former Italian Minister, worked with Mifsud to obtain approval to open a University of Malta branch in Rome. It was the first foreign university authorized to operate in Italy. The name was changed to LINK Campus University. Scotti is the President.
- Gianni Pittella is a very influential Italian Member of the European Parliament (MEP) because he leads the second-largest power block of politicians. He was a Visiting Professor of the LAD, helping to develop programs there, and a close friend of Mifsud's, even bringing Mifsud campaigning with him. Pittella is on a LINK steering committee with Scotti. Pittella, who called Donald Trump a 'virus,' said "I have taken the unprecedented step of endorsing and campaigning for Hillary Clinton because the risk of Donald Trump is too high." He spoke at the 2016 Democratic National Convention in Philadelphia. Pittella told Time magazine. "I believe it is in the interest of the European Union and Italy to have Hillary Clinton in office. A Trump victory could be a disaster for the relationship between the U.S.A. and Italy."

Following is a summary of Mifsud's rapid career rise after his entrapment of Papadopoulos and his disappearance:

On December 17, 2016, the King Faisal Center for Research and Islamic Studies held discussions in Riyadh with a delegation of top European academics and experts on foreign affairs Academics discuss ways to promote Saudi-European cooperation. Prince Turki Al Faisal is the chairman of the center and was at the discussion. Many distinguished people attended including the former Swedish prime minister; the former assistant to US Secretary of State Hillary Clinton; former Finnish prime minister; several members of the European Parliament; members of the European Council on Foreign Relations; and a number of ambassadors. Mifsud was a participant and his erstwhile director position of the then defunct LAD is clearly not in the same class as the very distinguished participants.

On December 27, 2016, the first annual Middle East Law Conference was held in Marrakesh, Morocco. Garoub of SLTC and Idris of LCILP organized the conference that was attended by 10 Arab justice ministers, 15 heads or members of supreme courts, plus judges, prosecutors and arbitrators. Mifsud was a speaker at the conference.

On January 27, 2017, the FBI interviewed Papadopoulos. Strzok interviewed Downer on August 3rd, immediately after the initiation of the Russia probe and found out about Papadopoulos's communications with Mifsud. Why did the FBI wait six months to interview Papadopoulos, and why did Strzok text Page in May 17, 2017 regarding his hesitation to join Mueller's team "You and I both know the odds are nothing. If I thought it was likely, I'd be there no question. I hesitate in part because of my gut sense and concern there's no big there there."?

Between February 8 to 12, 2017, the FBI interviewed Mifsud in Washington, D.C. Mifsud was in Washington to speak at the large annual conference for Global Ties U.S., an organization that has been a partner of the U.S. State Department for over 50 years. Several State Department officials also spoke at the conference. The FBI had Downer's information about Mifsud since July, and this information was used as the predicate to initiate the Russia probe. This begs the question: why didn't the FBI arrest Mifsud as a Russia spy seeking to influence the election?

On May 8, 2017, LINK Campus University and the Essam & Dalal Obaid Foundation (EDOF) signed a partnership agreement to establish the EDOF Centre for War and Peace Studies at LINK. The announcement stated that the "EDOF Centre will work closely with the various interdisciplinary academic departments at the Link Campus University as well as with international governments and organizations in order to support experts, academics, researchers, diplomats, governments, and civil society activists in their attempts to help countries in conflict, crisis and transition around the world." It said that Professor Joseph Mifsud will be appointed the Founding Director of the Centre for a period of three years. Mifsud was not qualified for the position. He received his PhD at Queen's University in Belfast in 1995, and his doctoral thesis was on educational reform. His work experience is unrelated to the Centre's mission.

On May 21, 2017, the Riyadh Forum on Countering Extremism and Fighting Terrorism took place in Saudi Arabia. Prince Turki Al Faisal's King Faisal Center for Research and Islamic Studies organized the conference. Mifsud chaired a panel on "The Terror/Crime Nexus." He has no expertise on this subject. Two of the distinguished speakers on his panel were Michael Hurley, a former CIA officer, the Senior Counsel on 9/11 Commission and director of the Commission's Counterterrorism Policy; and Katherine Bauer of the Washington Institute thinktank and a former adviser on Iran for the US Treasury. Many very distinguished people attended the conference such as Ashton Carter, the former US Secretary of Defense, and Richard Barrett, the former MI6 Head of Global Counter Terrorism Operations. Two things stand out about Mifsud's participation: 1) he was extremely unqualified, and 2) he could not conceivably be a Russian spy and attend this conference with so many high-level intelligence officials from around the world.

On July 27, 2017, Papadopoulos was arrested upon his arrival at Dulles International Airport.

On October 5, 2017, the Saudi King Salman visited Russia - the first ever state visit by a Saudi monarch. Mifsud was part of the Saudi delegation of more than 100 people. Mifsud participated in a seminar organized by Turki Al Faisal's Center for Research and Islamic Studies. The seminar focused on security challenges in the Gulf and the prospects for political resolution of the situation in Yemen.

On the same date, Papadopoulos pled guilty to lying to the FBI.

On October 19, 2017, Mifsud attended a Conservative party fundraising dinner where he was photographed next to Boris Johnson, the British foreign secretary, the most senior intelligence official responsible for running MI6, the UK's foreign intelligence service, and Government Communications Headquarters (GCHQ), the UK's signals intelligence and security organization. Prior to the dinner, Mifsud boasted he would be "meeting Boris Johnson for dinner re Brexit." Alok Sharma, a Conservative Member of Parliament, gave a public lecture at the LAD in 2015. Sharma admitted to have "briefly greeted" Mifsud at the fundraising dinner.

On October 30, 2017, Mueller's court documents were unsealed and news media reported that "George Papadopoulos Pleads Guilty in Russia's Mueller Probe." The plea agreement referenced a "professor living in London," who the Washington Post identified as Joseph Mifsud. Mifsud told the Washington Post that he had "absolutely no contact" with the Russian government.

November 1, 2017, Mifsud gives an interview to the Italian paper "Repubblica:"

> *"Joseph Mifsud is the Maltese professor who, according to the rumors and anticipations of the Russiagate investigation, has approached George Papadopoulos, an aide of Donald Trump during his presidential campaign, to help him to contact Russian authorities in the Kremlin, even for organizing a meeting between Trump and Putin. Mr. Mifsud is said to have given to the aide "dirty information" on Mrs. Clinton collected by the Russian. "This is nonsense", Mifsud comments, "friendship is friendship but Papadopoulos doesn't tell the truth. The only*

thing I did was to facilitate contacts between official and unofficial sources to resolve a crisis. It is usual business everywhere. I put think tanks in contact, groups of experts with other groups of experts", he states.

"I am a member of the European Council on Foreign relations", he adds, *"and you know which is the only foundation I am member of? The Clinton Foundation. Between you and me, my thinking is left-leaning."*

Ok. But what about the emails stolen from Mrs. Clinton? "The dirty job" offered to Papadopoulos? "I don't know. I strongly deny any discussion of mine about secrets concerning Hillary Clinton. I swear it on my daughter. I don't know anyone belonging to the Russian government: the only Russian I know is Ivan Timofeev, director of the think tank "Russian International affairs council." Which is based at The Ministry of Foreign Affairs of the Russian Federation. "But this is meaningless," Mifsud says.

Mifsud underlines that he and Papadopoulos met three or four times overall.

The same day, his friend, Gianni Pittella, also is interviewed by "Repubblica" saying *"Joseph is a dear friend of mine I cannot believe he is involved [with Russiagate]"*

November 10, 2017, CNN reported that "Mifsud has gone to ground. Last Thursday he disappeared from the private university in Rome where he teaches. Repeated attempts to reach him since have been unsuccessful.

January 2018, Stephan Roh and Thierry Pastor interviewed Mifsud. They wrote in a book that: *"Mifsud denied saying anything about Clinton emails to Papadopoulos. Mifsud stated "vehemently that he never told anything like this to George Papadopoulos." Mifsud asked rhetorically: "From where should I have this [information]?"*

Roh and Pastor wrote that Vincenzo Scotti, the president of LINK, told Mifsud to go into hiding. Roh said "I don't know who was hiding him, but I'm sure it was organized by someone. And I am sure it will be difficult to get to the bottom of it."

September 2018, In April 2018, the DNC filed a lawsuit against more than a dozen defendants, including Russia, WikiLeaks and the Trump campaign. In a September filing, the DNC said that "Mifsud is missing and may be deceased." A spokeswoman said "The DNC's counsel has attempted to serve Mifsud for months and has been unable to locate or contact him."

Stephan Roh, a close friend and adviser of Mifsud's, calls the allegation "nonsense." "I'm in a better mood today. I got it from really good sources. They say that he is alive, that he has another identity, and that he is staying somewhere, at a nice place," Stephan Roh told The Daily Caller News Foundation.[clii]

After the Papadopoulos entrapment, Mifsud was given a highly prestigious position at LINK Campus, an Italian university involved in training western law enforcement, intelligence services and the military. Vincenzo Scotti, a former Italian minster, told Mifsud to go into hiding when his name was revealed after Mueller's indictment of Papadopoulos. Mifsud no longer receives an income from his LINK Campus University job or from his frequent conference speaker engagements. Mifsud was a very successful and well-known academic. Why would Mifsud give up everything he worked so hard for when Scotti told him to go into hiding after the media discovered he was linked to Papadopoulos in the Mueller indictment. The only plausible answer is that Mifsud was a covert agent trying to entrap Papadopoulos and a government(s) quickly gave him a new identity, a nice place to live, and an income in order to hide its involvement with Mifsud and the intelligence operation to influence the 2016 US presidential election to help Clinton win. Which government(s)? One must wonder if former Italian Minister, Vincenzo Scotti's call for Mifsud to go undercover or

Saudi Arabia's sudden interest to help Mifsud's career provides any clues?

A4. Examples of Interview Topics for Gina Haspel

- Steele Dossier
- Christopher Steele meeting with FBI agent Gaetz from US embassy in Rome
- Covert agents used by the US or the UK to spy on the Trump campaign. For example, Stefan Halper, Azra Turk, Joseph Mifsud, others?
- Communications with John Brennan regarding spying and acquiring intelligence on the Trump campaign.
- The information that Robert Hannigan, then head of the UK's GCHQ, gave to John Brennan, and the "eyes only" information that Brennan disclosed to Comey, Clapper, and Lynch.
- Was George Papadopoulos a covert agent?
- Joseph Mifsud's meetings with George Papadopoulos
- London Centre of International Law Practice: Joseph Mifsud, Majed Garoub, George Papadopoulos, Nagi Idris
- Andrew Wood and Christopher Steele connection
- Alexander Downer meeting with Papadopoulos
- LINK Campus University in Rome: What were the interrelationships between Joseph Mifsud, Gianni Pittella, Vincenzo Scotti, Saudi officials, intelligence agencies, military, law enforcement and the university?
- Were any current or former British intelligence people involved in the Steele dossier or surveilling Trump campaign members? For example, Hakluyt associates such as Jonathan Clarke and Mike Reynolds, Sir Richard Dearlove, Chris Burrows, Robert Hannigan?

Endnotes

i McCarthy, Andrew C. "Rod Rosenstein's Resistance." Nationalreview.com. https://www.nationalreview.com/2018/09/rod-rosenstein-resistance-president-trump/ (September 23, 2018).

ii Office of the Inspector General, U.S. Department of Justice. "A Review of Various Actions by the Federal Bureau of Investigation and Department of Justice in Advance of the 2016 Election." Justice.gov. https://www.justice.gov/file/1071991/download (June 14, 2018).

iii Harding, Luke. "What we know – and what's true – about the Trump-Russia dossier." Theguardian.com. https://www.theguardian.com/us-news/2017/jan/11/trump-russia-dossier-explainer-details (January 11, 2017).

iv Solomon, John. "Collusion bombshell: DNC lawyers met with FBI on Russia allegations before surveillance warrant." Thehill.com. https://thehill.com/hilltv/rising/409817-russia-collusion-bombshell-dnc-lawyers-met-with-fbi-on-dossier-before (10/3/2018).

v Office of the Inspector General, U.S. Department of Justice. "DOJ OIG Announces Initiation of Review." Justice.gov. https://oig.justice.gov/press/2017/2017-01-12.pdf (January 12, 2017).

vi Circa. "The face of FBI politics: Bureau boss McCabe under Hatch Act investigation." Circa.com. https://www.circa.com/story/2017/06/27/the-face-of-fbi-

politics-bureau-boss-mccabe-under-hatch-act-investigation
(June 27, 2017).

vii Circa. "The face of FBI politics: Bureau boss McCabe
under Hatch Act investigation." Circa.com.
https://www.circa.com/story/2017/06/27/the-face-of-fbi-
politics-bureau-boss-mccabe-under-hatch-act-investigation
(June 27, 2017).

viii Circa. "The face of FBI politics: Bureau boss McCabe
under Hatch Act investigation." Circa.com.
https://www.circa.com/story/2017/06/27/the-face-of-fbi-
politics-bureau-boss-mccabe-under-hatch-act-investigation
(June 27, 2017).

ix Herridge, Catherine, and Pamela K. Browne. "FBI No. 2
did not disclose wife's ties to Clinton ally, records show."
Foxnews.com.
http://www.foxnews.com/politics/2017/03/15/fbi-official-did-
not-disclose-wifes-ties-to-clinton-ally-records-show.html
(March 15, 2017).

x Circa. "The face of FBI politics: Bureau boss McCabe
under Hatch Act investigation." Circa.com.
https://www.circa.com/story/2017/06/27/the-face-of-fbi-
politics-bureau-boss-mccabe-under-hatch-act-investigation
(June 27, 2017).

xi McCarthy, Andrew C. "The Clinton E-mails Are Critical to
the Clinton Foundation Investigation." Nationalreview.com.
http://www.nationalreview.com/article/441675/clinton-
foundation-fbi-investigation-loretta-lynch-obstruction
(November 1, 2016).

[xii] McCarthy, Andrew C. "The FBI's Defense of How the Clinton Interview Was Conducted Is Full of Holes." Nationalreview.com. http://www.nationalreview.com/article/440624/james-comey-testimony-fbi-defense-clinton-interview-doesnt-add (October 1, 2016).

[xiii] McCarthy, Andrew C. "Immunity for Witness in Hillary E-Mails Caper — So Is There a Grand Jury?." Nationalreview.com. http://www.nationalreview.com/article/432301/hillary-clinton-grand-jury-ijnvestigation-probably (March 3, 2016).

[xivxiv] McCarthy, Andrew C. "Why Hillary Clinton's E-Mail Scandal 'Lawyers' Are So Problematic." Nationalreview.com. http://www.nationalreview.com/article/440853/hillary-clintons-email-lawyers-cheryl-mills-heather-samuelsons-problematic?target=topic&tid=4571 (October 8, 2016).

[xv] McCarthy, Andrew C. "The FBI's Defense of How the Clinton Interview Was Conducted Is Full of Holes." Nationalreview.com. http://www.nationalreview.com/article/440624/james-comey-testimony-fbi-defense-clinton-interview-doesnt-add?target=topic&tid=4571 (October 1, 2016).

[xvi] Coffin, Shannen W. "The Curious Case of Cheryl Mills." Weeklystandard.com. http://www.weeklystandard.com/the-curious-case-of-cheryl-mills/article/2004156 (September 3, 2016).

[xvii] Ibid

[xviii] Ibid

xix McCarthy, Andrew C. "Why Hillary Clinton's E-Mail Scandal 'Lawyers' Are So Problematic." Nationalreview.com. http://www.nationalreview.com/article/440853/hillary-clintons-email-lawyers-cheryl-mills-heather-samuelsons-problematic?target=topic&tid=4571 (Date: October 8, 2016).

xx McCarthy, Andrew C. "Please Tell Me These FBI/DOJ 'Side Deals' with Clinton E-Mail Suspects Didn't Happen." Nationalreview.com. http://www.nationalreview.com/article/440697/hillary-clinton-email-scandal-side-deals-fbi-department-justice-politicized (October 4, 2016).

xxi Podesta, John. "Re: Fwd: Shelly." Wikileaks.org. https://wikileaks.org/podesta-emails/emailid/57309 (March 3, 2015).

xxii Zapotosky, Matt. "House Oversight Chair Asks for New Investigation of Deleted Clinton Emails." Washingtonpost.com. https://www.washingtonpost.com/world/national-security/house-oversight-chair-asks-for-new-investigation-of-deleted-clinton-emails/2016/09/06/357c5052-7445-11e6-8149-b8d05321db62_story.html?utm_term=.a3b581295a81 (September 6, 2016).

xxiii Watson, Kathryn. "DOJ Let Clinton Aides' Lawyer Limit FBI's Investigation." Dailycaller.com. http://dailycaller.com/2016/10/05/doj-let-clinton-aides-lawyer-limit-fbis-investigation/ (October 5, 2016).

xxiv McCarthy, Andrew C. "Please Tell Me These FBI/DOJ 'Side Deals' with Clinton E-Mail Suspects Didn't Happen." Nationalreview.com. http://www.nationalreview.com/article/440697/hillary-clinton-email-scandal-side-deals-fbi-department-justice-politicized (October 4, 2016).

xxv Ibid

xxvi Napolitano, Andrew. "Judge Nap: 'Inexplicable' That Clinton Staffers Were Granted Immunity by DOJ." Foxnews.com. http://insider.foxnews.com/2016/09/12/judge-napolitano-hillary-clinton-email-investigation-staffers-getting-immunity (September 12, 2016).

xxvii McCarthy, Andrew C. "Revealed: Eleventh-hour Subpoenas in the Clinton E-mails Investigation." Nationalreview.com. http://www.nationalreview.com/article/447209/hillary-clinton-e-mail-investigation-grand-jury-subpoenas (April 29, 2017).

xxviii Re, Gregg. "State Department provided 'clearly false' statements to derail requests for Clinton docs, 'shocked' federal judge says." Foxnews.com. https://www.foxnews.com/politics/state-department-provided-clearly-false-statements-to-derail-hillary-clinton-doc-requests-federal-judge-says (October 17, 2018).

xxix McCarthy, Andrew C. "Clinton Transmitted Classified Information to Her Lawyers." Nationalreview.com. http://www.nationalreview.com/article/441453/hillary-clintons-emails-lawyers-without-security-clearance-got-classified-information?target=topic&tid=4571 (October 26, 2016).

xxx McCarthy, Andrew C. "The FBI's Defense of How the Clinton Interview Was Conducted Is Full of Holes." Nationalreview.com. http://www.nationalreview.com/article/440624/james-comey-testimony-fbi-defense-clinton-interview-doesnt-add (October 1, 2016).

xxxi Office of the Inspector General, U.S. Department of Justice. "A Review of Various Actions by the Federal Bureau of Investigation and Department of Justice in Advance of the 2016 Election." Justice.gov. https://www.justice.gov/file/1071991/download (June 14, 2018).

xxxii Ibid.

xxxiii McCarthy, Andrew C. "Clinton–Obama Emails: The Key to Understanding Why Hillary Wasn't Indicted." Nationalreview.com. https://www.nationalreview.com/2018/01/hillary-clinton-barack-obama-emails-key-decision-not-indict-hillary/ (January 23, 2018).

xxxiv Ernst, Douglas. "Loretta Lynch's email alias as Obama's AG revealed: 'Elizabeth Carlisle'." Washingtontimes.com. http://www.washingtontimes.com/news/2017/aug/7/loretta-lynchs-used-elizabethe-carlisle-email-alia/ (August 7, 2017).

xxxv Office of the Inspector General, U.S. Department of Justice. "A Review of Various Actions by the Federal Bureau of Investigation and Department of Justice in Advance of the 2016 Election." Justice.gov. https://www.justice.gov/file/1071991/download (June 14, 2018).

xxxvi Watson, Kathryn. "DOJ Let Clinton Aides' Lawyer Limit FBI's Investigation." Dailycaller.com.

http://dailycaller.com/2016/10/05/doj-let-clinton-aides-lawyer-limit-fbis-investigation/ (October 5, 2016).

xxxvii Westwood, Sarah. "Issa: Clinton aides had immunity from destruction of evidence." Washingtonexaminer.com http://www.washingtonexaminer.com/issa-clinton-aides-had-immunity-from-destruction-of-evidence/article/2603077 (September 28, 2016).

xxxviii McCarthy, Andrew C. "Why Hillary Clinton's E-Mail Scandal 'Lawyers' Are So Problematic." Nationalreview.com. http://www.nationalreview.com/article/440853/hillary-clintons-email-lawyers-cheryl-mills-heather-samuelsons-problematic?target=topic&tid=4571 (Date: October 8, 2016).

xxxix McCarthy, Andrew C. "Clinton Transmitted Classified Information to Her Lawyers." Nationalreview.com. http://www.nationalreview.com/article/441453/hillary-clinton-email-classified-information-lawyers-security-clearance?target=topic&tid=4571 (October 26, 2016).

xl Coffin, Shannen W. "Did Hillary Commit a Felony?." Nationalreview.com. http://www.nationalreview.com/article/414835/did-hillary-commit-felony-shannen-coffin (March 4, 2015).

xli McCarthy, Andrew C. "The FBI's Defense of How the Clinton Interview Was Conducted Is Full of Holes." Nationalreview.com. http://www.nationalreview.com/article/440624/james-comey-testimony-fbi-defense-clinton-interview-doesnt-add (October 1, 2016).

xlii McCarthy, Andrew C. "The Democrats' Likely Nominee Appears to Be a Felon — This Is Not Business as Usual."

Nationalreview.com.
http://www.nationalreview.com/article/431254/hillary-clintons-e-mail-felony-violations-arent-stopping-her-running
(February 13, 2016).

[xliii] Coffin, Shannen W. "FBI Director Comey Is Wrong: The Case for Prosecuting Hillary Clinton Is Strong." Nationalreview.com.
http://www.nationalreview.com/article/437493/hillary-clinton-email-scandal-fbi-director-comey-built-strong-case-decided-against (July 5, 2016)

[xliv] McCarthy, Andrew C. "FBI Director Comey Is Wrong: The Case for Prosecuting Hillary Clinton Is Strong." Nationalreview.com.
http://www.nationalreview.com/article/437493/hillary-clinton-email-scandal-fbi-director-comey-built-strong-case-decided-against (July 5, 2016)

[xlv] Babbin, Jed. "Ratting Out Hillary." Spectator.org.
https://spectator.org/65703_ratting-out-hillary/ (March 7, 2016).

[xlvi] McCarthy, Andrew C. "The Clinton E-mails Are Critical to the Clinton Foundation Investigation." Nationalreview.com.
http://www.nationalreview.com/article/441675/clinton-foundation-fbi-investigation-loretta-lynch-obstruction (November 1, 2016).

[xlvii] McCarthy, Andrew C. "FBI Director Comey Is Wrong: The Case for Prosecuting Hillary Clinton Is Strong." Nationalreview.com.
http://www.nationalreview.com/article/437493/hillary-clinton-email-scandal-fbi-director-comey-built-strong-case-decided-against (July 5, 2016). 317

xlviii Sperry, Paul. "Despite Comey Assurances, Vast Bulk of Weiner Laptop Emails Were Never Examined." Realclearinvestigations.com. https://www.realclearinvestigations.com/articles/2018/08/22/despite_comey_assurance_vast_bulk_of_weiner_laptop_emails_never_examined.html (August 23, 2018).

xlix Powell, Sidney. "The FBI Deliberately Ignored 'Golden Emails,' Crucial Abedin Messages, and More." Dailycaller.com. http://dailycaller.com/2018/06/22/fbi-ignored-golden-emails-and-abedin-messages/ (June 22, 2018).

l Office of the Inspector General, U.S. Department of Justice. "A Review of Various Actions by the Federal Bureau of Investigation and Department of Justice in Advance of the 2016 Election." Justice.gov. https://www.justice.gov/file/1071991/download (June 14, 2018).

li Sperry, Paul. "Despite Comey Assurances, Vast Bulk of Weiner Laptop Emails Were Never Examined." Realclearinvestigations.com. https://www.realclearinvestigations.com/articles/2018/08/22/despite_comey_assurance_vast_bulk_of_weiner_laptop_emails_never_examined.html (August 23, 2018).

lii Weber, Peter. "4 things James Comey revealed about Hillary Clinton's email investigation." Theweek.com. http://theweek.com/articles/767677/4-things-james-comey-revealed-about-hillary-clintons-email-investigation (April 16, 2018).

liii ABC News. "Transcript: James Comey's interview with ABC News chief anchor George Stephanopoulos."

Abcnews.com. https://abcnews.go.com/Site/transcript-james-comeys-interview-abc-news-chief-anchor/story?id=54488723 (April 15, 2018).

[liv] Powell, Sidney. "The FBI Deliberately Ignored 'Golden Emails,' Crucial Abedin Messages, and More." Dailycaller.com. http://dailycaller.com/2018/06/22/fbi-ignored-golden-emails-and-abedin-messages/ (June 22, 2018).

[lv] Sperry, Paul. "Despite Comey Assurances, Vast Bulk of Weiner Laptop Emails Were Never Examined." Realclearinvestigations.com. https://www.realclearinvestigations.com/articles/2018/08/22/despite_comey_assurance_vast_bulk_of_weiner_laptop_emails_never_examined.html (August 23, 2018).

[lvi] Ibid.

[lvii] Ibid

[lviii] Powell, Sidney. "The FBI Deliberately Ignored 'Golden Emails,' Crucial Abedin Messages, and More." Dailycaller.com. http://dailycaller.com/2018/06/22/fbi-ignored-golden-emails-and-abedin-messages/ (June 22, 2018).

[lix] Barrett, Devlin. "FBI in Internal Feud Over Hillary Clinton Probe." Wsj.com. https://www.wsj.com/articles/laptop-may-include-thousands-of-emails-linked-to-hillary-clintons-private-server-1477854957 (October 30, 2016).

[lx] Barrett, Devlin. "FBI in Internal Feud Over Hillary Clinton Probe." Wsj.com. https://www.wsj.com/articles/laptop-may-include-thousands-

of-emails-linked-to-hillary-clintons-private-server-1477854957 (October 30, 2016).

lxi McCarthy, Andrew C. "The Clinton E-mails Are Critical to the Clinton Foundation Investigation." Nationalreview.com. https://www.nationalreview.com/2016/11/clinton-foundation-fbi-investigation-loretta-lynch-obstruction/ (November 2, 2016).

lxii McCarthy, Andrew C. "McCabe: Leaking and Lying Obscure the Real Collusion." Nationalreview.com. https://www.nationalreview.com/2018/04/andrew-mccabe-collusion-obama-justice-department-clinton-campaign/ (April 21, 2018).

lxiii McCarthy, Andrew C. "Spinning a Crossfire Hurricane: The Times on the FBI's Trump Investigation." Nationalreview.com. https://www.nationalreview.com/2018/05/crossfire-hurricane-new-york-times-report-buries-lede/ (May 17, 2018).

lxiv Harding, Luke, Stephanie Kirchgaessner and Nick Hopkins. "British spies were first to spot Trump team's links with Russia." Theguardian.com. https://www.theguardian.com/uk-news/2017/apr/13/british-spies-first-to-spot-trump-team-links-russia (April 13, 2017).

lxv Rybka, Nastya. "Photo of Nastya Rybka with Oleg Deripaska." Instagram.com. https://www.instagram.com/p/BaNoosxD_To/ (October 13, 2017).

lxvi Dyer, J.E. "How the FISA warrant on Carter Page enabled Obama Administration surveillance of the entire

Trump team, and why civil libertarians should be worried."
Tabletmap.com. https://www.tabletmag.com/jewish-news-
and-politics/256333/fisas-license-to-hop (March 6, 2018).

[lxvii] Ioffe, Julia. "Who Is Carter Page?." Politico.com.
https://www.politico.com/magazine/story/2016/09/the-
mystery-of-trumps-man-in-moscow-214283 (September 23,
2016).

[lxviii][lxviii] Dyer, J.E. "How the FISA warrant on Carter Page
enabled Obama Administration surveillance of the entire
Trump team, and why civil libertarians should be worried."
Tabletmap.com. https://www.tabletmag.com/jewish-news-
and-politics/256333/fisas-license-to-hop (March 6, 2018).

[lxix][lxix] Cleveland, Margot. "Why The FBI Needs Yet Another
Cover Story For Starting Spygate." Thefederalist.com.
http://thefederalist.com/2018/06/06/fbi-needs-yet-another-
cover-story-probe-trump-russia/ (JUNE 6, 2018).

[lxx][lxx] Ross, Chuck. "Cambridge Professor Spied on Trump
Campaign Advisers." Dailycaller.com.
https://dailycaller.com/2018/05/19/trump-papadopoulos-
page-halper/ (May 19, 2018).

[lxxi] Ibid.

[lxxii] Witte, Griff. "The rise and striking fall of Trump adviser
George Papadopoulos." Chicagotribune.com.
http://www.chicagotribune.com/news/nationworld/politics/ct
-trump-george-papadopoulos-20171210-story.html (December
10, 2017).

lxxiii Ross, Chuck. "Papadopoulos Told Feds He Received $10,000 from Foreign National He Believed Was a Spy." Dailycaller.com. https://dailycaller.com/2018/08/20/papadopoulos-foreign-payment/ (August 20, 2018).

lxxiv Ibid.

lxxv Ibid.

lxxvi Ross, Chuck. "DNC Said Joseph Mifsud Could be Dead – His Adviser Pours Cold Water on the Theory." Dailycaller.com. https://dailycaller.com/2018/09/10/joseph-mifsud-alive/ (September 10, 2018).

lxxviilxxvii McCarthy, Andrew C. "Outrageous Redactions to the Russia Report." Nationalreview.com. https://www.nationalreview.com/2018/05/russia-report-redactions-cover-fbi-missteps/ (May 7, 2018).

lxxviii McCarthy, Andrew C. "In Politicized Justice, Desperate Times Call for Disparate Measures." https://www.nationalreview.com/2018/05/clinton-email-trump-russia-probes-justice-department-double-standards/ (May 19, 2018).

lxxixlxxix Parry, George. "The Real Andrew McCabe." Spectator.org. https://spectator.org/the-real-andrew-mccabe/ (March 23, 2018).

lxxxlxxx Tapper, Jake. "Government Source Confirms Different Michael Cohen was in Prague." Twitter.com. https://twitter.com/jaketapper/status/819187673961287681?lang=en (January 11, 2017).

lxxxi York, Bryan. "Trump campaign vet: Informant used me to get to Papadopoulos." Washingtonexaminer.com. https://www.washingtonexaminer.com/news/trump-campaign-vet-sam-clovis-says-informant-used-him-to-get-to-papadopoulos (May 28, 2018).

lxxxii McCarthy, Andrew C. "The Rosenstein Memo." Nationalreview.com. https://www.nationalreview.com/2018/04/russia-investigation-rod-rosenstein-memo-mueller-probe-limits/ (April 4, 2018).

lxxxiii Hemingway, Mollie. "McCabe's Bogus Witch Hunt Of Jeff Sessions Confirms Worst Fears About FBI/DOJ Politicization." Thefederalist.com. http://thefederalist.com/2018/03/22/mccabes-bogus-witch-hunt-of-jeff-sessions-confirms-worst-fears-about-fbi-doj-politicization/ (March 22, 2018).

lxxxiv McCarthy, Andrew C. "The Rosenstein Memo." Nationalreview.com. https://www.nationalreview.com/2018/04/russia-investigation-rod-rosenstein-memo-mueller-probe-limits/ (April 4, 2018).

lxxxvlxxxv Vazquez, Maegan, Sarah Westwood and Boris Sanchez. "Former Trump operative Roger Stone met with Russian who wanted $2M for Clinton dirt." Cnn.com. https://www.cnn.com/2018/06/17/politics/roger-stone-henry-greenberg-michael-caputo/index.html (June 17, 2018).

lxxxvi Ibid.

lxxxvii Hemingway, Mollie. "New Book: McCabe Initiated White House Meeting That Led To Leak." Thefederalist.com. http://thefederalist.com/2018/01/29/new-book-mccabe-initiated-white-house-meeting-that-led-to-leak/ (January 29, 2018).

lxxxviii Ibid

lxxxix Sciutto, Jim, Evan Perez, Shimon Prokupecz, Manu Raju and Pamela Brown. "FBI refused White House request to knock down recent Trump-Russia stories." Cnn.com. https://www.cnn.com/2017/02/23/politics/fbi-refused-white-house-request-to-knock-down-recent-trump-russia-stories/index.html (February 24, 2017).

xc McCarthy, Andrew C. "Yes, the FBI Was Investigating the Trump Campaign When It Spied." Nationalreview.com. https://www.nationalreview.com/2018/05/trump-campaign-spying-obama-administration-investigation/ (May 30, 2018).

xci McCarthy, Andrew C. "Yes, the FBI Was Investigating the Trump Campaign When It Spied." Nationalreview.com. https://www.nationalreview.com/2018/05/trump-campaign-spying-obama-administration-investigation/ (May 30, 2018).

xcii Ibid

xciii McCarthy, Andrew C. "The Antithesis of Obstruction." Nationalreview.com. https://www.nationalreview.com/2017/06/trump-obstruction-narrative-comey-knew-it-was-fake/ (June 24, 2017).

xciv McCarthy, Andrew C. "Rod Rosenstein's Resistance." Nationalreview.com.

https://www.nationalreview.com/2018/09/rod-rosenstein-resistance-president-trump/ (September 23, 2018).

xcv Turley, Jonathan. "It's high time Rod Rosenstein recuse himself." Thehill.com. http://thehill.com/blogs/pundits-blog/the-administration/345538-opinion-why-its-high-time-rod-rosenstein-recuse-himself (August 7, 2017).

xcvi Ibid

xcvii McCarthy, Andrew C. "Mueller's Empire: Legions of Lawyers, Bottomless Budget, Limitless Jurisdiction." Amgreatness.com. https://amgreatness.com/2017/06/21/muellers-empire-legions-lawyers-bottomless-budget-limitless-jurisdiction/ (June 21, 2017).

xcviii Rosenstein, Rod, and Chris Wallace. "Rod Rosenstein addresses efforts to stop White House leaks." Foxnews.com. http://www.foxnews.com/transcript/2017/08/06/rod-rosenstein-addresses-efforts-to-stop-white-house-leaks.html (August 6, 2017).

xcix McCarthy, Andrew C. "Rosenstein Fails to Defend His Failure to Limit Mueller's Investigation Rod Rosenstein on Capitol Hill in June." Nationreview.com. http://www.nationalreview.com/article/450230/rod-rosenstein-mueller-investigation-special-counsel-fishing-expedition (August 7, 2017).

c Poulsen, Kevin and Spencer Ackerman. "EXCLUSIVE: 'Lone DNC Hacker' Guccifer 2.0 Slipped Up and Revealed He Was a Russian Intelligence Officer." Thedailybeast.com. https://www.thedailybeast.com/exclusive-lone-dnc-hacker-guccifer-20-slipped-up-and-revealed-he-was-a-russian-intelligence-officer (March 22, 2018).

ci Solomon, John. "Collusion bombshell: DNC lawyers met with FBI on Russia allegations before surveillance warrant." Thehill.com. https://thehill.com/hilltv/rising/409817-russia-collusion-bombshell-dnc-lawyers-met-with-fbi-on-dossier-before (10/3/2018).

cii Harding, Luke. "What we know – and what's true – about the Trump-Russia dossier." Theguardian.com. https://www.theguardian.com/us-news/2017/jan/11/trump-russia-dossier-explainer-details (January 11, 2017).

ciii Solomon, John. "Collusion bombshell: DNC lawyers met with FBI on Russia allegations before surveillance warrant." Thehill.com. https://thehill.com/hilltv/rising/409817-russia-collusion-bombshell-dnc-lawyers-met-with-fbi-on-dossier-before (10/3/2018).

civ Foreign Intelligence Surveillance Court. "MEMORANDUM OPINION AND ORDER." Documentcloud.org. https://assets.documentcloud.org/documents/3718776/2016-Cert-FISC-Memo-Opin-Order-Apr-2017-1.pdf (April 2017).

cv Eastman, John C. "The General Warrant and the Politics of Personal Destruction." Amgreatness.com. https://amgreatness.com/2017/06/20/general-warrant-politics-personal-destruction/ (June 20, 2017).

cvi Jacobson, William A. "Fusion GPS co-founders signal next phase in attempted Trump takedown has started." Legalinsurrection.com. https://legalinsurrection.com/2018/04/fusion-gps-co-founders-signal-next-phase-in-attempted-trump-takedown-has-started/ (April 22, 2018).

cvii McCarthy, Andrew C. "Clinton's State Department: A RICO Enterprise." Nationalreview.com. http://www.nationalreview.com/article/441573/hillary-clinton-corruption-foundation-was-key (October 29, 2016).

cviii McCarthy, Andrew C. "Susan Rice's White House Unmasking: A Watergate-style Scandal." Nationalreview.com. http://www.nationalreview.com/article/446415/susan-rice-unmasking-trump-campaign-members-obama-administration-fbi-cia-nsa (April 4, 2017).

cix Ibid

cx McCarthy, Andrew C. "FISAgate: The Question Is Not Whether Trump Associates Were Monitored." Nationalreview.com. http://www.nationalreview.com/article/446122/fisagate-monitoring-trump-associates-was-spying-abuse-power (March 27, 2017).

cxi McCarthy, Andrew C. "FISAgate and Russia: Comey and Nunes Stir the Muddy Waters." Nationalreview.com http://www.nationalreview.com/article/446024/devin-nunes-james-comey-break-no-new-ground-trump-russia-ties (March 23, 2017)

cxii Singman, Brooke. "Firm behind anti-Trump dossier also worked for Russia, Senate witness says." Foxnews.com. http://www.foxnews.com/politics/2017/07/27/firm-behind-anti-trump-dossier-also-worked-for-russia-senate-witness-says.html (July 27, 2017).

cxiii Harding, Luke. "What we know – and what's true – about the Trump-Russia dossier." Theguardian.com. https://www.theguardian.com/us-news/2017/jan/11/trump-russia-dossier-explainer-details (January 11, 2017).

cxiv Hall, Kevin G. "John McCain faces questions in Trump-Russia dossier case." Mcclatchydc.com. http://www.mcclatchydc.com/news/nation-world/national/article160622854.html (July 11, 2017).

cxv Scarborough, Rowan. "FBI possessed, studied anti-Trump dossier, says former top spy." M.washingtontimes.com. http://m.washingtontimes.com/news/2017/may/25/fbi-possessed-studied-anti-trump-dossier-says-form/ (May 25, 2017).

cxvi McCarthy, Andrew P. "FISAgate and Russia: Comey and Nunes Stir the Muddy Waters." Nationreview.com. http://www.nationalreview.com/article/446024/devin-nunes-james-comey-break-no-new-ground-trump-russia-ties (March 23, 2017).

cxvii McCarthy, Andrew P. "The Antithesis of Obstruction." Nationalreview.com. http://www.nationalreview.com/article/448940/trump-obstruction-narrative-comey-knew-it-was-fake (June 24, 2017).

cxviii Ibid

cxix McCarthy, Andrew C. "Explosive Revelation of Obama Administration Illegal Surveillance of Americans." Nationalreview.com. http://www.nationalreview.com/article/447973/nsa-illegal-surveillance-americans-obama-administration-abuse-fisa-court-response (May 25, 2017).

cxx Ibid

cxxi Turley, Jonathan. "The damaging case against James Comey." Thehill.com.

http://thehill.com/blogs/pundits-blog/the-administration/337160-opinion-the-damaging-case-against-james-comey (June 9, 2017).

cxxii Dyer, J.E. "How the FISA warrant on Carter Page enabled Obama Administration surveillance of the entire Trump team, and why civil libertarians should be worried." Tabletmap.com. https://www.tabletmag.com/jewish-news-and-politics/256333/fisas-license-to-hop (March 6, 2018).

cxxiii Rosiak, Luke. "Luke Rosiak Articles." Dailycaller.com. https://dailycaller.com/author/Luke+Rosiak (Various dates).

cxxiv Rosiak, Luke. "A History of Alleged Intimidation and Tampering in House Hacking Case Marked by Witnesses' Silence." Dailycaller.com. https://dailycaller.com/2018/03/18/imran-awan-house-hacking-intimidation-tampering/ (May 18, 2018).

cxxv McCarthy, Andrew C. "The Very Strange Indictment of Debbie Wasserman Schultz's IT Scammers." Nationalreview.com. www.nationalreview.com/article/450665/debbie-wasserman-schultz-it-scammers-indicted-mysteriously-narrow-and-low-key-way (August 21, 2017).

cxxvi McCarthy, Andrew C. "Debbie Wasserman Schultz and the Pakistani IT Scammers." Nationalreview.com. http://www.nationalreview.com/article/449983/debbie-wasserman-schultz-pakistani-computer-guys-bank-fraud (July 29, 2017).

cxxvii Rosiak, Luke. "Trump is Right: A 'Pakistani Mystery Man' has Documents Wasserman Schultz Didn't Want Prosecutors to See." Dailycaller.com.

https://dailycaller.com/2018/04/22/trump-pakistani-mystery-man-documents-debbie-wasserman-schultz/ (April 22, 2018).

cxxviii McCarthy, Andrew C. "The Very Strange Indictment of Debbie Wasserman Schultz's IT Scammers." Nationalreview.com. www.nationalreview.com/article/450665/debbie-wasserman-schultz-it-scammers-indicted-mysteriously-narrow-and-low-key-way (August 21, 2017).

cxxix Ibid

cxxx Ibid

cxxxi CrowdStrike Global Intelligence Team. "Use of Fancy Bear Android Malware in Tracking of Ukrainian Field Artillery Units." Voanews.eu. https://docs.voanews.eu/en-US/2017/03/23/13e4fe03-a7a7-47ab-b88a-9eb9a2449d19.pdf (December 22, 2016).

cxxxii Woodruff, Judy, Thomas Rid, and Dmitri Alperovitch. "Security company releases new evidence of Russian role in DNC hack." Pbs.org. http://www.pbs.org/newshour/bb/security-company-releases-new-evidence-russian-role-dnc-hack/ (December 22, 2016).

cxxxiii Kuzmenko, Oleksiy, and Pete Cobus. "Think Tank: Cyber Firm at Center of Russian Hacking Charges Misread Data." Voanews.com. https://www.voanews.com/a/crowdstrike-comey-russia-hack-dnc-clinton-trump/3776067.html (March 23, 2017).

cxxxiv Carr, Jeffrey. "The GRU-Ukraine Artillery Hack That May Never Have Happened." Medium.com. https://medium.com/@jeffreycarr/the-gru-ukraine-artillery-hack-that-may-never-have-happened-820960bbb02d (January 3, 2017.).

cxxxv Carr, Jeffrey. "Crowdstrike Needs to Address the Harm It Caused Ukraine." Linkedin.com. https://www.linkedin.com/pulse/crowdstrike-needs-address-harm-causedukraine-jeffrey-carr (January 16, 2017).

cxxxvi Stokel-Walker, Chris. "Hunting the DNC hackers: how Crowdstrike found proof Russia hacked the Democrats." Wired.co.uk. https://www.wired.co.uk/article/dnc-hack-proof-russia-democrats (March 5, 2017).

cxxxvii Ward, Vicky. "The Russian Expat Leading the Fight to Protect America." Esquire.com. http://www.esquire.com/news-politics/a49902/the-russian-emigre-leading-the-fight-to-protect-america/ (October 24, 2016).

cxxxviii Office of the Inspector General, U.S. Department of Justice. "A Review of Various Actions by the Federal Bureau of Investigation and Department of Justice in Advance of the 2016 Election." Justice.gov. https://www.justice.gov/file/1071991/download (June 14, 2018).

cxxxix Dyer, J.E. "How the FISA warrant on Carter Page enabled Obama Administration surveillance of the entire Trump team, and why civil libertarians should be worried." Tabletmap.com. https://www.tabletmag.com/jewish-news-and-politics/256333/fisas-license-to-hop (March 6, 2018).

cxl McCarthy, Andrew C. "FBI Director Comey Is Wrong: The Case for Prosecuting Hillary Clinton Is Strong." Nationalreview.com.

http://www.nationalreview.com/article/437493/hillary-clinton-email-scandal-fbi-director-comey-built-strong-case-decided-against (July 5, 2016)

cxli Babbin, Jed. "Ratting Out Hillary." Spectator.org. https://spectator.org/65703_ratting-out-hillary/ (March 7, 2016).

cxlii McCarthy, Andrew C. "Outrageous Redactions to the Russia Report." Nationalreview.com. https://www.nationalreview.com/2018/05/russia-report-redactions-cover-fbi-missteps/amp/ (May 7, 2018).

cxliii McCarthy, Andrew C. "Why Doesn't Trump Just Unmask the Unmasking?." Nationalreview.com. https://www.nationalreview.com/2017/08/obama-administration-unmasking-trump-should-declassify/ (August 3, 2017).

cxliv McCarthy, Andrew C. "Outrageous Redactions to the Russia Report." Nationalreview.com. https://www.nationalreview.com/2018/05/russia-report-redactions-cover-fbi-missteps/amp/ (May 7, 2018).

cxlv Barnes, Robert. "ANALYSIS: Constitution Compels Sessions Dismiss Mueller From Non-Campaign Cases." Lawandcrime.com. https://lawandcrime.com/opinion/constitution-jeff-sessions-dismiss-robert-mueller-non-campaign-cases/ (March 28, 2018).

cxlvi Ibid

cxlvii Harding, Luke, Stephanie Kirchgaessner and Nick Hopkins. "British spies were first to spot Trump team's links with Russia." Theguardian.com. https://www.theguardian.com/uk-news/2017/apr/13/british-spies-first-to-spot-trump-team-links-russia (April 13, 2017).

cxlviii Cleveland, Margot. "Why The FBI Needs Yet Another Cover Story For Starting Spygate." Thefederalist.com. http://thefederalist.com/2018/06/06/fbi-needs-yet-another-cover-story-probe-trump-russia/ (JUNE 6, 2018).

cxlix Strassel, Kimberly. "The Curious Case of Mr. Downer." Wsj.com. https://www.wsj.com/articles/the-curious-case-of-mr-downer-1527809075 (May 31, 2018).

cl Ibid

cli Ross, Chuck. "Papadopoulos Told Feds He Received $10,000 from Foreign National He Believed Was a Spy." Dailycaller.com. https://dailycaller.com/2018/08/20/papadopoulos-foreign-payment/ (August 20, 2018).

clii Ross, Chuck. "DNC Said Joseph Mifsud Could be Dead – His Adviser Pours Cold Water on the Theory." Dailycaller.com. https://dailycaller.com/2018/09/10/joseph-mifsud-alive/ (September 10, 2018).

67643005R00201

Made in the USA
Middletown, DE
11 September 2019